THE
EVERYTHING®
GUIDE TO
LIVING OFF THE GRID

Dear Reader,

Twenty years ago, my family and I left the hustle and bustle of living in Chicago and moved to a small farm in northwest Illinois. I remember the very first night in our hundred-year-old farmhouse, resting in my bed and being kept awake by the sounds of frogs and crickets—instead of the usual noises of the trucks and cars on the highway and the air-planes from O'Hare. We couldn't sleep because it was too quiet. A lot has changed since then.

During these years much of what we learned about a self-sufficient lifestyle was by trial and error. From chasing our escaped cattle down the road when I was eight months pregnant to trying to herd sheep in on a rainy day, I know we gave our more experienced neighbors good reason to shake their heads and laugh.

With this book, I'd like to take your hand and guide you through some of the things we learned, so you're not out there on your own. Instead, you'll have a friend to lean on. This book will send you in the right direction and give you the tools to learn more. Enjoy your journey to being self-sufficient. It's well worth the trip!

Terri Reid

Welcome to the EVERYTHING® Series!

These handy, accessible books give you all you need to tackle a difficult project, gain a new hobby, comprehend a fascinating topic, prepare for an exam, or even brush up on something you learned back in school but have since forgotten.

You can choose to read an *Everything*® book from cover to cover or just pick out the information you want from our four useful boxes: e-questions, e-facts, e-alerts, and e-ssentials.

We give you everything you need to know on the subject, but throw in a lot of fun stuff along the way, too.

We now have more than 400 *Everything*® books in print, spanning such wide-ranging categories as weddings, pregnancy, cooking, music instruction, foreign language, crafts, pets, New Age, and so much more. When you're done reading them all, you can finally say you know *Everything*®!

QUESTION

Answers to
common questions

FACT

Important snippets
of information

ALERT

Urgent
warnings

ESSENTIAL

Quick
handy tips

PUBLISHER Karen Cooper

DIRECTOR OF ACQUISITIONS AND INNOVATION Paula Munier

MANAGING EDITOR, EVERYTHING® SERIES Lisa Laing

COPY CHIEF Casey Ebert

ASSISTANT PRODUCTION EDITOR Jacob Erickson

ACQUISITIONS EDITOR Kate Powers

SENIOR DEVELOPMENT EDITOR Brett Palana-Shanahan

EDITORIAL ASSISTANT Ross Weisman

EVERYTHING® SERIES COVER DESIGNER Erin Alexander

LAYOUT DESIGNERS Colleen Cunningham, Elisabeth Lariviere, Ashley Vierra, Denise Wallace

Visit the entire Everything® series at *www.everything.com*

THE EVERYTHING®

GUIDE TO LIVING OFF THE GRID

A back-to-basics manual for independent living

Terri Reid

Avon, Massachusetts

*Dedicated to all of those who are willing
not only to dream big, but also have the
courage to make their dreams come true.*

An Everything® Series Book.
Everything® and everything.com® are registered trademarks of F+W Media, Inc.

Published by Adams Media, a division of F+W Media, Inc.
57 Littlefield Street, Avon, MA 02322 U.S.A.
www.adamsmedia.com

ISBN 10: 1-4405-1275-2
ISBN 13: 978-1-4405-1275-9
eISBN 10: 1-4405-2491-2
eISBN 13: 978-1-4405-2491-2

Printed in the United States of America.

10 9 8 7 6 5 4 3 2 1

Library of Congress Cataloging-in-Publication Data
Reid, Terri.
The everything guide to living off the grid / Terri Reid.
p. cm.
Includes index.
ISBN 978-1-4405-1275-9
1. Self-reliant living. 2. Sustainable living. I. Title.
GF78.R45 2011
640—dc22
2011010219

*This book is available at quantity discounts for bulk purchases.
For information, please call 1-800-289-0963.*

Contents

Acknowledgments

To my husband, Richard, and to my wonderful children, who make every day in this journey called life a delightful adventure. Thank you for your willingness to not only put up with, but go along with some of my "interesting" ideas. And thank you for believing in me.

Thanks to my parents and siblings for their encouragement and support.

Thanks to my writing "sisters," who sent encouragement, support, chocolate, and good vibes my way.

Thanks to my editor, Kate, for her swift responses and encouragement.

And, finally, thanks to my Heavenly Father for creating this magnificent world we get to live in, with all of the astonishing animals, plants, and natural wonders we have stewardship over. May we all remember to be grateful and wise stewards.

The Top 10 Reasons to Live
Off the Grid

1. To create a more self-sufficient lifestyle for you and your family
2. To be more conscious of the environment and your impact on it
3. To feel more secure away from the issues associated with urban areas
4. To be the master of your own destiny
5. To have a simpler, more satisfying lifestyle
6. To raise your own vegetables, fruit, and livestock
7. To live free from debt and learn how to be frugal
8. To know that no matter what happens in the world, your family is prepared
9. To learn to live off the land
10. To give your children a legacy of independence

Introduction

DO YOU WANT TO stop receiving electricity bills? Are you willing to spend money to make money? Do you want to have things like electricity and hot water at any time, no matter what's going on outside your property? Do you want to have more control over the things you eat, and know how they are processed? Do you want your family to be safe and secure from the worries of a bad economy, crime, and terrorism? If your answer is "yes" to questions like these, then living off the grid is something you need to consider.

Although living off the grid means hard work, the benefits you receive will make it all worthwhile. Just imagine how you will feel running your home using clean or renewable energy sources. Think of the pleasure of harvesting your own fruits and vegetables, or picking up fresh brown eggs from your own chicken coop. Envision enjoying the sounds of nature, rather than the noise of expressways, sirens, and airplane traffic.

But perhaps more important than these benefits are the groundbreaking steps you will be making for your children and their children. When you choose a self-sustaining, eco-friendly lifestyle, you are making the world a better place for future generations by decreasing your carbon footprint and by demonstrating that you can have a successful and happy life without all of the hustle and bustle of the city and suburbs.

When you move off-grid with children, you are allowing them to learn life lessons they will never forget. They will understand how to respect life by helping to raise livestock. They will understand the natural process by helping to plant seeds, weed gardens, and finally harvest produce. They will learn the value of hard work and the joy in a job well done. They will climb trees and run outdoors, rather than sit in front of a screen and play video games. You will work together as a family and create memories and bonds that will withstand generations.

Even though hundreds of thousands of people have managed to move off-grid, some people will only be able to incorporate part of the off-grid existence into their lives. You need to understand that any effort you make toward living a more self-sustaining life will help you and your family in the long run. Whether all you decide to do is put a solar panel on your roof, grow a small vegetable garden in your backyard, learn to cook using basic ingredients, or get out of debt; this book will help you.

However, if you are considering immersing yourself in an off-the-grid, self-sustaining lifestyle, this practical and informative guide will ease off-the-grid beginners into a more independent way of living and give you enough of an overview to be able to make initial decisions and move forward in the right direction.

CHAPTER 1

The Reality of Living Off the Grid

"Living off the grid" can refer to two different, but similar, ideas. On one hand, the term has become a catch phrase for a more self-sufficient lifestyle. But, taken literally, it means becoming energy independent, so you are not attached to a utility grid for any of your power needs. This book will focus on the first definition, with information that will help, if you so desire, to incorporate the second into your life.

Why Should You Move Off the Grid?

The answers are as varied as the individuals who choose this lifestyle. You may want to move off-grid because you're looking for a "greener" lifestyle and want to lessen your carbon footprint. You don't have to move out of town or even from your current residence to do this. You can install solar-energy shingles on your roof or a geothermal heating and cooling system in your home. There are even designs for low-impact wind turbines that generate electricity. You can install energy-efficient appliances and low-water-use toilets and showerheads. Implementing many of these measures will not only make an ecological statement, it will also save money in the long run.

ESSENTIAL

Go Green: ditch the bottled water. Bottled water has a huge carbon footprint; it's bottled at a central location in small plastic bottles and shipped all over. Try buying a reusable water bottle or canteen for your water. Many plastic water bottles are recycled, but most are not, making the footprint even bigger.

You may want to move off-grid because you are looking for a simpler, back-to-basics lifestyle. Perhaps the hustle and bustle of the city is too much. You want to raise your children at a slower pace in a place where they can grow up understanding the benefits of hard work and responsibility. You want to feel the pleasure of a pantry stocked with jars of your own homemade preserves and pickles. You want to walk outside in the early morning light and scatter feed to your chickens and collect farm-fresh eggs. You want to gather your own vegetables and grow your own meat. You enjoy the security you feel knowing your family would be able to get by, no matter what the machinations of the economy.

You may decide to move off-grid because you are concerned with security. You don't feel that the world is a safe place for you and your family, especially not in its large cities. You want to move to a place where you don't rely on power grids that can be destroyed in terrorist attacks. You don't want to be in a populated area where you might be a target for a biochemical or nuclear threat. You are moving off-grid for safety and to create an independent lifestyle for yourself and the ones you love. You have a sense of urgency, and the sooner you can relocate, the better.

ALERT

> In March 2010, the U.S. Congress heard testimony about a scientific study that appeared in the journal *Safety Science*. This study presented a model of how an attack on a small, unimportant part of the U.S. power grid might be able to bring the whole grid down. A second article came out in the journal *Nature* the following month. This article presented a model of how a cascade of failing interconnected networks led to the 2003 blackout in Italy.

Finally, you might be considering living off the grid as a necessary option because of a financial setback. Living a back-to-basics and no-frills lifestyle might be what you need as you look for new employment or get out from under an upside-down mortgage. Many of the things you will read in this book will help you save money and learn to economize. However, it is important to realize that moving off-grid is not an escape hatch for any financial bedlam you have created in your current life: you are still responsible for resolving any owed monies or loans in your name.

Depending on your resources and your motivation, living off the grid can be done quickly, or it can be done in a series of small steps. Either way, you need to be sure you have taken into account more than just solar power and dehydrated food. Moving from a life that is reliant on the ease and convenience of nearby malls and thermostat-regulated environments to one of making do or doing without, and chopping wood to heat your home, can be overwhelming. You need to be sure you prepare yourself physically, mentally, financially, and emotionally.

The good news is you can start today, no matter where you are or what you are doing. You can start looking at your finances to see where you can economize. You can look at your food preparation and substitute basic items for quickly prepared foods. You can take an inventory of how often you run to the grocery store, the coffee shop, or the fast-food restaurant and limit your exposure to any or all of them.

Can You Survive Off the Grid?

Any version of off-grid living takes some adjustment. If you are simply looking for a way to reduce your dependence on traditional energy sources, you will need to be sure your usage does not exceed your ability to create energy. Part of the equation is installing the necessary alternative energy sources, but another part is weaning yourself away from an energy-reliant life. You will need to perform an energy inventory on the appliances and other gadgets you have in your home and decide what can stay and what can go. There are a number of small electronics, like hair dryers, clock radios, and coffeemakers, you might use daily that may not work with your new lifestyle. These objects aren't always necessary, but sometimes it's hard to give up the small conveniences of life.

ESSENTIAL

You can use this formula to estimate an appliance's energy use:
Wattage × Hours Used Per Day ÷ 1,000 = Daily Kilowatt-hour (kWh) Consumption (1 kilowatt [kW] = 1,000 watts)

If you're looking at a completely self-sufficient lifestyle, get ready to be introduced to some muscles you didn't even know you had! Moving off the grid in this fashion is plain hard work. There is wood to cut, gardens to plant, livestock to take care of, and meals to prepare. The nearest McDonald's might be fifty miles away, so fast food is often off the menu. This is not the life for someone who does not want to sweat and does not understand that a few blisters are actually medals of honor. This is not the life for someone who *needs* that daily run to Starbucks, weekly trips to the mall, and monthly weekends at the spa (although you can install a solar-heated whirlpool bath in your home). Just as you would assess your power needs, you need to assess your physical abilities and decide how much off-grid living you can employ in your life.

The Different Levels of "Off-Grid" Living

What does off-grid mean to you personally? You can actually live off-grid in the middle of a suburb, if your version of off-grid is to be less dependent on traditional fuel sources. Installing a geothermal heating and cooling system along with solar panels and a battery array might be your solution for an off-grid existence. You can also live off-grid by purchasing 200 acres of land in the mountains of Kentucky and creating your own self-sufficient environment. You can live off-grid by buying a small farmette and learning to raise some livestock and some vegetables.

The beauty of your off-grid lifestyle is that you get to determine what you want to do and how far you want to go. However, every successful adventure begins with a plan. List your goals and set down intermediate steps. Do you want to eventually move away from the city, but still need the employment found there? Perhaps your next step would be relocating to a smaller town near enough to commute to the city, with a larger piece of property to begin your first garden. Do you want to have a green home? Perhaps your next step would be to look into the geographic advantages of the different options of alternative energy.

Each goal you make and each step you take will bring you closer to your final destination of living off-grid in your own way.

How Far Off the Grid Are You Able to Go?

For many, moving up to a secluded spot nestled next to Yellowstone National Park with nothing but the pine trees, bears, and moose as neighbors could seem ideal. But, you need to realistically decide how far off the grid you can go. Here are some things you need to consider:

Health Care

If you are newly married and are planning to have children, or already have children, you don't want to be 200 miles away from the nearest hospital, unless you have the kind of training or experience that makes you capable of giving emergency medical attention to your family members. And, even if you have that training, what happens if you are the one who gets hurt?

Cellular Phone Linkage

With modern technology and a good satellite provider, you can have Internet and television access almost anywhere in the world. The problem comes when you are trying to get cell phone linkage, because you need to be able to bounce off a tower. There are still many places throughout the United States and the world that don't have cell coverage.

Access to Mass Transportation

If you need to fly occasionally, you need to decide how close you want to be to an airport. Luckily, today there are a number of secondary airports that feed into major airports. Even a relatively small city like Dubuque, Iowa, has an airport that feeds into Chicago's O'Hare Airport. Depending on frequency of flights, you should decide how long you want to travel to get to an airport.

Access to "Civilization"

There are many other conveniences you might not want to sacrifice with your new off-grid lifestyle. Do you want to occasionally go to a movie or out to dinner? Will you need to go grocery shopping on a regular basis? Will your children take piano, ballet, gymnastics, or other lessons? Do you want to live near a library or in a college town? Remember, it's not realistic for you to believe that you could "commute in" for many of these activities. If you are living a completely off-grid lifestyle, you won't have time to spend several hours driving back and forth. You need to be brutally honest with yourself before you make any decisions!

All of these different variables are important for you to consider as you decide how far off the grid you want to live.

Keeping and Maintaining Relationships

Just because you are moving off-grid does not mean you have to leave your friends and family behind. Especially today, with the technology available, it is easy to keep in touch on a daily basis.

Social Networking

Facebook, Twitter, and blogging are wonderful ways to share information, post photos, and keep up to date on the comings and goings of your friends and family. A quick browse through your Facebook page can update you on any changes or events in the lives of any of your "friends." TechCrunch recently reported that Facebook, which currently has over 350 million users, is poised to become the most popular social networking site in the world. Over the past year, the number of users in countries outside the United States, particularly in Europe, Africa, and Latin America, has grown significantly.

Video Chat and Video Conferencing

There are a number of software programs that allow you, with the use of a webcam, to hook up with friends and family all around the world in a video chat and even a video conference. Some of these programs allow for multiple chats at the same time, so you can connect with several friends all across the country and visit together via video chat. You will need high-speed Internet and a computer with webcam capabilities, but beyond that, the software is user-friendly and you can "see" your friends and family whenever you desire.

Make Room for Visitors

When you decide on your off-grid property, make sure you've set aside space for visitors. A back-to-basics, out-in-the-country lifestyle appeals to many people, and even though they might not be able to choose this life for themselves, they are curious and eager to learn more. Most people who make the move find they often become a long-weekend destination for families and friends. Although the extra mouths to feed can be a little burdensome, these visits give you the opportunity to put your guests to work so they get a taste of what living off the grid is really like.

On the other side of the coin, living off the grid does not always mean staying off the grid. Getting back out and "on" again to visit family and friends is allowed!

Taking the First Steps

For many, just getting started seems overwhelming. You should start with baby steps to get you moving toward a more independent, self-sustaining lifestyle.

Reduce Your Energy Use

Look around you and unplug all of those unnecessary appliances. Use a hand-operated can opener instead of an electric one. Use a whisk instead of a mixer. Look for phantom electricity drains. The U.S. Department of Energy states, "Many appliances continue to draw a small amount of power when they are switched off. These phantom loads occur in many appliances, such as VCRs, televisions, stereos, computers, and kitchen appliances. This can be avoided by unplugging the appliance or using a power strip and using the switch on the power strip to cut all power to the appliance."

ALERT

In the average home, more than 50 percent of the electricity used to power electronics is consumed while the devices are turned off! In the United States alone, phantom load costs consumers more than $3 billion a year and adds up to the output of several full-size power plants.

Check the Energy Star ratings on your appliances and, if you can, replace older appliances with more efficient new ones. If you can't afford to do that, inspect your current appliances. Be sure that seals are in good repair, or replace them. Make sure your washing machine belts are tight so the engine doesn't have to work harder to get your clothes clean and the spin cycles draw out a majority of the water. Be sure that filters in your furnace, air conditioner, refrigerator, and dryer are all clean and allow free-flowing air. Also, check the air vents from your dryer to the outside to be sure they are clean and free of obstructions.

FACT

Energy Star is a joint program of the U.S. Environmental Protection Agency and the U.S. Department of Energy that helps us all save money and protect the environment through energy-efficient products and practices. You may see Energy Star appliances at your local home-goods store; that seal means they are certified energy-efficient products.

Plant a Garden

Whether you have a spot in your yard that can be tilled or some potting soil, a collection of containers, and a room on your patio or porch, you can plant a garden. Start with some tomato plants in a five-gallon pail or some herbs on a sunny kitchen window. Begin to learn the joy of growing your own.

Many of the more urban communities have been promoting "community gardens," or shared spaces in a public location, where residents can purchase a plot to use for gardening. This is a great solution if you live in a heavily populated city or simply don't have the yard space for a large garden. Just be sure to have the soil tested before buying, as lead and other toxic heavy metals are present in some community gardens.

Stop Eating Out

When you are busy and running late, it's so easy to fall into the habit of driving through, picking up, or eating out. To learn to be more self-sufficient and to have a healthier life, plan a menu and learn to cook from the basics. Make your own homemade pizza or taco salad. Substitute healthier alternatives to high-fat, high-sodium fast-food offerings.

Start Exercising

If you are planning to be self-sufficient, you need to be physically fit. Begin taking daily walks or working out for fifteen or twenty minutes in your home. Park your car farther away from the store, so you're forced to walk. Walk rather than ride, if possible. Have your family participate in outdoor sports together, rather than watch television.

FACT

A tip for a successful workout: prepare for your workout the night before by packing your gym bag or, if you work out at home, laying out your workout clothes so when you get home, you're ready to go. You'd be really surprised the amount of ways you can talk yourself out of a workout routine, so it is best to have everything ready.

Making exercise a family activity can get everyone in on the action, and allows you to spend more time together. An after-dinner walk on a spring evening or a weekend hike in the mountains are great ways of getting yourself in shape and setting aside some time to spend with your loved ones.

Start Studying

Now is the time to take a class at the local Cooperative Extension System office or community college, or borrow books from your library about alternate energy sources, gardening, livestock, or any other area you need to brush up on. Sign up for seed catalogs and browse through the varieties available and the advantages and disadvantages of each.

Organizations also occasionally offer workshops and classes on making the transition to a more self-sufficient lifestyle. Sign up for some, and make it a point to talk to the teacher—more likely than not, he or she lives off the grid and can give you some firsthand advice. Nothing beats the wisdom of experience!

CHAPTER 2

Getting Out of Debt

You might wonder why getting out of debt is one of the first chapters in the book. In order to truly have a self-sufficient lifestyle, you need to be debt-free or nearly debt-free. When you owe someone else, your choices are limited; you have to earn a certain amount of income to meet your obligations. Spending less than you make is vital to financial security.

What Is Debt?

When you are in debt, you have borrowed money from an outside source (for example, a credit card company, an automobile dealership, or a bank) with the promise to not only pay back the original borrowed amount (the principal) but also pay to the lender a charge for borrowing the money at a certain percentage rate (interest).

Three out of five U.S. households have an average credit card balance of more than $11,000. Paying only minimum payments at 24 percent interest, it would take twenty-two years to pay it off—and you would pay more than $47,000 in interest.

To help you understand more about money and how to get out of debt, you need to consider these areas:

- How interest works against you or for you
- Good debt and bad debt
- Creating a budget
- Sticking to a budget
- Refocusing your priorities

Famous American essayist Ralph Waldo Emerson said, "A man in debt is so far a slave." Getting into debt or living beyond your means does more than affect your credit rating, it affects your life. Statistics show one of the primary causes of divorce is financial problems. Choosing to spend today and pay tomorrow will indenture your future. As you gain control of your money, you will be free to move forward with the changes you want to make in your life.

The average college graduate has nearly $20,000 in debt; average credit card debt has increased 47 percent between 1989 and 2004 for twenty-five- to thirty-four-year-olds, and 11 percent for eighteen- to twenty-four-year-olds. Nearly one in five eighteen- to twenty-four-year-olds is in "debt hardship," up from 12 percent in 1989.

How Interest Works Against You or for You

Simple interest is the type of interest used for most consumer loans. The original amount of the loan is your principal. For example, if you bought a washing machine for $1,000 and put no money down, your principal would be $1,000. The interest accrued or accumulated is calculated by counting the number of days since your last principal payment multiplied by your daily interest factor on the outstanding balance. Here's an example:

Loan balance or principal = **$1,000**
Interest charge = **13%**
Your first payment = **$50**
Number of days since last principal balance payment = **30**
Daily interest factor ($1,000 x 13% /365) = **$0.36** (So, you pay 36 cents a day interest.)
Amount of interest owed (30 days x $0.36) = **$10.80**
Amount of your payment that goes toward the principal ($50–$10.80) = **$39.20**
New loan balance after payment ($1,000–$39.20) = **$960.80**

If you continue making payments of about $50 every month, it will take you approximately two years to pay off your loan and during that time you will have spent an additional $141 on interest payments. If, however, you make payments of $90 every month, it will take you half the time to pay off your loan and you will have only spent approximately $72 on interest payments.

FACT

The average American with a credit file is responsible for $15,788 in debt, excluding mortgages, according to Experian, a credit reporting bureau.

The longer you take to pay off your loans and the smaller the amounts you pay toward the principal, the more money you pay in interest. An amortization table can show you how long it will take you to pay off your loan and how much interest you will pay during that period. You can find amortization calculators online, and many banking websites also offer them. You can use these not only to determine how quickly you can pay off your current debt, but also to get a realistic grasp of how much it's actually going to cost you to borrow.

Interest can work for you, too. If you have a checking or savings account that earns interest, the money you have deposited in it is growing. However, before you start putting money into a savings account earning 4 percent interest, be sure you are not maintaining a balance on a credit card at 16 percent interest. You are actually losing money by not paying off the credit card first. Only after eliminating debt should you put your money into a savings account, with the exception of allowing a small amount to be saved in case of emergencies.

Good Debt versus Bad Debt

Are their good reasons to go into debt? Certainly! If you are investing in something that will increase in value, like a home, a business, or even student loans, that is good debt. If you take out a home equity loan to pay off a higher-interest credit card, that's a good debt because your home equity loan will generally have a lower rate and will be tax-deductible. However, be careful you don't spend your home's equity on bad debt like a vacation, new furniture, or other items that will not increase or retain value. Most consumer debt, i.e., credit cards, is bad debt. A good rule to live by is "if you can't afford to pay off your credit card at the end of the month, you can't afford to make a purchase."

ALERT

It's important to know your credit score. Your credit score will dictate how much borrowing money will cost you. Each of the three main credit bureaus offers free reports each year. To get a free report, go to the website set up in accordance with the Fair and Accurate Credit Transactions Act (FACT Act) (*www.annualcreditreport.com*).

Cars

Automobiles are another area where people make poor financial decisions. You should consider how much car you really can afford. You should also consider that over the first year of ownership, some cars depreciate at a rate as high as 35 percent. You can find the value of a car at websites like Kelley Blue Book (*www.kbb.com*) or Edmunds (*www.edmunds.com*).

Weigh the pros and cons of new car ownership; is a new car warranty worth the cost of depreciation? Can you find a used car that is still within the original manufacturer's warranty, yet because it's used, it will depreciate at a slower rate? How much money can you put down on the car, and how much will you have to borrow? What will the cost (interest) on the loan be? When you combine interest and depreciation, will your car be the value you thought it was?

QUESTION

What is the depreciation on a used car?
According to Safecarguide.com, the yearly rate of depreciation on a used car is anywhere from 7 percent to 12 percent. More specific information depends on the model and make of the car, as well as the mileage.

Creating a Budget

The first step to getting out of debt is to see where you spend your money. If you find you have more bills than money at the end of the month but don't understand where it all went, a budget is an essential step. However, a budget will do you absolutely no good if you create it and file it away. You need to make daily entries into your budget until you have better control of your finances.

The first step in creating your budget is to pull together all of your financial information. This includes paycheck stubs, bank statements, bills, and any other expense or income. Sort these into several piles: income, weekly expense, monthly expense, quarterly expense, and annual expense. The weekly expenses might be things like gasoline for your car, the cost of baby-sitting, or grocery shopping. A monthly expense might be a utility bill or credit card payment. A quarterly expense might be your garbage or water bill. And an annual expense might be your property taxes or vehicle registration.

First, create a list for income. In one column place the source of income; in the next column place the amount. If you are self-employed and your income can be variable, always use the most conservative amount. Don't forget to deduct self-employment taxes and any other fees you pay from your income. If you receive a regular paycheck, you should only count your net income, or the amount you receive after the taxes and other deductions are subtracted.

The next list will include your weekly expenses. This list will have three columns. In the first column, record the name of each expense; remember to include even the smallest items, like the cost of your morning coffee or the amount you spend for lunch each day. In the second column, record your estimated cost for these expenses. Fill in the third column at the end of the week, when you tally your actual expenses and compare them to the second column.

Create lists for your monthly, quarterly, and annual expenses in the same way. Remember to include things like car insurance, dry-cleaning costs, veterinary costs, entertainment, and anywhere else you spend money. Make sure to include every expense, no matter how small. Paying a few dollars a day for a coffee may not seem like a budget-buster, but it's small costs like this that add up to big numbers!

Look at your expenses and see which ones are fixed (the amount is always the same, like a mortgage payment) and which ones are variable (the amount is changing, like a grocery bill). Highlight the expenses that are variable.

Now, add up the columns. If you find yourself in a situation where your expenses exceed your income, you need to look at your variable expenses and see which ones can be altered. You can also look at some of the luxury expenses, like cable television, entertainment, or other non-essential charges, and decide which ones to eliminate. You need to put yourself in a situation where you are in control of your money, not the other way around.

If you find that you have eliminated all nonessential bills and have cut your variable expenses as much as you can, and you still have more expenses than income, you need to make some serious decisions. Talk to your creditors to see if you can reduce your payments for the time being. Most creditors will want to work with you if they know you are trying.

Look at alternatives in some of your expenses. When was the last time you had your insurance policy updated? Could there be a savings in switching providers? Are you shopping at low-cost, no-frills grocery stores? Are you purchasing expensive convenience foods, or are you buying less-expensive ingredients to make meals from scratch? Are you buying costly items like soft drinks, packaged bakery goods, and bottled water that you might be able to do without?

ALERT

Three in ten Americans age twenty-five and over report they have not saved any money for retirement (29 percent of workers and retirees). Of these, 79 percent of workers and 60 percent of retirees say this is because they cannot or could not afford to save.

Finally, you need to keep a daily record of any money you spend. A small notebook or even an index card is fine for this purpose. Every time you make a purchase, from a candy bar at the newsstand or a pair of nylons at the store or even giving the paperboy a tip; you need to write down the amount. At the end of the week, sort these amounts into the categories you've already created in your budget. Add the amounts to see if the estimate you placed in the first column when you created your budget is realistic or if you underestimated your spending habits. If you are like most people, you will be amazed at the amount of money that flows through your hand without conscious thought. If you are spending more than is budgeted, you need to curb your impulse spending, because that is the only way you are going to get out of debt.

Maintain your daily record keeping for at least a month, so you have a good indication of where your money is going.

Sticking to a Budget

Creating a budget is easy. Sticking to a budget is much more difficult. But, if you have a goal in mind, any sacrifices you make will be worth it.

First, be sure that both you and your spouse agree to the new budget. Your budget will not work if one of you is not on board. You need to support each other and work toward your goal together.

Be creative. Find new ways to save money and get excited about it. Rather than going to the movies, rent a movie and pop your own popcorn. Try shopping at resale shops rather than at the mall. Make a list when you go to the store, and stick to the list!

Be frugal. Look at the ways you might be wasting money. Do you leave the lights on in unoccupied rooms? Do you use energy-efficient lighting? Do you run hot water longer than necessary? Do you throw away leftovers every week when you clean out your refrigerator?

If your goal is to eventually live off-grid, you need to not only be frugal, but also resourceful. Think of ways you might be able to add to your income in order to get out of debt. Do you have a hobby or skill that could produce income? Are there part-time job opportunities that would work into your schedule? Are there items in your home that could be sold on Craigslist or eBay?

Make sure your budget is revisited often. The worst thing you can do is to create your budget and then forget about it. You need to be diligent and wise when it comes to your personal finances if you ever want to be independent.

Refocusing Your Priorities

Now that you've set up your budget, you need to work on a plan to ensure you get out and stay out of debt. First, you need to realize that until you are out of debt, you don't have extra spending money. Just because you paid off one bill does not mean the money budgeted for that bill is now free for spending. The next step is a debt elimination calendar.

To create a debt elimination calendar, go back to your budget and create a list of all of the bills that are creditors rather than monthly expenses. For example, a consumer credit card would be a creditor, and an electric bill would be a monthly expense. Decide which creditor you want to pay off first. You can determine that by either who would be the quickest to be paid off, or, perhaps, who has the highest interest rate.

Create a table, either on a piece of paper or in a spreadsheet, listing the creditor on top of the column and the payments needed to pay them off below. Then list all of your creditors in the order you would like to pay them off, in subsequent columns. Start them all off with at least the minimum payment due. If you have extra money, use it to pay off your first creditor. List the monthly payment underneath the creditor's name on the sheet. When the first creditor is paid off, move the payment amount from that column and add it to the payment amount for the next creditor. With the extra money going to the second creditor, calculate when that creditor will be paid off and add both sums (the first creditor's payment and the second creditor's payment) to the payment of the third creditor. Continue your calculations until you have finished your debt elimination calendar. If you are consistent in your payments and do not charge anything else on credit, you will be able to successfully pay off your debt.

Setting Reasonable Goals

As you pay off your debt, it is important for you and your spouse to set short- and long-term goals. By setting goals, you will remind yourself of the ultimate reward for getting out of debt. Every time you save money or eliminate a creditor, you are getting closer to your goal.

ESSENTIAL

Effective goals follow these basic rules: be positive in your goal statements, write down your goal and put it where you can see it every day, be specific when setting your goals so you can track your success, and set realistic goals.

Short-term goals are those you can accomplish within several months or under a year. As you read through the rest of this book, think about realistic goals you can set that will move you closer to your ultimate goal of living off the grid. A short-term goal could be learning to cook using basic ingredients, or attending an alternative energy fair. Create goals you can accomplish as you work your way out of debt.

Long-term goals generally take a year or more to accomplish. A long-term goal could be purchasing a piece of property or installing an alternate energy source in your home. You can have several short-term goals leading up to your long-term goal. For example, researching the costs of solar panels and how to install them could be a short-term goal that complements your long-term goal of installing an alternate energy source.

Long-term goals should excite you and give you the incentive to work hard and sacrifice in order to realize them. Long-term goals can be as soon as a year or two away, or can be as far as five years away. Setting a goal for more than five years can be a deterrent to your day-to-day efforts because the realization of the goal can seem so far away. If you believe you need more than five years to reach your goal, be sure to set some stepping-stone mid-term goals to help you stay on task and motivated.

Either way, it is important that you create goals you can reasonably accomplish, but also set goals that are challenging. Nothing takes the wind out of your sails faster than failing to meet a goal. You don't want to get discouraged and abandon the whole effort. Paying off the remainder of your thirty-year mortgage in two years is unrealistic and an unfair burden to place on yourself and your family. However, placing a goal like paying off your $5,000 credit card debt in five years makes a mockery of your efforts. Although you shouldn't be creating goals that will discourage you, goals should make you stretch and challenge you. Aim for the most you can do.

Off-Grid Living as an Escape Hatch

Although not many people take it to this extreme, it must be mentioned that moving off-grid is not an escape hatch for your financial or personal woes. Leaving the grid and living a self-sufficient life does not excuse you from any debt that you have accrued, or any problems that you have caused in your current life. You are ultimately responsible for credit cards, student loans, mortgages, child support, alimony, and all other debts (including any loans on which you were a co-signer), and it is vital that you resolve these issues before embarking on your new life.

If you are planning to move off-grid to avoid paying bills or eliminating your obligation to your debtors, think again, and think long and hard about your reasons. The fact that you no longer rely on public utilities and food sources does not forgive your previous debt; you are always obligated by law to repay what you have borrowed, and as such will suffer the penalties for nonpayment for any loans on which you have defaulted or ceased payment with no communication. The penalties can be as minor as a lien on your property until the debt is repaid, or as severe as jail. Living off-grid is all about self-sufficiency—you are not self-sufficient if you have obligations chained to you. Hiding off-grid does not eliminate previous debt. Knowing this, do you still want to make that life change?

If your finances are in trouble and you still want to pursue the off-grid life, but you are sensing no feasible way to do so in a timely manner, you should consult a professional financial planner or set up an appointment with a credit counselor. As said before, creditors may be willing to work with you if they know you are trying to resolve your debt honestly.

CHAPTER 3

Generating Income Off the Grid

Unless you have an ample pension or a large savings or investment portfolio, or if you are still going to keep a regular job, you are going to have to find some way to earn money even if you are living off the grid. The reality is, even if you are totally self-sufficient, there is no escaping expenses like property taxes. This chapter will give you ideas on creating income.

How Much Does It Cost to Go Off-Grid?

Many years ago the United States government offered free land in order to increase the population in certain areas of the county. But, under the Federal Land Policy and Management Act of 1976 (FLPMA), the federal government took over ownership of public lands and repealed all remaining traces of the Homestead Act of 1862, but it did grant a ten-year extension on claims in Alaska. However, there are communities in places like Kansas, North Dakota, Minnesota, and Nebraska that are willing to give up a parcel of land, provided you meet the right criteria. But these are parcels within a community, not farmland in the countryside.

FACT

Congress passed the Homestead Act and created the Department of Agriculture, the transcontinental railroad, and the land grant college system all within two months of one another (May–July 1862).

One of the first expenses you will encounter when you move off-grid is the purchase price of your land. The first three rules of real estate are location, location, and location. This is also true when estimating the cost of your property. You can spend from $25,000 to $2,500,000 depending on the number of acres, location of the property, and condition and size of the home.

Add to that initial expense any updating to the house, outbuildings, septic system, and alternate energy sources. Of course, these things don't have to happen all at once. But, you should budget enough to ensure your home is in good shape. You will also have to purchase supplies like seed, livestock, animal feed, and whatever equipment you decide is necessary to work your land. Be very realistic when you prepare a budget for your new move and then add 20 percent for those little surprises that always seem to crop up at the last moment.

The bottom line is this: it is not cheap or free to move off grid. Despite the view of "the simple life," an off-grid life needs to be built from the bottom up. Unfortunately, those who start out thinking they can move off the grid on a shoestring budget are often those who give up their dreams and move back to the city. With a little advance planning, however, you can successfully earn a good income while living off the grid.

Generating Income

When you're looking for a method of earning income as you begin your new off-grid life, you need to look out of the box. First, consider your current employer. Is there a way to take what you do for them to a home office? Perhaps you could commute to the office several days a month, but do the rest of your work at home. Perhaps you could transfer from being an employee to becoming a consultant. If you've done a good job and have a good work history, you might be surprised at some of the options employers are willing to offer you. A word of caution: if your employer is downsizing and looking for opportunities to lay off employees, don't explore this option unless you have something to fall back on if he says no.

Your next option is to do a self-assessment and consider the talents you have and how you might be able to market them. In today's world of virtual offices and rapid Internet connections, there is an amazing number of options for employment.

Are you Internet savvy? Website designers, graphic artists, copywriters, and even bloggers are just some of the Internet-based jobs available. Study a local Craigslist Help Wanted section to view the variety of virtual employment opportunities.

ALERT

If you are going to run your own business, don't forget business expenses: Keep receipts and good records of business travel and other expenses including office supplies, postage and shipping costs, dues, subscriptions, and anything else business-related, including computer software for your business and upgrades to your system.

Are there classes you can take, either online or through your local community college, to hone some skills in order to create an online consulting business?

Perhaps as you review your skills, you find you have skills that are more down-to-earth. Are you handy around the house? Do you have excellent carpentry, painting, remodeling, or plumbing skills? These skills are very much in demand, especially as baby boomers age and need help around their homes.

Are you an excellent cook or baker? Can you build a kitchen in your home that can be FDA certified so you can provide baked goods to local restaurants or gift shops? Can you start a catering business?

How about accounting skills? Do you have the background to start a bookkeeping service for local businesses?

As you look at these options, be sure you study the area where you are going to be relocating. Speak to the Chamber of Commerce and the local Extension office to get ideas about the needs of the community. Speak to the director of a nearby senior center to discern the need for a handyperson or other services the senior community might desire.

Be creative as you explore your options for income so it meshes with your new lifestyle.

Bartering and Dealing

One of the oldest methods of commerce is bartering. The late James Harvey Stout wrote that bartering was in its third cycle in the United States during the early 1980s. The first cycle was the colonial era: "During the seventeenth and eighteenth centuries, money was scarce, so the colonists relied primarily on bartering, with commodities such as beaver pelts, corn, musket balls, nails, tobacco, and deer skins (from which we get our modern slang, "buck," for the word "dollar"). Colonists also used the money of other cultures—the Native Americans' wampum (which consisted of beads made from shells), and the coins of foreign countries."

The second era of bartering happened during the Great Depression. During the 1930s, money was scarce, so people established barter groups like the Unemployed Citizens League of Denver (with 34,000 members) and the National Development Association. The League was developed by Charles Dunwoody Strong, a community activist whose own business, an architectural practice, folded in 1929. He modeled the League after a similar organization in Seattle. An excerpt from his biography at the Colorado Historical Society gives a little more insight into the League:

The organization sought to relieve the distress of the unemployed and underemployed through cooperative production. Meetings were held in mortuaries because schools were closed in the summer and churches were reluctant to open their doors to the unusual, and in some eyes, questionable organization.

Membership surged. In 1932, Strong met with the governor, labor leaders, and veterans' groups to plan an "economic takeover" of the state upon the reelection of President Hoover. With the election of Franklin Roosevelt, the initiation of his New Deal programs, and the subsequent relief of some economic suffering, interest and membership in the League wavered.

According to Stout, the third era of bartering began in the early 1980s. During the long recession, bartering resurfaced and was featured in many magazine articles and many new books. Barter clubs were created throughout the nation. More companies learned about the advertising industry's "trade-outs," international commerce's "countertrade," and the other possibilities for bartering in business.

ESSENTIAL

When you barter, have a clear idea of what you need ahead of time. Offer a concise description of the goods or services you need and the goods of services you can offer. Have your description slimmed down to a sentence or two.

Arguably, you can see a fourth era of bartering regaining popularity as websites like Craigslist.com offer items for trade, and e-mail services like Freecycle.com offer members the opportunity to trade for items no longer used or needed by other members. In an off-the-grid situation, you can barter produce, services, eggs, milk, or anything that has value with neighbors.

The key to successful bartering is to be sure that you offer equal value for whatever you are bartering for. Bartering does not have to be limited to your locale. An interesting experiment in bartering was documented at One Red Paper Clip blog. Kyle MacDonald started with one red paper clip and ends up with a house. Although this is not a common occurrence, you will be able to see how bartering can work, especially in today's economy.

Farmers' Markets and Other Local Produce

One of the first things you should do when you decide where you are going to purchase your off-the-grid property is to have a conversation with the local Extension agent. Through the Cooperative Extension System, you will be able to learn not only which crops grow best in your area, but also the specific type of seed you should use. You can learn which crops are cash crops in your area, those that you can sell to local restaurants and grocery stores or are in demand at farmers' markets. You will also learn whether there is an overage of certain crops on the market, so you'll know to only grow enough of those for your family.

FACT

According to the USDA, between the years 2009 and 2010 there was a 16 percent increase in the number of farmers' markets in the United States. The number grew from 5,274 to 6,132.

The Extension agent can also give you information about local farmers' markets, including the dates they start and the hours they run. Like anything else, you want to be sure you receive enough return on your investment. If the local farmers' markets do not offer a lot of foot traffic, you might want to look at markets in neighboring communities.

Many restaurants, and even grocery stores, will contract with local farmers for fresh eggs, local cheese, fresh produce, and even canned goods like preserves and relishes. Once again, your local Extension agent will be able to guide you in the right direction, but don't be afraid to make some contacts of your own; locally produced food is gaining more popularity.

When you bring your produce to the farmers' market, be sure it is presented in an appealing manner. You are competing with all of the other farmers, so be sure your produce is fresh, properly cleaned, and displayed to the best advantage. Little things, like placing your produce in baskets with gingham cloth on a clean table, can pull a potential buyer from another booth to your booth. Pay attention to the prices of the produce around you. You don't necessarily have to underprice your produce, but if your prices for the same produce are much higher, you won't get the sale. Look into the requirements in your area to be able to call your produce "organic." Some states require a several-year process showing that no chemicals had been used on your land. Other states' rules are not as rigid. Having organic produce will bring a premium price for you.

ALERT

Rich Pirog of the Leopold Center for Sustainable Agriculture reports that the average fresh food item on your dinner table travels 1,500 miles to get there. Buying locally produced food eliminates the need for all that fuel-guzzling transportation.

Craft Sales

Whether you are handy with a camera, a quilter's thimble, or a paintbrush, there is a demand for high-quality artisanal work. Some communities actually have stores that promote their local crafters and sell their work on consignment.

If you are an accomplished crafter, you can take samples of your work to local specialty and gift stores and see if they are willing to sell your products. You can also think of other places, like small cafés and beauty parlors that have the right demographic for your product, and ask if they would be willing to sell products for you. Remember, any of these places of business will expect a portion of the sales, so price your crafts accordingly.

Craft shows are another way to sell your work. Except for the dates of the show, there are no obligations regarding your time. You will find that one of the nice things about participating in arts and crafts fairs is the direct contact you will have with your marketplace. You can use a fair as a market research area to test new products, designs, price changes, and booth displays. If your work doesn't sell, you will have immediate marketplace data to help you hone your products.

You can do one or two events and walk away with a minimum of expense of time and money, or you can do shows every month and take up the craft-fair lifestyle, making it the mainstay of your business.

As opposed to selling through an Internet site, when you sell to the public you keep the entire amount of the sales, minus expenses. Most of the craft shows are held on weekends, so selling in this way would not interfere with any other job you might have or your time for creating new products.

You can find out about shows through several resources. One source, an online resource called Art & Craft Show Yellow Pages is at *www.artscrafts showbusiness.com*. It lists show listings, articles, and links. Other resources can be found by searching for "craft show locations" on the Internet. And finally, another source of art and craft shows will be your state arts council.

When you apply to a show, there is generally a booth fee associated with the application. To ensure you are not wasting your money, before you apply, you should visit a show, read reviews in the show guides, and talk to other crafters who have participated at the show. Some important information to gather is the size of the show (the larger the show, the larger the crowds), the facility provided (whether it is an indoor or outdoor show), the amount of promotion and how the show is advertised, the security arrangements, and the kinds of craft exhibited. The last point is very important, because if your crafts are high-end sculptures and the other crafts are crocheted toilet-roll covers, you are not going to find buyers interested in spending the kind of money that will make your time at the show worthwhile.

When selecting shows, be sure to choose the kind of event that will attract your kind of buyers. Shows vary greatly, from fine arts shows that might accept jewelry, but may not allow craft items, to juried art and crafts fairs.

A juried show is often the type that reaps the most benefit for you, because all entrants' work is submitted to be judged by a jury committee, which then selects the best products from the hundreds of entries. Because items are judged, the crafts displayed tend to be better quality and higher priced. Buyers realize they will be paying for premium quality work and therefore will pay top dollar.

Country craft fairs are on the other end of the spectrum. The crafts exhibited at these fair are moderately priced—from $2 to $50. These shows encompass things like local Christmas bazaars; they feature small, inexpensive gift items. You should try to find a local craft guild in your area to learn more about the local shows and to network with other crafters.

Online Store

When trying to sell products or services, you are no longer limited by geographic locale. The Internet provides a myriad of opportunities for you to showcase and sell your products. Creating your own website is a great idea if you have experience in web design and search engine optimization, or if you have the ability to pay someone who has those talents. Because the Internet is vast and many hosting services are providing websites either free or nearly free, new sites are popping up all over the place. Unfortunately, if you have a poorly designed website or a site that looks like an amateur created it, it will reflect badly on the products you are offering.

ALERT

Use social networking to help you sell! In a study conducted by social networking site myYearbook.com, 81 percent of respondents said they'd received advice from friends and followers relating to a product purchase through a social site; 74 percent of those who received such advice found it to be influential in their decision.

Search engine optimization (SEO) is the science of placing keywords throughout your site in order to have your site show up as one of the first responses to a search. For example, with SEO, if you sell homemade soap and someone searched for "homemade soap," you would be competing with about 470,000 entries. If your site appears even halfway up the list, chances are no one is going to find you. Search engine optimization enhances your ability to move up the list.

There are programs available that can help you set up a shopping cart on your site. The price of the software is often tied to the functionality of the product, but a simple shopping cart program can start as low as $20 a month.

Another thing you need to consider is how will you ensure a secure transaction once someone has placed an item in the shopping cart. There are only a small number of secure payment services that allow you to accept credit card and electronic check payments quickly and affordably. Because it is so easy to steal credit card and banking information, if you want to have an online store, you must have a secure payment area. You can also consider vendors like PayPal, but you should consider the cost of the service and how much that will take from your bottom line.

If you don't want to go to the expense of creating your own website, you can sell your products through a number of other sites. Although you may be familiar with eBay, you may not know about Etsy (*www.etsy.com*). Etsy specializes in offering handmade and vintage products from people all around the world. Founded in 2005, it now boasts thousands of sellers. One of the remarkable features of this website is the ability for buyers to find sellers in their own communities. So, not only can you reach out to the world, your local buyers can find you too. Etsy.com is also a good place to browse to get ideas for handmade items you could create and get a measurement of how you can price them.

There are a number of websites that offer services similar to Etsy.com. Just do a search on "buy and sell online craft stores" and decide which site, or which number of sites, works best for you.

CHAPTER 4

There's No Place Like Home

One of the biggest decisions you will make when choosing to move off grid is where, exactly, you are going to move. Many details should factor into this decision: price, climate, location, geographical issues, and population. This is not a decision to be made lightly because this, hopefully, will be a place where you will stay for the rest of your life. This chapter will explore the particulars of choosing the right piece of property for you and your family.

The Perfect Piece of Land

When you are looking for a piece of property, make a list of the features you will need. Are you planning on growing crops or raising livestock? Do you need some acreage in trees to feed your wood-burning stove? Do you need level fields for planting, or hilly pastures for grazing? Do you want a water source, like a pond or creek, on your property? Does the property have out-buildings like a barn or stables on it already, or are you willing to build your own?

Determine the acreage needed for tillable land and pasture. Make sure you understand the soil composition in your prospective property—is it sandy, clay, silty, or loamy? This will make a difference in the kinds of crops you decide to grow. Look to the future. As you consider your property, ask yourself if there is room for eventual expansion, should you choose to add to your property.

Understand your water rights. In many states, even though the water runs through your property, you don't own the rights to it. You may also find you don't own the rights to drill for water on your property. Obviously, these are good things to know before you buy. Last, but not least, consider your alternative energy needs. Is this property in an area that has enough sunlight for solar, enough wind for turbines, or is it located in an area where geothermal heating is an option?

Some other areas you should consider as you look for your ideal piece of property are:

- Geographical perks
- Geographical warning signs
- Paying for your property
- Temporary housing
- Building your own shelter

Once you've read through these topics and developed a realistic budget, you should be able to start your search.

Geographical Perks

As you look for your property, you can also look for extra geographical perks that give you more for your money. Many of these perks will make life for you and your family much easier.

- **Natural gas wells:** Did you know there is land all across the United States that has private natural gas wells that have been in use for decades? These wells have been used to not only supply heat and cooking fuel, but they also can be leased to natural gas companies and earn an income for the property owner.
- **Microclimates:** A microclimate is the climate of a section different from the surrounding sections. It may be warmer or colder, wetter or drier, or more or less susceptible to frosts. The USDA Hardiness Zone Map will often show you if your potential property is located within a microclimate. But you also need to be aware that you can have even smaller patches of microclimates in different parts of your property. For example, a protected spot on the south side of your house may actually be a zone warmer than an exposed spot on the north side. Talk to your Extension agent to learn more about the microclimates in your area.

FACT

San Francisco is a city with microclimates and submicroclimates. Due to the city's varied topography and influence from the prevailing summer marine layer or winds that come off the ocean, weather conditions can vary by as much as 9°F (5°C) from block to block.

- **Artesian aquifer:** An artesian aquifer is an aquifer, or underground river, that is confined between layers of rock. Because it is confined, the water is under pressure, which causes the groundwater to flow upward through a well without the need for pumping. If the pressure is high enough, the water may even reach the ground surface, and then it's called a flowing artesian well.

- **Natural boundaries:** Mountains, rivers, forests, and lakes can be wonderful "fences" to secure the edges of your property. Not only do natural boundaries protect your real estate investment and ensure you will not have encroaching neighbors, they also provide a natural secure periphery to your property.

Geographical Warning Signs

As you decide on your property location, the general feel of the land and condition of the house and outbuildings are not the only things about which you should be concerned. You should look at any geographical threats in your area.

- **Active earthquake faults:** You can find out about earthquakes and faults all over the world by accessing the U.S. Geological Survey website at *earthquake.usgs.gov/earthquakes/world/*.
- **Floodplains:** The Federal Emergency Management Agency (FEMA) is the agency in the United States that maps and delineates floodplains. Just because your piece of property hasn't experienced a flood in the past doesn't mean it won't in the future. Although you might have heard about 100-year floods, flood risk isn't just based on history anymore. Unfortunately, many of our wetlands have disappeared due to urban spread. Because those places the water used to naturally flow into are gone, the water is forced to seek other outlets further upstream. You can go to the FEMA website to order floodplain maps (*www.fema.gov*).
- **Landslides, mudslides, avalanches, and alluvial fans:** Hillsides, hilltops, and basins are very popular places for building homes; unfortunately there are some geographical hazards to watch for in these areas. Landslides are caused by several factors: water saturation, slope degeneration due to construction or erosion, soil deterioration due to freezing, thawing or the loss of cover vegetation, trembling from earthquakes and aftershocks, and volcanic eruptions. Mudslides are fast-moving landslides generally associated with steeper terrain. Mudslides start out as shallow landslides, but gain momentum and debris as they race downhill. Unfortunately, it is common for mudslides to pick up rocks, boulders, trees, and even cars.

Avalanches develop or build up on slopes between 25 and 55 degrees and start on slopes that have reached between 35 and 45 degrees. Avalanches generally occur after a significant snowfall covers a steeply inclined mountain that already has a considerable snowpack. If the new layer of snow does not bond to the original layer, there is a danger of an avalanche. Not every new snowfall triggers an avalanche; other factors include temperature, angle of the mountain, wind direction and speed, and type of snow.

ALERT

Landslides can vary in size. They can be as small as the movement of a single boulder in a minor rockfall or as big as thousands of tons of earth and debris that fall to the bottom of a slope or a cliff. Every year, landslides in the United States cause approximately $3.5 billion in damage, and kill between twenty-five and fifty people.

One of the best ways to determine whether your property has the potential for any of these geographical hazards is to look for an alluvial fan. From the sky, alluvial fans look like a river of sediment—sand, silt, gravel, and often larger objects—running down the side of a mountain that end up fanning out at the base of a mountain or hill. Sometimes these fans are so large, it's hard to see them from the ground, and so you should use something like Google Earth to view your prospective piece of property. Alluvial fans are geographical markers indicating that a landslide, mudslide, or avalanche has occurred in that area, and, if the conditions are repeated, can occur again.

Paying for Your Property

Now that you've located your property of choice, how do you plan on buying it? If you are looking at a piece of land and are planning to build, you need to understand that in today's financial climate, getting a loan for a piece of land is often much harder than getting a loan for a home. For land purchases you have three options:

Cash

The best way to purchase land is to have cash. Not only are cash purchases clear-cut and uncomplicated, you also have more bargaining power when you can pay in cash. If you pay with cash, you will not have a loan payment or additional interest added to the cost of the property.

Seller Financing

Quite often, when a seller is offering a piece of land, unlike a home, he has some financial options in the sale. Often sellers are willing to finance your purchase. This transaction works well for both of you; the seller will be able to earn a higher rate of interest than he would at most banks and you will be able to make payments to the seller rather than to a bank. Although seller financing might seem like a nice, friendly transaction, both you and the seller should be sure that expectations and terms are very clear and in writing. You need to have a lawyer help you with the purchase documents to ensure, for example, that you hold title to the land, but the owner holds a lien on your property. You need to have in writing who is responsible for any property taxes and what happens to the property should you default, or if either seller or buyer should die. Seller financing can offer you some interesting and beneficial options, but be sure to protect yourself and your investment.

Bank Financing

If you are going to approach a bank about financing land, you will need to have detailed information about your plans for the land. You will need to have information about zoning, soil samples, easements, and your building plans. A local bank is going to be your best chance at financing land. Local banks invest in their communities and can be more open to the needs of their customers. However, if you plan to finance your land, you will need a fairly substantial down payment. Many banks will require anywhere from 20 to 50 percent down. You will also be subject to higher interest rates than you would with a mortgage because land financing is riskier. Once you build your home, you can approach the bank about refinancing the loan as part of a traditional mortgage.

Traditional Mortgages

If you find that you will not be able to pay cash or come up with a large down payment, your credit isn't strong enough for conventional financing, and your seller is not interested in holding a note, another option is to buy a piece of property that has an existing home on it. That way, it will be easier to get financing. If you are in a rural area, you might be eligible for certain United States Department of Agriculture (USDA) Farm Service Agency (FSA) loans. Even if the home is not exactly what you want, you can either renovate the existing home or build another on the same property. Before you start looking for property, you should visit with a trusted banker and see what kind of loan and the amount of loan the bank would be willing to make to you. Having this information in hand gives you better bargaining power because you are prequalified. Sellers are more apt to go with a lower bid on property if they are assured the buyer will be able to get financing.

Temporary Housing

Once you buy your property, you might need some temporary housing until you've finished building your new home. Whether you've hired a contractor to build your home for you, or you've decided to build it yourself, you should always assume the worst when it comes to a building schedule. It's better to count on not getting into your house until the spring than to be living in insufficient temporary housing midwinter.

The first step in finding temporary housing is to determine your budget and your needs. If you are building in a temperate climate you might be able to get along with a less substantial shelter. However, if you are facing a cold winter or damp spring, you will want to be sure your temporary housing is well insulated and suited for your conditions.

Recycled Options

Recycling can not only save you money, but it also diminishes your carbon footprint by reusing and repurposing items already created. Consider using 20-foot or 40-foot shipping containers for housing. Solid and often insulated, these large metal boxes can provide you with many options for housing. There are a variety of websites with images and ideas for shipping-container homes. One that has garnered a lot of attention is the site run by Keith Dewey, owner and designer of Zigloo.ca, at *http://zigloo.ca/zigloo _domestique_hd*. A website called Greenupgrader.com gives directions for creating a home from pallets (*http://greenupgrader.com/2387/recycled-pallet-house-disaster-relief-housing*) for temporary housing. There are also prefabricated temporary shelters made from recycled materials that can be purchased for under $10,000.

FACT

Shipping containers can be readily modified to accommodate a range of creature comforts and can be connected and stacked to create modular, efficient spaces for a fraction of the cost, labor, and resources of more conventional materials.

Mobile Homes and Trailers

Mobile homes and trailers are another option for temporary housing while your home is being built. You can purchase a used mobile home or trailer and move it to your property and have all the comforts of home. There are websites that advertise used mobile homes across the country, like MHBay.com at *www.mhbay.com*. There are also companies that rent mobile homes and trailers, like Pope Housing (*www.popehousing.com*), that specialize in temporary housing for people whose houses have been destroyed by fire or natural disaster or who are building a new home and want to live on their property.

Tents and Yurts

Depending on your location, you might be able to temporarily live in a large tent, like an army surplus tent. Tents are often used for temporary housing after a disaster. Many new tents offer cut-outs that allow you to place a small stove and stack within the tent. Some off-gridders in Hawaii have successfully lived in tents for years.

A yurt is a round structure, somewhat like a tent, that is generally made of a feltlike material laid over a frame lattice of wood or bamboo. Yurts were traditionally used by nomadic tribes in Central Asia and can be used in all climates. Yurts vary in cost, depending on the manufacturer and your specific needs, but a 30-foot-diameter yurt can cost less than $10,000. To learn more about yurts, go to Yurtinfo.org at *www.yurtinfo.org*.

QUESTION

Can I stay warm in a yurt?
Yes. The shape of the yurt is very thermally efficient. A large yurt can be easily kept warm using a small wood-burning stove down to 23°F without any additional insulation. In Central Asia, layers of thick felt keep the yurt warm as the outside temperature drops well below -40°F.

Building Your Own Shelter

The first thing you need to decide when it comes to building your shelter is whether you are going to do it yourself or hire a contractor. If you have the skill set to do the job, including experience in the construction trades, building your own home can be a fulfilling experience. If you do not have the experience, you can make costly mistakes. However, there are many sources available to help you work through the process of building your own off-grid home.

Since you are building to live off-grid, you want a home that is energy efficient and as green as possible. Earthship Biotecture *(http://earthship .com)* provides an entire website explaining how to use recycled materials to create a self-sustaining green home. Using used tires as a base for foundations and walls, the architects at Earthship have developed technologies from solar lighting to geothermal heating to wastewater management that can be built into your off-grid home.

Greenhomebuilding.com *(www.greenhomebuilding.com)* offers potential off-grid homeowners "a wide range of information about sustainable architecture and natural building." Through this website, you can learn about alternative, natural building materials like sod, compressed earth, plaster, straw, tires, recycled paper, cans, bottles, cordwood, and even corn cobs. You can also find building plans and reviews of books about green and recycled building options.

If done correctly, your off-grid home will not look like a traditional home found in most neighborhoods. Off-grid homes are often built into the land to take advantage of passive geothermal heating and cooling. They often have windows on the south side of the house, to add in passive solar capture, but don't have windows on the north side because of heat loss. Very often, off-grid homes are more compact, so you are not heating extra space. However, off-grid homes can also be works of architectural beauty, expressing your unique tastes.

CHAPTER 5

Family Needs

When you move off the grid with your family, there are many things you need to consider. Schooling is probably the primary cause for concern. Are you able and willing to homeschool your children or are you going to rely on the local public school system for your child's education? Many places that are suitable for off-grid living don't have the best educational systems. Do you have a predetermined social group like a church or even extended family who can provide moral support and socialization? Have you considered the other support services you will need like health care and legal services? In this chapter, you will be offered an overview of the needs of your family when you move off-grid.

Socialization for Kids and Adults

Loretta F. Kasper, PhD, writes: "Socialization helps to shape and define our thoughts, feelings, and actions, and it provides us with a model for our behavior. As children become socialized, they learn how to fit into and to function as productive members of human society. Socialization teaches us the cultural values and norms that provide the guidelines for our everyday life."

Kasper explains that the family has primary importance is shaping a child's attitude and behavior because it provides the context in which the first and most long-lasting relationships are formed. Further studies show that the family determines a child's identity in terms of race, religion, social class, and gender. However, Kasper continues, even though we begin the process of socialization within the context of the family, a child's school offers more objective social relationships: "School is a social institution, and as such, has direct responsibility for instilling in, or teaching, the individual the information, skills, and values that society considers important for social life. In school, children learn the skills of interpersonal interaction. They learn to share, to take turns, and to compromise with their peers."

Children need to interact with peers to develop the ability to interact in the world. As you consider your off-grid location, you need to consider how you can provide some kind of socialization for your children.

You might think children are the only ones who need socialization. However, in a recent University of California study, researchers have identified a distinct pattern of gene expression in immune cells from people who experience chronically high levels of loneliness. The study's findings revealed that feelings of social isolation can cause inflammation, the immune system's first response, which can lead to an increased risk of heart disease, viral infections, and even cancer.

It's a good idea for you to become part of a community of people who share similar values and beliefs. Whether you can find that through a church, a fraternal organization, or like-minded individuals on an emergency preparation forum, you need to reach out beyond your nuclear family to develop relationships that will bring you support and a sense of belonging.

The ABCs of Off-Grid Schooling

Off-grid schooling can encompass either homeschooling or public or private schools in the nearest community. Many rural areas have school systems that bus children from out in the country into town to meet their educational needs.

If you are considering a public or private school, you should go to a site like GreatSchools.org *(www.greatschools.org)* to compare test scores, class size, teacher involvement, administrative involvement, and parent reviews. These kinds of sites can help you decide if the public school in your area is going to meet your needs.

FACT

Homeschooling may be the fastest-growing form of education in the United States (at 7 percent to 12 percent per year). Home-based education is also growing around the world in many nations. There are about 2 million homeschooled students in the United States.

You may decide to homeschool your children for a number of reasons. You might like the idea of incorporating your new lifestyle into your child's school curriculum. You might feel the time spent commuting to and from school is too long. You might feel the public education system does not meet your child's needs. You might have a differing point of view about what should be taught at school.

The website Free Home Education *(www.freehomeed.com)* is a great resource with links to free homeschooling resources on the Internet. You also need to research your state's particular laws about homeschooling. The Home School Legal Defense Association website *(www.hslda.org)* can provide you with resources about the laws within every state in the United States, resources and information about homeschooling, and support groups for you.

You will find that living an off-grid lifestyle is a wonderful way to incorporate teaching experiences with real life. When you plant a garden, you can teach your child botany. When you cook with your child, you can teach mathematics and chemistry. As you raise livestock, you can teach biology.

Most educators agree that a "hands on" learning experience makes more of an impact than just reading something from a book.

There are many resources to help you decide on a teaching method at Julie Shepherd Knapp's website "Homeschool Diner" (*www.homeschool diner.com*). The site provides information about seventeen different popular methods and philosophies of homeschooling. Knapp writes, "Each approach is given a brief description, and you will find links to additional books and websites so you will be able to research the methods you think you and your child might enjoy. Under each approach you will find curriculum options, brief reviews of some popular commercial products, free online resources, and a listing of important websites and books."

Support Groups and Assistance

The Internet has opened up the world to us. We can chat with people on the other side of the world with just a few clicks of a mouse. This is a boon for people who are living off-grid who want to still have a community of friends and mentors.

From homeschooling to emergency preparedness, there are forums on the Internet that can provide not only basic information, but also a community of like-minded people who will understand and support you.

On Timebomb2000.com, A World's Events Focus Group and Forum (*www.timebomb2000.com*), members are encouraged to not only share information and opinions about world events, but also to participate in sub-forums like Preps, Alternative Living, Homemaking and Homesteading, Granny's Kitchen, Alternative Medicine, Firearms Hunting and Fieldcraft, and Mechanics. In these forums, members share their experiences and are willing to help novices with counsel and advice.

Many online forums are recognizing a need for their members to actually meet, so they arrange local events where members can get together. Timebomb2000.com actually has a forum that is divided into geographical locations, so members can communicate with one another about local events and even plan local get-togethers.

To locate a group that meets your needs, start with an Internet search in the subject area that you are interested in. Then spend some time on the various forums as a guest. Observe the interaction of the members with each other. Is there a lot of hostility or is there good-natured disagreement? Do many of the views reflect your beliefs? Does the information seem solid or does it seem extreme? Is there a cost to be a member? Who is the owner of the forum and what is the forum's goal?

Once you feel comfortable, join the forum and venture into the conversations. Introduce yourself and ask some questions. Don't be a wallflower, but don't be a know-it-all either. Slowly make you way into the fold of the forum, respecting others' opinions and sharing some of your own.

Of course, choosing an off-grid lifestyle does not necessarily mean that you will be isolated and limited to interaction on the Internet. Visit the nearest town and learn about opportunities to volunteer in areas that interest you. Join local groups, especially groups like 4-H or Scouting programs for your children. Become a member of a local church, not only for religious instruction, but for the support you can receive from members of a religious community.

Do You Still Need Health Insurance?

Health insurance is used to cover the cost of private medical treatment for any illness and injury that is curable and short term.

Without insurance, you will be responsible for the cost of any health care treatment you or your family requires. These costs, at times, can be astronomical. As you look at your budget, you need to ask yourself what will happen if you can't afford the premiums. How will you be able to afford the treatment?

With new legislation on the horizon, many of the old "Charity Care" safety nets for health care may be gone. Charity Care was federally funded, but each state has its own version of it. The Hill-Burton program, initiated between 1946 and 1974, was one initiative. Through Hill-Burton, federal funds were used to improve state medical facilities. In return, those facilities had to provide health care to those who could not afford it.

How do you know if you fit under the "can't afford it" label? To qualify for services, an applicant's income must fall within the annually published Poverty Guidelines of the U.S. Department of Health and Human Services.

QUESTION

What is considered "income" under the Hill-Burton program?
Gross income (before taxes), interest/dividends earned, and child support payments are examples of income. Assets, food stamps, gifts, loans, or one-time insurance payments are examples of items not included as income when considering eligibility. For self-employed people, income is determined after deductions for business expenses.

There is a chance, in the near future, that having health insurance will be legislated in the United States and you will not have an option. If this is a concern to you, you need to research legislation and find out what it means to you in your particular situation.

Building a Strong Community

Why would building a strong community be an important task for someone who lives off-grid? Even back when the original pioneers and homesteaders settled this country, they built communities in order to support one another. Communities were created for protection, to share the cost of communal needs like teachers, doctors, and pastors, and to share knowledge and skills. There was always one woman in town who was called to assist in childbearing, one man in town who understood blacksmithing, or another person who understood how to use medicinal herbs.

The same is true today, but the skill sets have changed. Perhaps someone is an expert in solar heating panels or running electric lines, another might be knowledgeable about agriculture, still another has a background in alternative medicine. If you can gather up an off-grid community in which you complement one another, you will be much better off.

But how can you accomplish setting up a community when you are trying to concentrate on getting your family ready to go off-grid? Through the forums you participate in and through the research you've begun, you can start watching for like-minded people who have already moved off-grid or are in the same position you are. If they've already moved off-grid, perhaps you could find your piece of property in the same vicinity as theirs. If they haven't moved yet, perhaps you can share information and see if the areas you have been researching are appealing to them.

You probably don't want to set up a commune or a joint venture; there may be too many potential problems of owning property with someone else. You just want to create a support system where shared skills benefit the community.

You should also visit the towns near the areas you are considering for your off-grid home. Read their local newspaper, either online or by subscription to the print edition. Learn about the community, its strengths and its weaknesses. Visit the community during a vacation and see how you are welcomed. Determine whether you and your family can become part of the community and "fit" well with the other residents. If not, look for another community.

Where to Find Legal Advice

As you take steps to buy your property and move your family off-grid, there are things you should consider to safeguard yourself and your family.

Be sure you have legal representation when you buy your property. Buying is expensive, and you don't want to make any mistakes.

Make sure a search has been done to ensure that the property is free from mortgage, unpaid taxes, or any other financial liens. If there is a lien on the property, you need to be sure that either the seller has paid the lien or the purchase price includes the amount that you will pay to the lien holder to free the property of encumbrances.

Be sure you and your spouse have an updated will and power of attorney. Because wills are legal documents that provide instruction on how your assets are to be distributed and who will become caregivers for any children, dying without one will take those choices away from your spouse and give them to the state or province in which you lived.

A power of attorney is a document that gives someone the right to act in your name, if you are unable to do so. The most common powers of attorney are for medical care and for financial matters. A medical or personal care power of attorney gives someone else the right to make decisions for you if you are unable to do so yourself. For example, if you are in a coma, the person holding the power of attorney would represent you and your wishes. A financial power of attorney allows someone to make financial decisions for you when you are unable to make those decisions for yourself. Financial powers of attorney often come into play as people age and can no longer handle the day-to-day duties of their finances. However, your power of attorney would also allow for your financial matters to be seen to if you were in a coma or in other ways incapacitated.

ESSENTIAL

To search for a lien, get the correct address of the property and contact the county assessor or local tax board. These departments will have public records pertaining to ownership of the property, taxes paid or owed, and the last sale date of the property. They will also know if there is a lien on the property and can direct you to the lien holder.

There are places on the Internet where you can download a basic power of attorney form and fill it in yourself. Be sure that you and your witness sign these documents in the presence of a notary public, who witnesses and verifies the document signatures with her stamp.

You can receive all kinds of legal advice and information on the Internet. There are places where you can pay a minimal expense to have documents like wills, trusts, and powers of attorney created for you by people with a legal background. However, even if you decide to have these documents created online, it's a good idea to have a relationship with a local lawyer you know and trust.

CHAPTER 6

Power Supplies

The basic idea of off-grid living is to be self-sustaining, so no matter what happens in the outside world, you and your family will be fine. One example of the importance of having your own power source is the ice storm that hit Canada in January 1998. Over the course of six days, freezing rain covered Ontario, Quebec, and New Brunswick with three to four inches of ice. The ice coating caused electric wires to become brittle and break. The power outages lasted for as long as a month. More than 3 million people were without power in Quebec, and over 1 million in eastern Ontario. About 100,000 people went into shelters in school gymnasiums and churches. If you were living in a self-sustaining house with your own power source and heat source, you would not be one of those forced to relocate. As a matter of fact, if the grid went down, it would not affect your life at all.

Geothermal Power

The word "geo" means earth, and "thermal" means heat. So, geothermal means heat from the earth. If you were to dig ten feet below ground level, almost anywhere in the world, you would find the temperature to be between 50° and 60°F (10° and 16°C). No matter what the temperature outside, the readings ten feet below the earth remain fairly constant. Geothermal heat pump systems use that constant temperature to either heat or cool your home. Using pipes that are buried in the ground near your home, fluid, like antifreeze, is circulated through the heat pump system. In winter, heat from the warmer ground travels through the heat exchanger of the pump and sends warm air into your home. In summer, the cooler temperatures travel through the heat exchanger and cool the air in your home.

ESSENTIAL

To determine whether or not your location has enough sun or wind to supply energy, you can study maps at WindSolarEnergy.org (*www .windsolarenergy.org*) that show you how much solar or wind power you can expect. In some cases, you might need to use a combination in order to live off-grid.

Geothermal heat pumps use much less energy than conventional heating systems, since they draw heat from the ground and only have to potentially bring the temperature up several degrees. For example, with other heat sources, you have to maintain the fuel source to reach the internal home temperature of your choice. With geothermal, your heat source is already at 60°F and so only has to be heated another ten or so degrees to reach your comfort level. The same is true for air conditioning, where the 60°F temperature can bring your home down to the level you desire without using excess energy. Geothermal heat systems can also heat your home's hot water.

Since the first geothermally generated electricity in the world was produced at Larderello, Italy, in 1904, the use of geothermal energy for electricity has grown worldwide to about 7,000 megawatts in twenty-one countries around the world. The United States alone produces 2,700 megawatts of electricity from geothermal energy. Using that amount of electricity is comparable to burning 60 million barrels of oil each year. Source: *http://geothermal.marin.org/pwrheat.html.*

Solar Power

There are two different kinds of solar energy—passive and active. Passive solar energy means you are not using any mechanical devices to harness the energy of the sun. For example, using south-facing windows to provide natural light would be passive solar energy. Having a sunroom with a brick floor that would absorb the heat during the day and release it at night is another example. Even heating the water in a swimming pool in the sun is an example. When you build your home, you will want to take advantage of passive solar energy because it is a free gift from the sun.

Active solar energy uses mechanical devices in the collection, storage, and distribution of solar energy for your home. Active solar energy works by taking energy from the sun and, using solar panels, converts that energy into electricity. A component called an inverter works with the solar panels to convert the electricity from your panels into AC (alternating current) electricity. This electricity can be used right away or stored in a battery array in your home for future use.

There are five main components to an off-grid solar electric system:

- **Solar panels:** may also be referred to as PV panels or modules. PV is short for photovoltaic ("light-powered"). A group of PV panels is called an array.

- **Mounting rack:** metal support structures that hold an array of solar panels in a tilted position facing the sun. There are some mounting racks that can track the movement of the sun and shift the panels to collect as much energy as possible.
- **Charge controller:** monitors and manages the electricity between the solar panels and the battery array.
- **Battery array or battery bank:** a group of batteries, wired together, to capture the energy captured by the solar panels. These batteries can then be drawn on for electrical use.
- **Inverter:** changes the battery power to AC power for everyday electrical use.

You will need to determine your power consumption before you can get started with any type of solar installation.

FACT

The idea of solar energy has been around for quite a while. A Swiss scientist, Horace de Saussure, invented the world's first solar energy collector or "hot box" in 1767. In the 1830s, British astronomer John Herschel used a solar energy collector box to cook food during an expedition to Africa. Albert Einstein won the Nobel Prize in 1921 for his experiments with solar energy and photovoltaics.

Wood Burning

Mankind has been using wood for fuel ever since fire was invented. Burning wood can be an inexpensive way to heat your home. However, you need to be sure you have a source for the wood you want to use. Does your land have several acres of hardwood? A good rule of thumb is that you need about ten acres of hardwood to produce enough wood to heat a home every year.

If you are able to cut, gather, and stack your own wood, you can really save money. Keep in mind, though, that the saying "when you cut your own wood, it heats you twice" is very true. Harvesting wood is hard work, and caution must be maintained when using a chain saw.

If you have to have someone cut and deliver your wood, find out how much he or she charges. In some places, paying for wood is more expensive than using fossil fuels.

If you decide to use wood for heating, you have several options: a fireplace, a wood stove, or a wood furnace.

QUESTION

Is heating with wood bad for the environment?
Biomass fuels, such as wood or corn, are "carbon neutral," which means they do not generate a net increase in greenhouse gas emissions. In fact, heating an average home with wood can save enough nonrenewable fossil fuel to operate an automobile for a full year.

Fireplaces

Using a fireplace is the most inefficient way to heat your home. Although charming, an open fireplace draws much more air than needed for combustion. This causes the warm air from the burning wood to be drawn up the chimney. Between 80 percent and 90 percent of the heat produced by wood burned in an open fireplace is lost up the chimney. The other drawback is that a fireplace will steal heated air from other parts of your home, because it will be drawing the air for combustion. This draw actually pulls cold air into your home through any unsealed areas, like windows and doors.

If you have a home with an existing fireplace, you can purchase a fireplace insert that is designed to fit into your fireplace. An insert has a firebox that is surrounded by a steel shell. Air flows into the shell and radiant heat from the burning wood warms the air, which is then redistributed back into your home. This prevents the majority of the heat from escaping up the chimney and prevents the air draw in your home.

Wood Stoves

A wood stove is considered a "space heater" because, unlike a furnace that pushes heat through a duct system, it will heat a specific area in your home. New designs in wood stoves and tighter-built homes now make it possible to heat a home with a single wood stove. However, the stove needs to be centrally located, so it can radiate heat throughout the area, and you must provide a way for heat to move through the rest of the home.

Wood stoves come in a variety of materials. Three of the most popular materials are cast iron, steel, and soapstone. Cast iron was the original material because the casting process was perfected long before steel and welding. You might even hear some people refer to wood stoves as "cast iron" stoves. The original Ben Franklin stoves from the 1700s were cast iron. Steel-plated stoves are another choice. Steel stoves heat up quickly and start radiating heat faster than cast iron. But when the fire is reduced to coals, there is little or no residual radiated heat. On the other hand, a cast iron stove might take a few hours to start radiating heat, but when the fire is reduced to coals you will continue to have residual heat for several hours. Soapstone is a relatively soft metamorphic rock. It was used in early New England because residents found that not only could it be easily cut and polished, but it would also absorb the heat and then provide a gentle and steady radiant heat. You can stand near a soapstone stove without feeling overwhelmed by the heat, in comparison to a cast iron stove, which can overwhelm you with the force of the heat it generates.

Wind Power

Once you've found that your particular piece of property is appropriate for wind power, you should research the different costs of wind systems and which will meet your energy needs. Some are actually hybrid systems that include not only the wind system, but also solar panels and a generator to ensure an ample supply of power to your home.

A small off-grid wind system is actually quite simple. It generally consists of a wind turbine that generates electrical power; a battery bank that stores the power; and an inverter, which, just like the inverter in the solar power system, changes the power into usable electricity.

You need to place the wind turbine on a tower that is approximately 100 feet high. At this height the winds are generally faster and less turbulent. Two or three blades are attached to the turbine. When the wind blows over the blades, they rotate. When they rotate, a shaft inside the turbine converts that movement into electricity.

Smaller vertical wind turbines have recently been developed for use in home power. These turbines take up less space than traditional horizontal turbines, and some can capture wind movement from all directions.

A relatively new product on the wind-power market is a vertical spire. One such product, marketed as Windspire, generates power when wind blows against the vertical airfoils, causing them to spin. This power is then converted to AC electricity and is immediately available to provide energy to your building. These spires are only 30 feet tall and 4 feet wide. In 11 mph annual average winds, each spire will generate about 2,000 kWh per year.

Hydro Power

Did you know that hydroelectric power is the most widely used renewable energy source in the world today? Worldwide, it accounts for approximately 16 percent of all electricity production. Much of the same technology used for massive hydroelectric plants can be used in powering your home.

Micro–hydro generators can use average water flows to generate electricity. The reason hydro power often surpasses solar and wind power in side-by-side comparisons is that water can generate power constantly, unlike sun and wind. If you've ever seen images of areas that have been flooded, you immediately understand the power of water.

The force of water is so powerful that it only requires six inches of water on a flooded street for you to lose control of your car. That same force, multiplied by four to equal two feet of water, can actually float your car downstream.

Although most commercial hydroelectric power plants use a dam, for residential power generation you will typically use a pipe to collect water from a stream or river. The water from the pipes increases in power or energy as it flows downhill from the source to the turbine. The water hits the turbine and causes it to spin, which generates electricity.

Before you can choose the correct hydro system for your home, you need to measure the amount of energy available in your water supply. To do this you need to determine two important numbers—flow and head. Hydro-electric installers will work with you to estimate these numbers, but you will want to have a general idea of how the process works.

The flow is the amount of water available to turn your turbine; the more flow, the more energy. Flow is measured in cubic feet per second. So, if you were to use a pipe to divert water from your source, how much would be diverted in one second?

Head is the pressure of the water when it hits the turbine. To determine head, you need to estimate the distance the water will fall (go downhill) before it reaches your turbine; the further the fall, the higher the energy.

In order to use hydroelectric power efficiently, one or both of these numbers—flow or head—has to be fairly high to make the investment worth your while.

Alternative Energies

Several centuries ago, many German farmers and their families lived in housebarns. These buildings were comprised of the barn on the ground level and the home on the second and sometimes third level. The primary reason for this arrangement was that the warmth from the animals would rise up and help heat the home. That was one of the first uses of an alternative energy source called *biomass*.

FACT

One cow's waste can produce enough electricity to light two 110-watt light bulbs twenty-four hours a day.

Biomass is organic material made from plants and animals that can be processed in order to provide energy. Biomass is processed by burning and by fermenting. The most common type of biomass that is burned is wood; however, garbage and wood waste can also be burned to produce energy. Another common biomass product is methane gas.

The Central Vermont Public Service corporation (*www.cvps.com /cowpower*), an electric utility company, offers its customers the option to power their homes using CVPS Cow Power. Local dairy farmers gather cow manure into specially designed holding tanks called methane digesters that keep the manure at a certain temperature. The manure releases methane gas, which is piped into a generator that creates electricity.

Unless you decide to build one for yourself, methane digesters are only available for larger agricultural facilities. However, as more people explore the benefits of methane gas, small residential units may be available in the future.

CHAPTER 7

Developing Your Green Thumb

There is nothing more satisfying than eating vegetables from your own garden. Not only do they taste better because they're fresh, but you know exactly what kinds of chemicals (if any) were used when growing them. In order to have a successful garden, you need to do some research on the type of soil you have, which planting zone you live in, and how best to make use of the garden space you have available to you.

Planning Your Garden

One of most important parts of your garden is the planning. You can pore over seed catalogs all winter long to look for the seed varieties you'd like. You can meet with your Extension agent to find out the particulars of gardening in your area. You can even meet with a master gardener who can answer many of your questions. But as you begin to plan your garden, you should ask yourself the following four questions.

Where Will Your Garden Be?

Generally, plants like lots of sun and well-drained soil. Look for places that are not shaded with trees or outbuildings. Try to find ground that is not rocky or sandy. Think about your water source. Is there a convenient way to transport water to your garden? How big do you want your garden to be? If you are planning to grow enough produce for your entire family, you should count on about 50 square feet of garden for each person, not counting paths.

How Will You Arrange Your Plants?

Are you going to use raised beds or use tilling? If raised beds, how are you going to place them? Are you going to plant single rows, double rows, or broadcast your seed over an area? How wide will your paths between rows be? If you use a rototiller or cultivator, you will want to plan your rows so it can easily be run up and down the paths. If you draw your garden on graphing paper, you can give each square a value—for example, each square is equal to 6 square inches—and plan your garden accordingly.

ESSENTIAL

Raised bed gardening refers to gardening in soil that has been mounded or contained at a higher level than the surrounding soil. Raised bed gardening is an old gardening practice, but it's currently growing in popularity again because it offers several advantages over simply growing your plants in level ground.

What to Plant?

Once you've decided where and how, deciding what to plant will help you with the placement of your plants. For example, if you are planting corn, you'll want to place it in an area where it won't shade other plants. If you are planting pumpkins or winter squash or watermelons, you'll want to plant them in an area where they have plenty of room to spread out. Companion plant by using flowers and herbs that discourage insects. Make the most out of your garden space by growing leafy vegetables like lettuce or chard alongside semi-shading plants like tomatoes. Plant what your family will eat. You might be able to get a bumper crop of radishes, but if your family won't eat them, they won't do you any good.

When to Plant?

Your average local spring and fall frost dates are available from your county Extension agent and online through most seed websites. When you pick out seeds, you should also take into account your climate zone, because that will show you how long your average growing season will be. For example, someone in North Carolina will have a longer growing season than someone in North Dakota. Some plants, like peas and spinach, can be planted early in the spring, while frost-tender plants, like tomatoes and peppers, need to be started later in the season.

FACT

The USDA Hardiness Zone Map divides North America into eleven separate zones; each zone is 10°F warmer (or colder) in an average winter than the adjacent zone. If you see a hardiness zone in a catalog or plant description, chances are it refers to the USDA map.

A Solar Greenhouse

A greenhouse allows you to buy seeds and start your own plants early. If you have priced vegetable plants you can see how much better it is to spend $2 for a packet of thirty tomato seeds than $4 or $5 per tomato plant.

If you are building your own off-grid home, you should consider adding a greenhouse to the south end of your home. It will not only help with passive solar energy, it will also allow you to tend your plants without having to leave your home.

You can construct a solar greenhouse out of many different materials and you can even use recycled materials, like used and discarded windows and old framing timber. If affordability is an issue, you can construct a fairly good-sized greenhouse with some PVC pipes, framing timbers for a foundation, and heavy-duty plastic. The cost is about $400. Alberta Home Gardening (*www.albertahomegardening.com/how-to-build-an-inexpensive-hoop-style-greenhouse*) has a step-by-step guide to building this kind of greenhouse. If you need to create a greenhouse for under $400, you can do that too. You can actually build a working greenhouse from two-liter plastic bottles. ReapScotland.org.uk offers a PDF along with photos on how this greenhouse is built. You can find the directions at *http://reapscotland.org .uk/Plastic_Bottle_Greenhouse_Instructions_2004.pdf.*

You can also create a "cold frame" to extend your gardening season on either end. A cold frame is a large wooden bottomless rectangular box— 8 inches tall on one end and 12 inches tall on the other. You lay glass frames or even plastic over the top of the frame to keep in the heat. Cold frames actually create a microclimate that can be a zone and a half warmer than your garden's zone.

QUESTION

Where did cold frames come from?
Cold frames were originally designed as an adjunct to a heated greenhouse. The concept was that once the seedlings had been grown in the heated greenhouse, they could be hardened off in the adjoining unheated cold frame.

The correct creation of the frame is important. You want to be sure it's positioned so the back of the frame is cut higher than the front in order to catch the angles of the winter sun. Placing your frames in an area where they have full sun is best. Surprisingly, even in cold weather, on a sunny day your cold frame could absorb too much sun. You should keep the internal temperature of your cold frame near 60°F. You can vent the frame to prevent overheating. Venting simply means lifting one edge of the glass frame in order to let a little cold air circulate inside the frame until the desired temperature is reached. There are temperature-activated ventilating arms available if you are unable to watch the frames yourself.

You can start some of your hardier plants in your cold frame in the spring and in the fall you also can grow vegetables, like spinach and certain lettuce varieties, that thrive in the cold. You can actually have vegetables, depending on your climate, through mid-December.

Preparing the Land

To produce soil that yields the best garden, you should begin with a soil test. You can order a soil test from most online gardening sites, or buy one at a local garden store. The test will measure the pH level of the soil as well as the amounts of nitrogen, phosphorus, and potash the soil contains. Each of these components plays an important role in the health of your garden:

- **pH:** Soil pH determines whether or not plants are able to consume nutrients. If the pH is too high or too low (too alkaline or too acidic), the nutrients in the soil cannot be absorbed into your plants.
- **Nitrogen:** Nitrogen produces the abundant growth of stalks, stems, leaves, and grasses. Too much nitrogen creates beautiful green plants with no fruit or seed formation. In other words, you would have beautiful-looking tomato plants with no tomatoes. Not enough nitrogen weakens plants, making them more susceptible to disease.
- **Phosphorus:** Phosphorus is necessary for the basic formation of the plant. It stimulates root formation, accelerates maturation, and promotes blooming and seed formation.
- **Potash or Potassium:** Potash stimulates early root or tuber formation, which is essential for vegetables like carrots, potatoes, radishes, and peanuts. Too much potash diminishes a plant's resistance to weather extremes and postpones plant maturity.

Once you determine the nutrient needs of your soil, you should apply the proper fertilizer to meet those needs.

Tilling the soil before planting breaks up the ground, works fertilizer into the soil, and fights weeds. It allows the young sprouts of the seeds you plant to break through the soil. In addition, when you till in last year's leftover vines and stalks, you are adding what's called *green manure* to your garden and increasing the nutrients in your soil.

ALERT

Weeds are the adversary of every gardener. Your initial tilling will destroy the weeds that have taken root by early spring, and with continued tilling, you will keep the weed seeds from taking root.

Another source of green manure is a *cover crop*, which is a crop planted specifically to be tilled into the soil. Usually green manure is planted in the fall, after your garden has been harvested. But you can also plant green manure on areas of your garden that are troubled with an influx of weeds. Cover crops help choke out the weeds and leave the soil ready for planting. There are two types of green manure: legumes, like alfalfa, clover, and soybeans; and non-legumes like ryegrass, buckwheat, and oats. It's a good practice to use more than one kind of green manure and rotate your choices from year to year.

If you plant cover crops in the fall, till them into the ground in the spring before you begin to plant. If you plant cover crops during the spring to help choke out weeds, you can till the cover crops in just before you want to use the area for another crop.

Animal manure is another way to add nutrients into your soil. The most common is cow, sheep, and chicken manure. You need to be sure that any manure you apply to your garden has aged at least six months to a year. You want to age manure for several reasons. First, fresh manure is "hot" (it has high levels of nitrogen) and it will burn your plants. Chicken manure is especially known for being hot and should be aged for a year. Also, fresh manure can carry bacteria that can cause illness and may have live weed seeds in it, especially if it's cow or sheep manure. Spreading this on your garden will be like planting weeds among your vegetables.

You will want to avoid manure from pigs, domestic animals like dogs and cats, or human manure. These all have a potential for carrying disease.

Planting Your Garden

Now is the time to put all of your planning to work. Using the garden layout you drew up for your garden, place stakes to mark out where different rows will be planted. The next step is for you to build any trellises or string lines, or set in solid stakes, for any climbing plants like peas, zucchinis, or beans. In the area where you have dedicated space for your spreading plants, like pumpkins and watermelons, build mounds several feet apart from each other, depending on the need of the specific plant variety. Be sure to create specific pathways right away, so you aren't tromping all over the garden and compacting the soil and you won't inadvertently step on your seedbed.

The day before you plant, water your garden thoroughly. Start planting by reading the back of the seed packet to ensure you understand the planting depth and seed spacing. Seeds planted too deep or too close together will not do well. Be sure to place a marker at the end of each row with the name and variety of seed you have sown. If you change varieties in the middle of a row, place a marker there too.

Stretch a string between the two stakes you set to mark the row and create a V-shaped furrow with the corner of your hoe. Make sure the depth of the furrow corresponds with the planting depth recommended on the seed packet. Tear the corner of the seed package and carefully tap the package as you move down the row, dispensing the seeds evenly. Larger seeds can be placed individually in the row at the appropriate spacing. Plant some extra seeds in each row to allow for failed germination. You can thin these out later if needed.

When you cover the seeds, make sure the soil is fine, with no large clods or rocks. Pack the dirt lightly over the seeds. After you have finished planting all of the seeds in one section, water the garden thoroughly using a gentle spray so you soak the ground, but don't disturb the seeds.

If you started your seeds indoors in pots and have bedding plants, you should follow the same steps you did with the seed sowing by stretching a string between the two stakes you set to mark the row. Using the string as a guide, dig small holes at the recommended spacing that are slightly wider and deeper than the root ball of the new plant. Water the plant thoroughly before planting to lessen the shock of transplanting it. Holding the base of the plant with one hand, carefully maneuver the pot to loosen the roots and remove the new plant. Sometimes the roots may be compacted.

Gently loosen the outer roots before you plant. Place the plant into the hole and pack the soil in around it, making certain that there is good soil/root contact.

Keep your garden watered to ensure good plant growth and germination. Once the seedlings emerge and develop their second or third set of true leaves, thin them so the strongest plants remain at the spacing directed on the seed package. Thinning early will prevent you from disturbing the roots of the remaining plants.

Composting

Compost is one of nature's best mulches and soil modifiers. It is cheap, you can use it instead of fertilizers, and it's better for your soil. Compost is simply decomposed organic material. The organic material can be plant or animal matter.

FACT

Compost improves soil condition; it loosens clay soils and helps sandy soils retain water. When you add compost to your soil, you improve fertility and stimulate healthy root development.

Here are several tips for composting:

- **Kitchen scraps.** Kitchen scraps are like gold. Don't throw them away—add them to the compost pile! Kitchen scraps, generally high in nitrogen, help heat up the compost pile and speed up the composting process. Eggshells, coffee grounds, fruit and vegetable peels, and table scraps are excellent things to add to your compost pile.
- **Bigger is better.** When you are dealing with a compost pile, you want the pile to be fairly large, because a larger pile builds up heat, which helps break down the composting material. However, there are some limits. You probably don't want your compost pile to get much bigger than 3' × 3'. An excellent way to set up a compost pile is to use four pallets on their ends, forming a square container.

- **Air is your compost's friend.** It is important to keep your compost aerated. Oxygen is another key ingredient to breaking down the composted materials. Tumbling composters, which are shaped like large balls, make aerating easy. Just turn the composter whenever you add new material. If you are composting a pile, just be sure to mix up the contents with a shovel or pitchfork to keep the mixture decomposing.
- **Keep it moist.** The microorganisms in your compost pile need water to live. Water just enough to maintain compost as moist as a wrung-out sponge. Too wet is almost as bad as too dry.
- **Variety is the spice of composting.** If you have all leaves, all grass clippings, or an overload of any other single type of material, it will throw off the balance of the pile. In general, too much of any one material will slow down the composting process. Make sure you have a good mix of both green (plant) and brown (manure) material.
- **What to compost.** You can compost kitchen waste, thin layers of lawn clippings, chopped leaves, shredded branches, disease-free garden plants, shredded paper, weeds, straw or hay, newspaper, wood ash, and tea leaves. Do not compost meat scraps or fatty trash, excessive wood ashes, sawdust, kitty litter, or ashes from coal or charcoal.

Harvesting

The harvest is the reward after all of your months of hard work. Red, ripe tomatoes bursting with flavor. Sweet ears of corn, just waiting for a pat of butter. Juicy, flavorful watermelon ready to be sliced and served. In order to receive the fullest benefit out of your garden, you need to be aware of when to harvest your bounty. Some of your vegetables will be ready for harvest in a little over a month after sowing; others will take the whole season. The following is vegetable harvesting criteria for judging when your garden will be ready for harvest.

- **Asparagus:** Begin harvesting when spears are six to eight inches tall and about as thick as your small finger. If you snap them off at ground level, new spears will continue to grow. Stop harvesting about four to six weeks after the initial harvest, to allow the plants to produce foliage and food for themselves so they'll bear well again the next year.

- **Beans (Snap):** Pick beans before you see the seeds bulging. Beans should easily snap in two. Check the beans often because if they are not picked when ready, they can become tough.
- **Beets:** Harvest the green tops when you thin out the rows. Beets are ready to be harvested once you see their shoulders protruding at the soil line.
- **Broccoli:** Harvest when the individual buds are about the size of a match head.
- **Brussels sprouts:** The sprouts mature from the bottom up. Harvest once the sprouts are an inch in diameter. Twist or cut the sprout from the stem.
- **Cabbage:** Harvest when the head feels solid when gently squeezed.
- **Carrots:** Harvest carrots after a light frost for added sweetness. To judge the carrots' length, measure the diameter appearing at the soil line and compare to the specifications listed for that variety. If the diameter looks right, the length is probably good too. However, to be certain, you will need to harvest one of the carrots. Carrots can be left in the ground once mature.
- **Cauliflower:** Harvest when the head looks full and while the curds of the head are still smooth.
- **Corn:** About three weeks after the silks form, they will turn dry and brown. The kernels should exude a milky substance when pricked.
- **Cucumber:** Fruits should be firm and smooth. Check frequently against maturity date of seed packet.
- **Eggplant:** Fruits should be firm and shiny. Cut rather than pull from the plant.
- **Garlic:** Tops will fall over and begin to brown when the bulbs are ready. Dig, don't pull, and dry before storing.
- **Kale:** Kale flavor is best in cooler weather, although deep green leaves with a firm, sturdy texture can be harvested throughout the season.
- **Kohlrabi:** Harvest once the bulb has reached two to three inches in diameter.
- **Leeks:** You can harvest leeks as small mild vegetables or as larger one-inch-diameter plants later in the fall.

- **Lettuce (Head):** You don't want to let your lettuce sit out in the sun once it is ready to be harvested because it can quickly go to seed. Pick the heads when they feel firm.
- **Lettuce (Leaf):** The wonderful thing about leaf lettuce is that you can harvest throughout the growing season and sometimes even into the fall. Just pick the outer leaves when they are about four inches tall (depending on variety) and allow the inner leaves to continue to grow.
- **Muskmelon:** When you are harvesting melons, the best way to tell if they are ripe is to smell them. They should smell "melon-y" near the stem end. The other way is when you lift the vine, the fruit will easy detach.
- **Onions:** You can actually harvest onions throughout the growing season—when they are younger, they are milder and sweeter. If you want onions for your root cellar, wait until the tops have browned and have fallen over. Then you can dig them up and let them dry in the sun to harden.
- **Parsnips:** There are a few vegetables that actually develop a "sweeter" taste if they are allowed to stay in the ground until after a frost. Parsnips are among these vegetables. You can even leave some in the ground over the winter and harvest them in the spring if you've planted enough. If you live in a particularly cold area, be sure to mulch over the parsnips for protection through the winter.
- **Peas:** Peas are very susceptible to heat, so you want to harvest them early in the season, when the pods look full. You should pick a pod and open it, to make sure the peas are fully developed and sweet.
- **Potatoes:** When your potato plant begins to flower, you can harvest sweet, little "new" potatoes. Keep the potatoes in the ground until the tops brown and dry out for larger, regular-size potatoes. Be careful as you harvest that you dig underneath and sift through the dirt, rather than digging in from the top.
- **Pumpkins:** Pumpkins will turn from green to orange as they get ready to be picked. You will want to harden the skin before you store it. The skin is hard enough if you can poke it with your fingernail and it doesn't crack. If you are expecting a hard frost, bring the pumpkins in.

- **Radishes:** When you can see the tops of the radishes break through the soil, you can begin to harvest them.
- **Rutabaga:** Rutabaga is another one of those vegetables that sweeten after a frost and can be left in the ground through the winter, if they are properly mulched. For a fall harvest, they are ready when they are about three inches in diameter, usually three months after you set them out.
- **Swiss Chard:** You can harvest Swiss chard throughout the season. Just cut the outer leaves and allow the center to continue growing.
- **Spinach:** Be sure to harvest your spinach before it begins to flower. You want to harvest the spinach leaves when they are still young and tender. Just cut the entire plant off, so the remainder is only about an inch tall. The plant will grow back.
- **Squash (Summer):** Summer squash usually grows very quickly. Check your plants often. Pick summer squash when it is young and glossy green. If you wait until they are larger, they are dry and seedy.
- **Squash (Winter):** The best indicator for harvesting your winter squash is its color. The squash should turn the color it's supposed to be before harvesting. Frost will damage winter squash, so bring the squash inside before a hard frost.
- **Tomatoes:** Watch your plants carefully and harvest the tomatoes when they have reached full color and are no longer hard. If you still have green tomatoes on the vine at the end of the growing season, you can pick them and use them for relish or fried tomatoes. Don't wait too long to harvest your tomatoes; they can overripen on the vine.
- **Turnips:** If you have planted turnips for greens, you can cut the outer leaves when they are a few inches tall. If you make sure the inner leaves are left untouched, you can still harvest the root in the fall. Just like rutabagas, turnips taste better after a frost. Be sure to keep them well-mulched to protect them. They should be about two inches in diameter when you harvest them.
- **Watermelon:** When harvesting a watermelon, you can look for a couple of signs. Thump on the side and listen for a hollow sound. The white spot on the bottom, where the melon rested as it grew, will actually change to a creamy yellow when the melon is ripe. Once you pick a melon, it will not continue to ripen.

CHAPTER 8

Starting an Orchard

Although Johnny Appleseed might have made planting and growing fruit trees look easy, you have to have the necessary knowledge about soil needs and the maintenance fruit trees require. But once you've taken the time to learn about having your own orchard, the benefits are innumerable. Not only will you benefit from the fruit harvest, but trees forestall erosion, they provide oxygen and remove carbon dioxide, they offer places for birds to nest, and later in life, they provide fuel for our wood stoves. An orchard is not like a garden that lasts three months; an orchard is a promise for the future.

Best Location for an Orchard

Fruit trees need full sun for proper growth and quality fruit production. When looking at a site for an orchard, seek land that has good water drainage and does not lie low in the terrain. Low areas are often frost pockets, because cold air settles into low areas, and the flowers on the fruit trees are very susceptible to a late freeze.

FACT

Johnny Appleseed was a real person. His name was John Chapman and he was a nurseryman who realized that there was a real need for service in supplying seeds and seedlings. In order to assure stability of the newly established homesteads, the law required each settler to plant fifty apple trees the first year. Johnny sold and gave away trees to the pioneers.

The early morning sun is particularly important since it dries the dew from the leaves, thereby reducing the incidence of diseases. Fruit planting sites should have good air circulation.

Fruit trees grow well in a wide range of soil types. They prefer soils with a texture of sandy loam to a sandy clay loam. Ideal soil pH for fruit trees is 6.5.

ALERT

Cedar-apple rust is a common disease of apple and crabapple trees. The fungus that causes the disease must spend a phase of its life cycle as a parasite on *Juniperus* species, such as red cedar or ornamental junipers. Cedar-apple rust can be very severe on apple trees. Infections of apple fruit result in lower fruit quality and early fruit drop.

What Size Trees Do You Use?

The common sizes available for fruit trees are dwarf, semi-dwarf, and standard. The size you choose depends on how long you want to wait for your first harvest, how much space you have for your orchard, and how much you want your harvest to yield.

Dwarf

Dwarf fruit trees can flourish in an 8-foot-diameter plot. Because of their size, they are easy to prune and harvest. However, even given their smaller stature, the fruit is normal size. Dwarf trees are not as hardy as standard or semi-dwarf trees. Part of the reason they are not as hardy is that they have fairly shallow roots, so a hard frost can kill them. For this reason, dwarf trees should not be grown in USDA zones 3 or 4.

You should plant dwarf trees at least 8 feet apart, but no further than 20 feet apart to ensure pollination. They should also be staked because of their lack of root depth. Dwarf trees can produce one to two bushels a year in about two years, and they will live about fifteen to twenty years.

Semi-Dwarf

Semi-dwarf are medium-sized trees that require a growing area of about 15 feet in diameter. They need annual pruning to keep the height down and the shape balanced. They are sometimes called semi-vigorous. Semi-dwarf apple trees will grow about 15 to 20 feet tall. They are hardier than dwarf trees, but still not as hardy as standard trees and should not be grown in USDA zone 3. Semi-dwarf trees should be planted at least 10 to 20 feet apart. However, in order to ensure pollination, do not plant them more than 20 feet away from another variety. A good semi-dwarf tree should live about twenty to twenty-five years and produce about five bushels of apples within three to four years.

Standard

If you have an older fruit tree on your property, it probably is a standard. Standard apple trees will grow about 25 feet tall, and even taller if they are never pruned. Standards were the only choice before the smaller hybrids were developed. They are hardiest and will adapt to a variety of soils and climates. Standard trees should be planted at least 25 to 30 feet apart. However, do not plant them more than that distance from another variety in order to ensure pollination. A standard tree should live fifty years or longer and produce about eight bushels of apples a year within five to six years.

Pruning Basics

Pruning is the removal of a portion of a tree to correct or maintain the tree structure and to optimize fruit production. Pruning is most often done during the winter, when the sap is not running through the tree; this commonly is referred to as *dormant pruning*. Lawn-and-Gardening-Tips.com (*www .lawn-and-gardening-tips.com*) advises that there are unique pruning instructions for different types of fruit trees depending on the structure of the tree itself. Here are the basics and some general instructions about pruning, as suggested on the website:

- **The Central-Leader System:** This is used for pruning apple trees, pear trees, and sweet cherry trees. A "central leader" is the main stem or trunk of the tree, from which other, lateral branches develop. Fruit tree pruning instructions for this method are based around thinning the lateral branches.
- **The Open-Center System:** Used for peach tree pruning, as well as pruning plum trees, nectarine trees, apricot trees, and sour cherry trees where there is no dominant, vertical trunk or central leader. Open-center fruit tree pruning instructions are based around three or four main limbs set at wide angles with about five lesser branches on each.
- **The Modified-Leader System:** Used for nut-bearing trees, but can also be applied when pruning apple trees and pear trees. Modified-leader fruit tree pruning instructions are based upon giving the central leader and three or four lateral branches equal importance.

Here are some general fruit tree pruning instructions to give you an idea of the process:

- Always use sharp shears or saws so your cuts are clean. Use pruning shears on young trees and limbs less than ½-inch in diameter, and lopping shears for your bigger cuts. For mature fruit trees, use a pruning saw.
- Begin by removing dead wood and broken branches. Then cut out any wood that crosses or rubs against any other branches. This opens up the middle so the sun can get to all the fruit.

- Make your cut close to a bud, to a joint in the branch, or to the trunk; never leave a stub. The pruning cut should be just above a bud. Make the cut at a backwards angle of about 30 degrees.
- Prune stems just above a pair of opposing strong shoots or buds. If shoots or buds are staggered, choose a strong one and prune just above it.
- Keep more horizontal branches, and prune more vertical branches.
- Remove suckers (shoots) from around the base of the tree.
- Get rid of all debris that can harbor pests and disease.

Fruit Trees

As you decide which trees you'd like for your orchard, you need to take into account a number of variables.

Consider Your Planting Zone

First, which varieties do best in your planting zone? You can ask your county Extension agent, the nursery owner, or your neighbors to see which trees have produced the best fruit for them. Determine whether you have a microclimate on your property where warmer-zoned trees might thrive.

The Dirt on Your Dirt

Second, you need to match the kind of tree you want to the kind of soil you have. Some fruit trees, like plums, do well in damp soil conditions. Other fruit trees, like apples, need well-drained soil. Some varieties might be more drought resistant than others, or more frost resistant. When you meet with your local nursery, garden center, or county Extension agent, describe the area you have in mind as your orchard location and have an expert help you pick out trees that would work best in that location.

The Buzz on Pollination

Make sure, if needed, you provide pollinators for your trees. Some trees are self-pollinating, like most varieties of peaches and nectarines, but others, like apricot trees, require another tree of the same type for pollination.

Be sure that you match your tree with the correct pollinator. Just because you have two apple trees does not mean they are pollinators for each other. Check with either your Extension agent or the nursery where you purchase your trees to be sure your have the right varieties.

Tyoes of Fruit Trees

While you choose various types of fruit trees, you should also look at the kind of varieties within each group. Apples have early harvesters and late harvesters, fruit that is excellent for eating, and fruit that is better for cooking. There are some fruits that store better than others. Decide on your needs and get a variety to extend your harvest.

Look for Healthy Tree Stock

You will want to purchase trees that have a straight trunk and no low branches, with branches evenly spaced around the tree. If you're selecting a bare-root tree, you want roots of quality and quantity. Roots should be numerous and healthy, as opposed to few and scrawny. If a tree has a cluster of branches or only one branch, those will not become good producers. You should also avoid any trees with a curved or bent trunk.

Planting Your Fruit Tree

Once you have decided about the size of the tree and soil type, it is time to plant your fruit tree. Soak the tree roots before planting. Dig a hole that is about 10 inches wider than the size of the root ball of the tree and deep enough to completely cover the roots. Be sure the graft union or graft line of the tree lies slightly above the level of the ground. The graft line can be identified as a diagonal scar on the trunk or as a lump a few inches above the soil level mark on the tree.

After digging, loosen the soil around the hole, so that the tree can easily expand its roots. Put some soil at the bottom of the hole in order to make a mound in the center. Carefully place the root ball of the tree on top of the mound. After placing the tree in the hole, fill it up with soil. Gently firm the soil around the tree and then water to settle the soil around the roots. Apply a layer of mulch or organic material like compost or leaves around the base of the tree to help retain moisture, ensuring that you do not place the material near the graft line of the tree.

Check with your local nursery or county Extension agent to find out when fruit trees should be planted in your area.

Berry Bushes

It's a good idea to have several varieties of berries in your garden, as well as a thriving fruit orchard. Strawberries will bear in June, raspberries in July, and blackberries and grapes in August and September. You can have fresh berries all summer long!

FACT

Strawberries have a history that goes back more than 2,200 years; they grew wild in Italy as long ago as 234 B.C. The first Europeans to land in Virginia found strawberries there when their ships arrived in 1588. Early settlers in Massachusetts enjoyed eating strawberries grown by local American Indians, who cultivated the fruit as early as 1643. After 1860, strawberries were widely grown in many parts of the country.

Strawberries

Plant your strawberries in a sunny location for the sweetest berries and the healthiest plants. If you have a spot on a south-facing slope, that would be ideal. Strawberry plants are usually planted in early spring in the north, but in the south, the fall works best. Strawberries love fertile, slightly acidic well-drained soil. If your soil is a heavy clay, you might want to consider raised beds for your berries.

Select plant varieties that do well in your area. Ask your local Extension agent or a good local strawberry grower which ones do best. There a two basic types of strawberries, June-bearing and everbearing. Plant varieties of each to extend your harvest. Strawberries are usually sold in bunches of twenty-five, and one or two bunches is enough if you are starting a bed.

Plant as early as you can and only use dormant plants. Soak roots in water as your make a furrow in the row where the strawberries will be planted. Plant in rows 4 feet apart. Trim roots so they are 4 to 5 inches long. Put some soil at the bottom of the row in order to make a mound in the center. Carefully place the trimmed roots over the mound of soil and then add soil on top of the roots. Be sure the base of the crown is just at the soil surface. Firm the soil around the plant and water well.

Mulch and fertilize your strawberries. During the first season, do not allow your plants to produce fruit; pinch off all the blossoms. This will allow the plants to put their energy into developing runners. Be sure to protect your strawberries in the winter. A 6-inch layer of straw over the plants will help insulate them from the freezing and thawing cycles.

Grapes

Green grapes are nice for straight eating, but don't do well in many areas of the country. Purple grapes are better for preserves and juice, and seem to thrive in all zones. Grapes should be planted in an area that gets full exposure to the sun. Grapes love well-drained, fertile soil. Remember, as you plan where to plant your grapes, they will need to be supported by a trellis or even fencing.

Grapevines can be planted in the spring as soon as the soil dries out enough to be worked. Prepare a small hole and set the plants to the same level as in the pot in which you purchased them. Clip the top off the vine, leaving only two buds near the soil line. Plant the grapes at least 8 to 10 feet apart. Mulch them to help keep the roots moist.

Bramble Berries—Red and Black Raspberries and Blackberries

Brambles prefer full sunlight and grow best in well-drained, sandy loam soils rich in organic matter. Berries prefer a soil pH of 5.6 to 6.2. Avoid low areas that remain wet late into the spring. However, you should ensure that the plants receive plenty of water during dry periods.

You should also be aware of what was planted prior to putting in the brambles. Certain vegetables like tomatoes, potatoes, peppers, and eggplants carry a fungus called *Verticillium*. This fungus lives in the soil for four to six years and attacks plants from their roots. Brambles are highly susceptible to *Verticillium*.

You will want to plant your brambles in the early spring, but wait until any danger of frost has passed. When you are planting the individual canes, be sure to keep them moist during the process. Dig a small hole; it should be large enough for the roots to spread out, but not so large that the plants would be set deeper than they were in the nursery.

FACT

The ancient Greeks utilized blackberries as a remedy for gout, and the flowers and fruit were also used to treat venomous bites. Eating the berry was known to stop looseness of the bowels, and the young shoots, combined with a little alum, were eaten in a salad to fasten loose teeth.

Make sure the soil around both the roots and the plant is firm. Then generously water each plant.

ALERT

Blueberries contain significant quantities of both antibacterial and antiviral compounds, and have a reputation in northern Europe of fighting infections. They may also help protect against heart disease.

Blueberries

Blueberries prefer full sunlight and grow best in well-drained, sandy soils rich in organic matter with a soil pH of 4 to 4.5. When planting, dig a hole 18 inches deep and 18 inches wide. Mix equal amounts of peat moss with top soil and pour into the hole until it is filled 4 inches from the top. Set the plant and cover the roots with the remaining peat–soil mix.

Space plants 5 feet apart in rows 10 feet apart. Apply 4 inches of sawdust or wood-chip mulch in a 2-foot-wide band after planting. Beginning the next year, maintain a 4-inch mulch depth in a 4-foot band over the life of the planting.

Blueberry bushes need at least one to two inches of water per week. In dry seasons, supplemental watering is essential to obtain good yields of high-quality fruits. Once you reach early fall, however, do not apply extra water unless the soil is very dry.

Remove blossoms that appear in the first year of planting and second year after planting to stimulate vigorous growth.

Wild Fruit

Mulberries, elderberries, and wild raspberries are just some of the bounties of nature that can be found throughout the countryside. These berries often have unique qualities and should be considered part of your harvest.

Mulberries

Mulberries resemble blackberries in shape and size and also have many seeds. They're fully ripe when black and soft. They are less tart and less pleasant-tasting than blackberries, but they are healthy to eat. One way to harvest mulberries is to spread a sheet of cloth or plastic underneath the tree, and then shake the branches so the fruit will fall onto the blanket. Mulberries will stain anything and everything they touch, so you should wear gloves while you harvest them. You need to process mulberries immediately, either by preserving them in a jelly or freezing them.

Elderberries

Elderberries resemble chokecherries, only they are smaller. Elderberries grow all over the United States, usually by the side of country roads. The black elderberries are the sweetest and can be used for juices and dried for baking. Elderberries grow in clusters, like grapes. The best way to harvest them is to hold a bowl underneath the cluster and snip the cluster from the tree. Elderberry blossoms are used for teas. Elderberries are also used for medicinal purposes.

Black elderberry extract has been found to be effective against the H5N1 strain of avian flu in humans. Black elderberry extract can help protect healthy cells and deactivate viruses. When given to patients, scientists have found the black elderberry extract has the ability to ward off flu infections.

Wild Raspberries and Blackberries

These berries are usually found in wooded areas. If you decide to go berry picking in the wilderness, be sure you examine the area around you closely—berries are also a favorite treat for bears. Wild berries are usually smaller than their domestic counterparts, but often sweeter. Wear long sleeves and gloves to protect yourself from the thorns surrounding the fruit. For harvesting, slip a bucket underneath the bush and as you pull the berries off the bush, and let them drop down into the bucket. You can use these berries as you would domestic raspberries and blackberries in preserves and jellies. You also can freeze them.

CHAPTER 9

Canning and Preserving Food

You will find that there is nothing as satisfying as looking at row after row of jars on the shelves in your kitchen that contain the literal fruits of your labors. Canning and preserving was the way our ancestors stored foods for the winter months. But there was more to it than just storing; they harvested their produce at the peak of freshness and captured it in a jar. Opening a jar of peach preserves on a cold winter's morning can transport you back to summertime. Knowing that your family will be well fed with nutritious and delicious food will give you a wonderful sense of well-being.

Canning Your Harvest

Whenever you can your harvest, you want to start out with fresh and unspoiled food. Remove any spots of decay. Wash foods thoroughly in clean water. Keep cold foods, especially meats, cold until you are ready to can them.

How you will can your food depends on it's pH content. The more acidic the food, the less heating time or less heat is required to destroy bacteria. Foods with less acidity need more time or more heat in order to be safe. Most fruits are more acidic and can be canned using a water-bath method. However, vegetables like corn and beans are less acidic and so must be canned using a pressure cooker. Tomatoes have always been in the middle, and it was recommended that water-bath canning was fine. But recently researchers discovered that the acid content of tomatoes depends on where they were grown as well as their variety and ripeness.

It is imperative that you can your foods for the correct amount of time in the correct manner.

ALERT

Botulism is caused by a certain kind of bacterium, *Clostridium botulinum,* that is practically everywhere in the soil. The bacteria themselves are not poisonous in their dormant state. However, when heated, the spores in the bacteria begin to grow and form a toxin. The spores are resistant to heat and thrive in an airless, low-acid, and low-sugar-content atmosphere. They are killed, however, by the 240°F temperatures achieved by heating under pressure.

Botulism toxin is one of the most deadly poisons known on earth. If you merely touch a finger to it and touch that finger to your lips to taste, you could get enough toxins to kill you. Luckily, the number of botulism cases are rare, but one death is too many. This isn't meant to frighten you away from home canning, because hundreds of thousands of people successfully home can their produce every year. This is to remind you that you cannot take shortcuts when it comes to preserving your food.

Before you begin canning look at your equipment, especially your jars. Most canning jars are made to be used year after year. Throw away any chipped or cracked jars. Canning lids are meant to be used only once. Throw away any old canning lids. Rings can be used over and over again, unless they don't fit tightly. Check your pressure cooker; usually your Extension System office will have information on pressure cooker checkups in the spring.

The U.S. Department of Agriculture offers a twenty-five-page booklet through the Extension service that explains what you need to know about canning, including a section titled "How Much Should I Can?" You can find that booklet at *extension.usu.edu/files/publications/publication/pub__1510735.pdf.*

Water-Bath Canning

For water-bath or steam-bath canning you need jars, lids, rings, a canning kettle, a rack, and a jar lifter. Place the prepared fruit in sterile, clean hot jars, covered with either water or syrup depending on your recipe. Put the lid and ring on immediately and tighten. Lower the jar into your kettle of boiling water. You will need a rack on the bottom of your kettle for the jars to sit on. Without a rack, the jars could break. The kettle has to be tall enough and the water deep enough so the water will cover the jars by at least 1 to 2 inches at all times. If the processing will take a long time, have an auxiliary kettle filled with boiling water waiting to replace the evaporated water. Once you have filled the kettle with your jars, make sure the water is at a boil, place the lid on the kettle, and set your timer.

Once the correct amount of time has passed, remove the jars with a jar lifter and place them on top of a towel or wooden board on your table or counter. As they cool you will hear the sound of popping, which indicates the lids have sealed.

Start timing your next batch once the water has come to a boil again.

Pressure-Cooker Canning

Pressure canning is not only a wonderful way to preserve vegetables, it's also a great way to preserves meats, poultry, and fish.

Unlike a water-bath canner, the jars do not need to be completely covered with water in a pressure canner. The directions that come with your specific brand of pressure canner tell you how many cups of water to add in order for it to generate the right amount of pressure.

ESSENTIAL

Modern pressure canners are lightweight, thin-walled aluminum or stainless-steel kettles. Most have twist-on lids fitted with gaskets. They have removable racks, a weighted vent port (steam vent), and a safety vent. They also have either a dial gauge for indicating the pressure or a weighted gauge that rattles when the appropriate pressure has been reached.

Place the specific amount of water into the canner, along with the rack. Place the canner on the burner and bring the water to a boil. Place the filled jars, already fitted with lids, on the rack in the canner. Place the canner lid on the canner and twist to seal it down. Initially leave the pressure weight off the vent port until the water boils and steam escapes strongly from the open vent. Let the steam flow for ten minutes. Place the weight on the vent. Once the pressure gauge has indicated the proper pressure, or the weight has begun to rattle, you can start timing your jars according to the recipe you use. Adjust the stove temperature to maintain the desired pressure. Once the time has elapsed, turn the heat off and allow the canner to cool down until the pressure is vented.

ALERT

DO NOT try to open the canner while there is still pressure inside. This can cause a serious scalding.

Once the canner has cooled, lift off the weight, open the top, and remove the jars. Carefully place the jars onto a towel or wooden board.

Drying Food

Perhaps the oldest method of preserving food is drying it. Drying is the process of removing water from food to prevent the growth of microorganisms and decay. Air-drying food is more applicable to people living in a warm and dry climate, but with today's countertop dehydrators, even leftovers can be chopped into smaller pieces, placed into a dryer, and packaged for later.

ESSENTIAL

You might be surprised to learn that drying foods actually saves more of the nutrient value. Because drying foods is achieved at a lower temperature, the digestive enzymes, which break down food in the course of digestion, and other nutrients are not destroyed. Drying is more economical than canning or freezing, saves space, and provides nutrition.

Drying foods is not as precise as canning and freezing because it involves so many factors, including type of food, water content, climate, and humidity. However, there are some basic guidelines that should be followed. Start with fresh, unblemished, unspoiled food. Cut food into small, thin slices. Place food so it does not overlap. Turn food frequently to ensure a consistent dehydration. Store dried foods in a closed container at room temperature and use within one year.

You can dry many different kinds of fruits, vegetables, herbs, and meats. You are primarily looking for denser material that does not hold a lot of liquid. For example, watermelon is not a good fruit to dry. It's a good idea to start off with a small batch of whichever food you want to dry to see if you are satisfied with the taste, texture, and color of the finished product.

You might want to see which foods are commercially dried, like cherries, apples, herbs, and beef, to give you an idea of some of the things you might want to dry at first. Then feel free to use your knowledge and experiment with other foods, following the appropriate safety standards.

Air-Drying

The process of air-drying is very easy. You gather the produce you want to air-dry, hang it in a clean, dry area that has good air circulation, and check on it occasionally to view its progress. Air-drying is often done with herbs.

FACT

Air-drying is not only the easiest and least expensive way to dry fresh herbs; the slow drying process doesn't deplete the herbs of their oils. This process works best with herbs that don't have high moisture content, like bay, dill, marjoram, oregano, rosemary, summer savory, and thyme.

To dry herbs, gather clean herbs together by their stems, place them in a paper sack with holes punched in it for air circulation, and hang them upside down in a warm, airy room. You can also air-dry small red peppers by threading them onto floral wire or twine and hanging them in a warm room.

Electric Drying

Electric food dehydrators come in a variety of models and have many capabilities. Dehydrators with multiple trays will save you time because you will be able to process more produce at the same time. Dehydrators with higher wattage will also save time because the higher temperature will decrease the drying time. Because fruits, vegetables, and meats should be dried at different temperatures, an adjustable thermostat that gives you the freedom to select different temperatures is useful.

Pickling

Pickling is one of the oldest methods of preserving foods and is a process that can be applied to vegetables, meats, eggs, and fruit. Pickling is the preserving of food in an acid, such as vinegar, and it is this acidic environment that prevents growth of undesirable bacteria.

The varieties of pickled and fermented foods are classified by ingredients and method of preparation. Regular dill pickles and sauerkraut are fermented and cured for about three weeks. Refrigerator dills are fermented for about one week. Fresh-pack or quick-process pickles are not fermented; some are brined several hours or overnight, then drained and covered with vinegar and seasonings. Fruit pickles usually are prepared by heating fruit in seasoned syrup acidified with either lemon juice or vinegar. Relishes are made from chopped fruits and vegetables that are cooked with seasonings and vinegar.

FACT

Most pickled foods are salted or soaked in brine first to draw out moisture that would dilute the acid used to safely preserve the food.

As mentioned before, the safety of canning relies on the acidity of the contents of the jar. The level of acidity in a pickled product is as important to its safety as it is to taste and texture. Make sure you are using vinegar with a 4 to 6 percent acid to be safe, although many food safety professionals are now advising 5 percent. Do not alter vinegar, food, or water proportions in a recipe and do not use vinegar with unknown acidity. Use only recipes with tested proportions of ingredients. Select fresh, unspoiled, and unblemished fruits or vegetables. Use canning or pickling salt. White vinegar is usually preferred when light color is desirable, as is the case with fruits and cauliflower.

Freezing

Freezing food is an excellent method of food preservation. It allows many foods to be stored for weeks or even months longer than they can be in the refrigerator and to be defrosted as needed, with no or very little loss of quality and nutrients.

Freeze food as quickly as possible after harvest. Never freeze food that has even the smallest degree of spoilage. When freezing non-liquid foods, such as vegetables or loose berries, fill your freezer containers as full as possible, because air dries out food. For example, when freezing blueberries you should clean the berries and air-dry them. Then pack them tightly into containers, being sure not to crush them, but filling the container to capacity. If you're freezing liquids, remember to leave expansion space in the containers. To keep items from freezing into one big block of produce, spread them out on cookie sheets and initially freeze them this way. When frozen, transfer to a container.

FACT

Freezing doesn't entirely halt the action of enzymes that break down food, so anything stored longer than twelve months should be thrown away.

The National Center for Home Food Preservation offers an online manual for the blanching times for certain fruits and vegetables before freezing. This process is done to inhibit destructive enzymes that break down food over time. You can find that information at *www.uga.edu/nchfp/how/freeze/blanching.html*.

CHAPTER 10

Building a Root Cellar

Root cellar storage keeps vegetables and fruits fresh longer because of the temperature and climate in the cellar. Planning your root cellar starts when you plan your garden and your orchard. Grow foods that store well in a cellar. Apples, beets, late cabbage, carrots, celery, onions, parsnips, potatoes, sweet potatoes, salsify, turnips, and winter squash can be stored without canning. In a root cellar, the flavor and texture of vegetables change very little, and the foods retain most of their nutritional value. Storing produce in a root cellar preserves more nutritional value than any other type of food preservation. The advantages you have in using a root cellar are the reduced dependence on electricity and less food processing time for you.

Choosing Crops for Fall Storage

Root crops, including potatoes, carrots, beets, turnips, rutabagas, winter radishes, kohlrabi, and parsnips, adapt to root cellar storage. This group stores best at near-freezing temperatures with a high relative humidity.

Onions can also be stored near freezing, but need a low relative humidity to discourage neck rot. Leafy crops such as celery and cabbage may also be stored. Store them by themselves—they give off ethylene gas while in storage, which has proven to cause other vegetables to spoil quicker.

Pumpkins and winter squash store longest at 50°F to 60°F and a low relative humidity.

ESSENTIAL

If you're planning on storing apples, look for firm, long-lasting apples. These are usually thick-skinned, tart apples like Rome apples. Melrose, Fuji, and Granny Smith are other examples of winter apples that will last well into the early spring when stored properly.

Apples need to be stored at near freezing with high humidity, and should not be stored near potatoes because the ripening apples give off the same ethylene gas that celery and cabbage produce. This gas will also make your potatoes sprout prematurely.

When selecting vegetables for storage, discard any unsound produce. This includes immature, damaged, or diseased specimens. Keep a fairly close eye on your produce and remove any that has begun to spoil. You will find that the old axiom "one bad apple will spoil the bushel" is true.

Harvesting and Preparing for Storage

When you are planning to harvest for your root cellar, the later you harvest, the better. Your root crops will store best if they are kept in the ground until there is a danger of soil freezing.

Also, if your crops remain in the ground, they are easily accessible if you need them. And you don't want to start storing them until the temperature in your root cellar is near freezing.

However, be sure to dig your root crops out of the earth before the soil freezes. Once harvested, remove any plant tops, clean roots by brushing off any excess dirt, and put them into storage.

Do not harvest winter squash and pumpkins until the vines are frost-killed and the skin is hard to the thumbnail. Leave stems on the fruit to protect against disease invasion. Parsnips will actually withstand freezing. Harvest some of your crop for use during the fall and winter, but leave a portion of the crop in the ground and dig in the spring. You will find the flavor will be greatly enhanced.

ESSENTIAL

You can actually postpone your harvest by hilling soil over the shoulders of carrots and beets to protect them from freezing. If you want to delay the harvest even further, you can pile straw and soil over the row as insulation.

Onions can be harvested as soon as their tops fall over. Pull up the onions, remove the tops, and dry the onions in mesh bags or crates where they have good air circulation until the necks dry down. You can tell when they are ready to be stored—they rustle when you handle them.

Kale and collards can be left in the garden long after the first fall frost. Harvest as needed until the foliage finally succumbs to cold weather. Celery and late cabbage may be harvested after the frost has stopped their growth. Pull celery with its roots attached. Cut cabbage and remove the loose outer leaves.

When harvesting apples, pick and handle the fruit carefully to prevent unnecessary damage. Sort through the apples during harvest and discard bruised or cut ones. You will also want to discard apples that show insect or disease problems. Separate the apples by size. Use the largest apples first, as they don't store as well as the smaller fruit.

Root Cellar Options

A root cellar is really nothing more than some sort of underground containment that maintains a certain temperature and humidity. The book *Root*

Cellaring: Natural Cold Storage of Fruits & Vegetables by Mike and Nancy Bubel has some expanded information about creating a root cellar to meet your needs.

FACT

A root cellar doesn't have to be fancy; a container buried in the ground will work. You can even bury a garbage can and cover it with straw and a layer of plastic.

If you have the time, space, and means to build a root cellar, you need to decide on its size and location.

How big of a cellar should you build? A 5' × 8' root cellar will store 30 bushels of produce; an 8' × 8' cellar should hold plenty for the average family; and a 10' × 10' cellar should take care of everything you can produce. Shelves should be kept several inches away from the wall to increase ventilation and should be made of rot-resistant or pressure-treated wood to stand up to the humidity and weight load from your crops.

FACT

Many older homes will have areas in the basements that already have earthen floors, designed for vegetable storage in the basement. You may already have a root cellar built in! Be sure to check before you start making plans.

Three examples of common root cellars are those built into the ground, into a hill, or built into the basement of your home. There are advantages and disadvantages to each. If you build your root cellar into a hill, you can easily find the door even if there's three feet of snow on the ground. There also will be less chance of food damage from flooding or melting snow. Your cellar can be graded so any water that should run in or seep in will run out the door. However, a cellar in the side of a hill can be much more difficult to excavate.

A cellar built into the ground is easier to excavate, cheaper to build, and can be done in most landscapes. Also, a shelter can be built above it to make it more accessible in inclement weather.

You may find that the advantage of having a root cellar as part of your home is the convenience. You don't have to leave your house to obtain your produce.

However, before you construct a cellar, you have to be sure that you can maintain the humidity and the temperature needed in order to preserve your crops.

Ideal Root Cellar Conditions

You want the temperature of your root cellar to stay near freezing. Depending on where you live, that might not be a problem during winter months. But, a couple of sunny days might bring the temperature up as winter turns to spring. To avoid too much heat, borrow colder temperatures from the ground. Earth, even two feet down, has a remarkably stable temperature. The farther down you go, the more stable it is. You must go down a full ten feet before complete temperature stability is reached, and for the average builder, depth is limited because of the expense of excavating. You can also borrow cool temperatures from the air. Often the nighttime air temperature will be cooler than the air in your cellar, so open a vent to take advantage of the cooler air. You should also think about the location of your root cellar in regard to passive solar heat. Build your root cellar in a place that is shady throughout the day, on the north side of your property, and use insulation to keep out the heat.

Your second most important consideration is humidity. Even if kept cool, vegetables will soften and shrivel up in a low-humidity environment. Most vegetables require high humidities. A typical underground root cellar will generally maintain a high humidity all by itself if it has an earth or dirt floor.

Because the vegetables in your cellar give off gasses that often are conducive to either spoilage or sprouting, you need to plan for good air circulation. Have an inlet vent and an outlet vent.

Keep shelves a couple inches away from the walls of the cellar to encourage air movement. Use wooden bushel baskets to hold your produce; they were actually invented for this purpose and they allow air to circulate from top to bottom.

Spoilage

Once produce is harvested it begins to decay. That's just part of the natural process. Certain microorganisms like bacteria, viruses, yeasts, molds, and protozoans cause the spoilage process. Microorganisms occur everywhere on the skin, in the air, in the soil, and on nearly all objects. It's important for you to remember that some of the conditions that accelerate spoilage, such as inappropriate temperature and moisture control, also encourage the growth of microorganisms that cause foodborne illness. Consequently, spoiled food is not just an issue of quality; it is also often a question of food safety.

The most common cause of spoilage in a root cellar is improper ventilation. Root cellars must have ventilation! This is one of biggest mistakes people make when designing and installing them. Proper ventilation moves the ethylene gas that encourages spoilage away from the produce, increasing your storage time and the quality of the items in storage. It also slows down molds and mildews that thrive in dark, damp, still environments.

Although root cellars need to have some humidity, if temperatures start to rise, moisture coupled with heat will also cause plant deterioration and spoilage. Your root cellar needs to stay moist and at a temperature near freezing (32°F) for most of your root vegetables. If you get much of a temperature fluctuation in your cellar, humid air will condense on the ceiling, walls, and the food you stored as the air cools past its dew point. Excess water on produce can also encourage spoilage. Cover vegetables with burlap, towels, etc., to absorb condensation, and open the vents to get the air moving and remove the excess moisture.

CHAPTER 11

Saving Seeds

Marc Rogers, in his book *Saving Seeds: The Gardener's Guide to Growing and Storing Vegetable and Flower Seeds*, wrote this: "A seed is much, much more than it appears to be. The hard, dry, distinctively shaped particles that we plant in our gardens are really dormant embryos—tiny, already formed plants encased in a protective coating. While we may think of seeds as a beginning, they are really links between generations of plants, vehicles of both the survival of the planet species and the spread of new life."

Why Save Seeds

When you look at a seed, especially an heirloom seed, you see more than the potential for a tomato plant or a head of lettuce. Rather, you can see generations of farmers cultivating, planting, and selecting the best of the yield—not to eat, but to save in order to harvest the seeds for the following year.

FACT

Seeds were so important to our ancestors that at weddings, both the bride's and the groom's families would present the newlywed couple with a gift of some of their own family's seeds.

When immigrants set out to the New World and were limited in the things they could bring across the ocean, they often smuggled seeds with them, not only as a means to begin a new life, but also as a way to connect back to the old one.

If not for generations of seed savers, we would not have the variety of seeds available to us today. And, if not for dedicated seed savers today, many of the wonderful and unique heirloom plants would have become lost forever.

In most cases, you can save seeds from plants classified as annual (those whose life cycle lasts only one year) and biennial (plants whose life cycle lasts two years). The seeds you save from your garden have already become accustomed to your climate, your soil, and even the insects in your area.

Saving garden seeds at the end of each growing season can be a great cost-saving measure. It also assures you that the delicious tomatoes you loved from your garden, or the beans that produced so well, will still be around next year.

The Difference Between Hybrid and Heirloom Seeds

When you purchase heirloom seed, you are getting seed produced from plants that have been saved and grown fifty years or more, their seed passed down from generation to generation.

Hybrid seeds are created by plant breeders. These plant breeders select two similar plant varieties and crossbreed them to create a new plant variety that features traits from the two parent plants. For example, a plant breeder might select one plant that is frost resistant, and another that has a sweeter taste. The new plant—the offspring of the two varieties—is now a unique hybrid variety that is both frost resistant and has a sweeter flavor.

FACT

An heirloom is open-pollinated, which simply means the plant is capable of producing seeds that will grow a new plant identical to the parent plant the seed came from.

Hybrid seeds are not bad in any way. They have helped increase crop yield and made it easier for many gardeners to be successful. However, hybrid seeds are not open-pollinated. If you save their seeds, the forthcoming plant will not be identical to the parent plant. It might not be sweeter or frost resistant. Many hybrid seeds can be sterile and will not germinate. In order to have the same success you had with the initial offspring, you have to buy your seeds from the plant breeder again.

The beauty of an heirloom seed is the ability of the plant to change on its own. When you save heirloom seeds you select the one that ripened the fastest, was frost resistant, or was sweetest, and save its seeds. So, in time, the seed works through the same process as the hybrid, but it's a natural process. The offspring of that open-pollinated seed will produce the same results, or better, over and over again.

Collecting Seeds

As you work in your garden, you need to watch and see which of your plants you want to choose for seed saving. Once you choose the plant, you should do something to identify it, so you don't accidentally harvest it. Whether you decide to place a certain-colored stake next to it, or tie a piece of ribbon around its stem, be sure you share your plan with the other members of your family.

You want to pick the vegetable or fruit at the peak of maturity, so your seed has the best chance of reproducing. There are three basic types of seed-bearing garden plants: fleshy fruits, seed crops, and those that scatter their seeds. When collecting the seeds for fleshy plants, like tomatoes and peppers, you should allow the fruits to ripen, or even overripen slightly, before you collect the seed. But you don't want the fruit to blemish, mold, or shrivel around the seeds. You are still looking for a healthy parent plant.

ESSENTIAL

In nature, the vegetables and fruit we eat are, in reality, merely the food supply for the seeds inside. As the plant matures, the seeds inside become stronger and ready to survive on their own.

When you collect from the seed crops, like corn, wheat, and beans, you want the plant to mature. These seeds will not deteriorate or blow away if the crop is left on the stalk or vine, as long as they remain dry.

Lettuce, onions, and broccoli are part of the group that scatters seeds. To be sure you capture the seeds from these plants, you can either watch them every day, collecting small amounts as they become available, or fashion a bag made of cheesecloth around the seed head to capture the seeds as they mature.

Extracting and Drying Seeds

When you extract the seeds from seed-containing fleshy fruits, you need to separate the seed from the pulp. If you've ever carved a pumpkin and cleaned it out, you will understand the process exactly. Once you've separated the seeds, wash them thoroughly and spread them out to dry. Large seeds can take up to a week to dry, smaller seeds half of that.

The best way for you to separate tomato seeds is to ferment them. The easiest way to do this is to slice open the tomato and squeeze the contents into a glass jar. Then you can add water to about halfway up the jar, stir, and set aside for a few days. A moldy residue will collect on the top of the water, as well as some tomato seeds. The tomato seeds that float to the top are worthless seeds. After about four days the water will clear and the good seeds will sink to the bottom of the jar. Discard the bad seeds and tomato pulp and place the good seeds on a paper towel to dry. Once dried, they can be removed from the paper and stored.

To extract the seed crop seeds, wait until the plants are fully dried and then twist them or pull their stalks through your hands to separate the kernels. Make sure they are dried and then store them.

The seeds you collected from the group that scatters seeds can be shaken through a hardware screen to ensure that pieces of chaff are not stored with them, and then dried and stored. Be sure to give your seeds a long enough drying period. Storing seeds with a high moisture content will cause them to germinate poorly the following year.

Storing Seeds

You should store seeds in conditions that are cool, dark, and dry. Temperature fluctuations, especially heat, and humidity are seeds' worst enemies. Seeds do best at a moisture content of about 8 percent.

One way for you to ensure moisture content is to use a desiccant (a product used to remove excessive humidity) with your seed packets and seal them together in an airtight jar. A standard canning jar and lid, along with some silica gel, will do the trick. Add the silica gel to the jar; add the seeds, still in their packets, to the jars, and seal. Small seeds will dry down to 8–10 percent moisture overnight, while large seeds may take several days. Seal the dried seeds in a new, dry jar and label it clearly. Then place it in a dark, cool place. You can even store seeds in your refrigerator or freezer.

Testing Seeds

After you've done all you can to identify, collect, extract, and store, you will want to be sure your seeds are viable for the next season before you plant them in the ground. The sure measure of success is a germination test. This test can be performed at the start of the regular growing season, so you don't waste your time and your land on seeds that are unprofitable.

A good germination test will provide the seeds with model conditions of moisture, air, temperature, and light.

Select ten or more seeds from the group to be checked. Spread out the seeds on a damp paper towel. Roll up the paper towel, thoroughly moisten it, and seal it in a polyethylene bag (like a Ziploc bag). Be sure to label the outside of the bag with the seed type. The inside of the bag should be moist, but not wet. Place the bag in a warm area (about 70°F).

Occasionally check the bag to ensure that the towel remains damp. Judge the germination test by the guidelines generally acceptable for the particular seed tested. If most of the seeds germinated in the time suggested, your seeds are worth planting. You can judge how thickly you should plant your seeds by the percentage of seed that germinated during the test.

CHAPTER 12

The Buzz about Beekeeping

People have been keeping bees for over 150 years. Bees are an essential part of agriculture, necessary for pollinating plants to ensure a better fruit set and bigger crops. Poorly pollinated plants produce fewer, often misshapen, fruits and lower yields of seed with inevitable consequences upon quality, availability, and price of food. One of the few farm activities that can actually increase yields, rather than simply protect existing yields from losses, is managing bees to encourage good pollination.

Is Your Location Right for Bees?

Honeybees can be kept almost anywhere there are flowering plants that produce nectar and pollen. Choose a site for beehives that is discrete, sheltered from winds, and partially shaded. Avoid low spots in a yard where cold, damp air accumulates in winter.

FACT

Bees pollinate about one-sixth of the world's flowering plant species and some 400 of its agricultural plants.

The best beehive location is one where your best source of pollen and nectar is within two square miles of your hive, the closer the better. Because bees actually use pollen and nectar to produce their own energy, the farther they have to travel for it, the more they have to consume themselves. In contrast, if you can place them closer to their food source, you can collect more honey.

Position your hive so the entrance faces east. This way the early morning sun will alert them to the new day.

FACT

Because flower nectar will often evaporate in the morning hours during the summer, the sooner bees are out of their hive foraging, the more honey they will produce.

The best position for a hive is where it will also have afternoon shade, shielding the hive from the summer sun. Shade, rather than sunlight, will give the bees more time to concentrate their effort on making honey, because they won't need to work on carrying water back and forth to cool the hive.

Basic Equipment

A manmade hive is built to imitate the space that bees leave between their honeycombs in nature. The dimensions are fairly standard and should be copied exactly if you decide to make you own beehives. The following equipment is used within a hive:

- **Bottom board:** a wooden stand that the hive rests upon. Bottom boards can be set on bricks, concrete blocks, cinder blocks, or any stable base to keep the hive off the ground.
- **Hive body or brood super:** a large wooden box that holds eight to ten frames of comb. In this space, the bees rear their brood and store honey for their own use. Up to three brood supers can be used for a brood nest.
- **Frames and foundation:** frames hang inside each super or box on a specially cut ledge, called a rabbet. Frames keep the combs organized inside your hive and allow you to easily and safely inspect your bees. Frames hold thin sheets of beeswax foundation, which is embossed with the shapes of hexagonal cells. Foundations help bees to build straight combs.
- **Queen excluder:** a frame made with wire mesh placed between the brood super and the honey super, sized so workers can move between the brood super and the honey super but keeps the queen in the brood super, so brooding will not occur in honey supers.
- **Honey supers:** shallow boxes with frames of comb hanging in it for bees to store surplus honey. The honey supers hold the honey that is harvested from the hive.
- **Inner cover:** placed on top of the honey super to prevent bees from attaching comb to the outer cover. It also provides insulating dead air space.
- **Outer cover:** placed on top of the hive to provide weather protection.

The following equipment is personal gear:

- **Smoker:** a beekeeper's best friend. A smoker calms bees and reduces stinging. Pine straw, sawdust, chipped wood mulch, grass, and burlap make good smoker fuel.
- **Hive tool:** looks like a small crowbar. It is ideally shaped for prying apart supers and frames.
- **Bee suit or jacket, veil, gloves, and gauntlet:** this is all protective personal gear worn when working with bees.

ALERT

Generally you need light-colored over-gear to keep your clothes clean and to create a barrier between you and the bees. Bees are not threatened by light colors, so the color of the suit makes a great difference as to whether the bees will attack or not.

Thin, plastic-coated canvas gloves, rather than the stiff, heavy leather commercial gloves, are supple and allow you more movement. Gauntlets are long cuffs that slid over your gloves to keep bees from climbing up your sleeves.

- **Ankle protection**—elastic straps with hook-and-loop attachment to prevent bees from crawling up your pants leg.
- **Feeders**—hold sugar syrup that is fed to bees in early spring and in fall.

How to Purchase Bees

Usually the best way to start keeping bees is to buy established colonies from a local beekeeper. Often a local beekeeper might even have a colony he or she wants to give away. It's better to get two colonies at the beginning, because that allows you to interchange frames of both brood and honey if one colony becomes weaker than the other and needs a boost.

Have the beekeeper open the supers. The bees should be calm and numerous enough that they fill most of the spaces between combs.

Moving a hive is a two-person job. It's easiest to move a hive during the winter when they are lighter and populations are low. The first thing you want to do is close the hive entrance. You can accomplish this with a piece of folded window screen. Then look for any other cracks and seal them with duct tape. Make sure the supers are fastened together and the bottom board is stapled to the last super. Remember to open hive entrances after the hives are relocated.

ALERT

If you are buying the colonies, realize that the condition of the equipment usually reflects the care the bees have received. If you find the colonies housed in rotting hives, don't purchase them.

Installing Packaged Bees

You can also buy packaged bees and queens. Bees are commonly shipped in 2- to 5-pound packages of about 10,000 to 20,000 bees. Keep the packages cool and shaded when they arrive. To transfer bees to their new hive, set up a bottom board with one hive body and remove half of the frames. Spray the bees heavily with sugar syrup (one part sugar to one part water) through the screen on the package; the bees will gorge themselves with syrup and become sticky, making them easy to pour.

The next step is to move the queen, which will be in a separate cage. Pry off the package lid, remove the can of syrup provided for transit, find and remove the queen suspended in her cage, and reclose the package.

ESSENTIAL

The queen cage has holes at both ends plugged with cork. Under the cork at one end you will see that it is filled with white "queen candy." Remove the cork from this end and suspend the queen cage between two center frames in your hive. Workers bees will eventually eat through the candy and release the queen.

Shake the original package lightly to move all bees into a pile on the bottom. Take the lid off the package again and pour the bees into the hive on top of the queen. As they slowly spread throughout the hive, carefully return the frames to their original positions. Replace the inner and outer covers on the hive. You have successfully created your first colony. You must now feed the bees sugar water until natural nectar starts to appear.

Managing Your Hive

You want your bees to be at their maximum strength before the nectar flow begins. This way, the created honey is stored for harvest rather than used to build up their strength. Feeding and medicating your bees should be done in January through February. Because the queens will resume egg-laying in January, some colonies will need supplemental feeding of sugar syrup.

By mid-February, you should inspect your hives. You should be looking for population growth, the arrangement of the brood nest, and disease symptoms. If one of your colonies has less brood than average, you can strengthen it by transferring a frame of sealed brood from your other colony.

If you use two brood supers and find that most of the bees and brood are in the upper super, reverse the supers, placing the top one on the bottom. You want to do this because it relieves congestion. When a colony feels congested it swarms, looking for another place to live. If you only have one brood super, you will need to relieve congestion by providing additional honey supers above a queen excluder.

Annual requeening can be done in early spring or in the fall. Most feel that requeening is one of the best investments a beekeeper can make. Young queens not only lay eggs more prolifically, but they also secrete higher levels of pheromones, which stimulates the worker bees to forage.

In order to requeen a colony, you must find, kill, and discard the old queen. Then you need to allow the colony to remain queenless for 24 hours. After that period of time, you can introduce the new queen in her cage, allowing the workers to eat through the candy in order to release her.

By mid-April your colonies should be strong enough to collect surplus nectar. This is when you should add honey supers above the hive bodies. Add enough supers to accommodate both the incoming nectar and the large bee population. Adding supers stimulates foraging and limits late-season swarming.

During late summer and early autumn, the brood production and the honey production drop. At this point, you should crowd the bees by giving them only one or two honey supers. This forces bees to store honey in the brood nest to strengthen the hive. Colonies are usually overwintered in two hive bodies or in one hive body and at least one honey super. Be sure that if you overwinter in one hive body and a honey super, you remove the queen excluder so the queen can move up into the honey super during winter. If your colony is light on stores, feed them heavy syrup (two parts sugar to one part water). Bees should have between 50 to 60 pounds of stores going into winter. A hive with a full deep frame weighs 6 pounds and full shallow frame weighs 3 pounds. You can pick up the frame to estimate the weight of the hive and stores. Never allow stores to drop below 12 to 18 pounds.

Common Problems

The common problems you encounter when raising bees are swarming, stings, and diseases and pests that can affect your hive.

Swarming

You cannot prevent bees from swarming all of the time. You can, however, make a swarm less likely by requeening your colony with a younger queen. You can also have a "bait hive" in place in case a swarm occurs. Bees will cluster within 100 feet of their old hive while the scout bees search for a new hive. A bait hive is simply an attractive home waiting for a swarm to discover.

Stings

If you keep bees, you are going to get stung. You can reduce stinging greatly by taking precautions and wearing protective gear, using a smoker, and handling bees gently. However, the likelihood is that you're still going to get stung. If there is a chance you are allergic to bee stings, you do not want to keep bees. If you are not allergic, you probably will find, as most beekeepers do, that although stings still hurt, after a few bites there is generally less of a reaction.

Honeybee Diseases and Pests

Honeybee brood and adults are attacked by bacteria, viruses, protozoans, fungi, and exotic parasitic mites. Additionally, bees and beekeeping equipment are attacked by a variety of insects. Some insects, like the wax moth, lay eggs on the equipment and their larva gnaw boat-shaped indentations in the wooden frame or hive body to attach their silken cocoons. With heavy infestations, frame pieces may be weakened to the point of collapse. Some insects, like spiders, actually eat bees. Disease and pest control requires constant vigilance by the beekeeper. Contact local beekeepers to learn about the diseases and issues prevalent in your area and how to prevent and cure them.

Gathering Honey

It's best to harvest your honey on a sunny, windless day, since bees are calmest then. Remove the bees from the hive by blowing smoke into the hive opening. After a few minutes, pry the outer cover loose and lift it off. Blow more smoke through the hole in the inner cover. Now you can remove the inner cover. After the inner cover is removed, once again blow smoke into the hive to finally drive the bees downward and out of the way.

Remove the super and pry the frames loose with the hive tool. Be careful not to crush any bees. A crushed bee releases a scent that stimulates other bees to attack. Gently brush off any bees that are clinging to the frames. A comb that is ready to be harvested should be about 80 percent sealed over.

Uncap the combs in a bee-proof location, like a tightly screened room. Bees will want to take the honey, if they can get to it. Slice off the comb tops with a sharp knife warmed in hot water. A heavy kitchen knife is fine. It's best to use two knives, cutting with one while the other is heating. Once the honey is extracted, return the emptied combs to the hive for the bees to clean and use again. With care, combs can be recycled for twenty years or more.

Legal Requirements

All states have laws that pertain to keeping bees and registering hives. You need to understand the laws of your state before you begin beekeeping. Now, because of parasitic bee mites and the Africanized honeybee, some states have even more stringent laws. For specific legal information, you can contact your county Extension agent or your state department of agriculture.

CHAPTER 13

Raising Your Own

Raising your own livestock can be a wonderful experience. You can delight in the daily gathering of fresh brown eggs or frothy goat's milk. The meat and poultry on your table will never taste better. You will know, with certainty, what went into the food you are eating. And you will learn to respect not only the process of raising your own, but also the animals that provided it for you.

Can You Afford It?

The late Carla Emery, author of *The Encyclopedia of Country Living*, wrote that animals had four basic rights—treatment when injured or diseased, freedom from extreme physical discomfort, sufficient and nourishing food and water, and care that minimizes fear and stress. If you meet those needs, you will have success in raising livestock.

However, you also need to be sure that your own needs are going to be met as you consider raising livestock. These are the areas you need to think about:

- Your lifestyle
- Your location
- Your return on investment
- Your livestock options
- Your shelter options
- Your animal husbandry experience

Once you've looked through these initial considerations, you can decide on the kind of livestock you want for your sustainable lifestyle. This chapter gives you an overview of your options; you will still need to learn more about the requirements of your specific animal.

Your Lifestyle

A dairy farmer gets up every morning at 4 A.M. and goes out to the barn to start his milking process. He can't sleep in because the cows are used to getting milked at a certain time every day. If he is late the cows can develop mastitis, a disease that blocks the teat and can eventually cause infection and death. Once the cows are milked in the morning, he does the other chores throughout his day and returns to his herd in the afternoon to repeat the process. Dairy farmers don't take vacation days. They don't skip milking for the holidays. They are tied to their farms.

As an owner of livestock, you will not be able to take a vacation or an overnight trip without considering the needs of your animals. If you have dairy cows or goats, you have an every-day, year-round responsibility. If you have chickens that are egg layers, you have a little more flexibility. You can stay away from them for a few days, as long as you have seen to their needs before you leave. However, if you are raising meat chickens, they need daily tending. Some people have been lucky enough to work out arrangements with friends in similar circumstances, and they take turns tending each other's livestock. Just remember, as you consider the kind of animals you want to raise and the size of your herd, that these animals depend on you every day.

Your Location

Your location will determine the kind of animals you decide to purchase. Check with your local zoning laws to be sure you can keep animals on your site. (If you are living in the country, this shouldn't be an issue. But it never hurts to check.) Find out what was raised on your acreage before you purchased it. There are some diseases that cross from one type of animal to another through soil contamination. (Talk to your veterinarian about how to vaccinate against the possibility of exposure.) Size matters! When an animal is raised in conditions that don't allow enough space to graze and move around, it becomes stressed. Stressed animals are more susceptible to disease.

FACT

Diseases like tetanus, botulism, and blackleg are caused by the family of bacteria known as *Clostridia*. These bacteria can remain viable in the soil for years. They are resistant to heat, cold, drought, ultraviolet radiation, and chemical disinfectants.

Your Return On Investment

It will generally cost you more to raise your own meat and dairy than it would to go to the nearest grocery store and purchase it. However, the meat, eggs, and milk you grow will more than likely taste better and be healthier. The cost of raising animals includes the initial purchase price, their feed, their shelter, equipment needed to raise them, any vet fees, and slaughtering fees (unless you are going to process them yourself; see Chapter 15). If you can grow your own feed, then you've cut down your costs considerably. Remember, animals that graze won't have access to their pasture through winter and spring in many areas. Also, even grass-fed animals need grain supplements. Equipment can be used year after year, so in the long run your equipment costs will be negligible.

As you add up the cost for raising your animal, don't forget that what you see "on the hoof" is not what you will get in your freezer. For a typical steer you can estimate that half of its live weight will be lost during the initial slaughtering process. Then, when the butcher processes it into various cuts, you will lose another one-third of the weight. In other words, with a 1,200-pound steer, you will end up with approximately 400 pounds of meat.

ESSENTIAL

Processors charge a "kill," or "slaughter," fee and charge a price-per-pound processing fee on the dressed weight, or hanging weight, of the animal. For example, if the kill fee is $40, the processing fee is .65/pound, and you have a 1,200-pound steer, your processing cost would be 600 (approximate dressed weight in pounds) x .65 = $390 + $40 (kill fee) = $430.

Your Livestock Options

Depending on the kind of animal you raise and your long-term goal, the cost of an animal can vary greatly. A purebred bull can cost over $10,000, depending on the breed and lineage, but you can also purchase a sale barn steer for $25. If your goal is to create a herd that can be sold for breeding purposes, a purebred bull is the way to go. If you are only thinking about filling your freezer in eighteen months, the sale barn steer will do the trick. As you consider your livestock options, take into account your geographic location and the hardiness of the varieties you choose. You will also want to research the length of time to slaughter. For example, it only takes meat chickens about eight weeks to be ready for slaughter. This amount of time gives you chickens that are dressed out (ready for consumption) and weigh about 4 pounds. Turkeys take much longer before they can be processed, about twenty weeks, and they will, therefore, consume more food. But you will also end up with about five times more meat. Your local Extension agent will be able to give you information about the varieties that thrive in your particular area.

Your Shelter Options

Good shelter from weather and predators is essential for raising any kind of livestock. Lambs and calves can die from exposure. Chickens are easy prey to foxes, raccoons, coyotes, and the neighbors' dogs. You need to protect your investment with a shelter that is secure and clean. You can be creative with recycled building materials to create the right shelter for your livestock, but keep two things in mind as you draw up the design—manure removal and animal control. A clean shelter is essential for healthy animals, and efficient manure removal will make the chore much easier. Animal control encompasses being able to move your livestock from one area to another with the least amount of trouble and getting access to the animal when you need it. This might seem insignificant, but when you are trying to give a 1,500-pound steer a shot of antibiotics, for example, you will be glad that you built a small holding pen in your barn.

QUESTION

Where can I go for more information about building a barn or shelter?
The books: *Building Small Barns, Sheds & Shelters* by Monte Burch; *Practical Pole Building Construction: With Plans for Barns, Cabins, & Outbuildings* by Leigh Seddon; and *Low-Cost Pole Building Construction: The Complete How-To Book* by Ralph Wolfe.

Good fences are essential for raising any kind of livestock. You have probably seen photos of chickens wandering loose all around the barnyard. But what those photos don't show you are the chickens devouring every last grape on the vine just before you were going to pick them for grape juice. You will also find that larger animals, like steers and goats, will be very willing to take advantage of any weaknesses in your fencing. There are also livestock, like pigs, who root underneath a fence and will need a fence line that is planted at least several inches below the ground.

Your Animal Husbandry Experience

Raising animals on a farm is vastly different from owning a dog or a cat in the city. You might never consider giving your pet vaccinations on your own, but on the farm it is common practice to give your animals shots. Although you can order your vaccines in bulk by mail or online, buying through your local veterinarian has the added benefit of the vet's free advice. Most farmers also keep antibiotics on hand for common maladies, but if you are inexperienced, the safest route is to call the veterinarian and allow her to diagnose the problem.

Other routine animal husbandry procedures are:

- **Dehorning:** removing the horn button on young animals so a horn does not grow
- **Castrating:** removing an animal's testicles when he is young
- **Hoof trimming:** removing part of the "toenail" of the animal to prevent foot problems
- **Shearing:** removing the fleece of an animal
- **Livestock reproduction:** everything from artificial insemination to helping with birthing

The sooner you master these tasks, the better. Books like *The Encyclopedia of Country Living* can give you a lot of good information, but the best way to learn is through experience. Volunteer to help a livestock-raising neighbor with these tasks in order to get some on-the-job training.

FACT

Rocky Mountain oysters are actually bull testicles. They are usually peeled, coated in flour, pepper, and salt, sometimes pounded flat, and then deep-fried. This delicacy is most often served as an appetizer.

Raising Poultry

Poultry is raised for egg or meat production or a combination of the two. You can learn a lot about different breeds and their production strengths by going to hatchery websites like Murray McMurray Hatchery (*www .mcmurrayhatchery.com*).

Chickens

If you are raising chickens for meat you will find the most efficient feed-to-flesh conversion ratio with the Cornish Rock broiler. These hybrid chickens grow quickly and produce broad breasts and big thighs (think white meat and dark meat.) But if you are buying chickens in order to create a flock that self-propagates, these are not the chickens for you. First, because they are hybrid, the chicks will not turn out like the parents. Second, because these chickens have been bred to grow so rapidly, they have been known to have heart attacks after three or four months. There are slower growing breeds that are both egg laying and meat producing. These breeds are a wonderful choice for growing a small farm flock. The meat growth will take more time and you will have a lower feed-to-flesh conversion ratio, but you will not have the expense of buying new chicks year after year because you will be able to hatch your own. Generally in these situations, you take the roosters (males) and grow them for meat, because you only need one rooster (and perhaps a backup rooster) for your flock.

Egg layers are often divided into two divisions, Bantams and Standards. Bantams are very small birds and come in a variety of colors and types. They require less room and less feed than Standards, but they produce smaller eggs (three Bantam eggs equal two regular eggs in a recipe). Bantams are often raised as pets because they have great personalities, but don't let that fool you into thinking they aren't producers. Bantams make the best brooders (hens that sit on their eggs so they hatch), and soon you'll have a good-sized flock of Bantams.

Standards range from heavy breeds to light breeds. They include many of the breeds you might be familiar with—Wyandotte, Rhode Island Red, White Plymouth Rock, and Barred Rock. Standards also include fairly unknown breeds like Turkens (naked-necked chickens that look like turkeys); Crested Breeds, which have tufts of feathers around their heads; and Feather-Footed Breeds. They can produce brown eggs or white eggs and some can even produce colored eggs. No matter what color is on the outside of an egg, the inside is the same. However, if you are thinking about selling some of your excess eggs, brown eggs will bring you more money per dozen. If you are raising a self-propagating flock, look for breeds that are good brooders.

Another resource you can use as you plan your first flock is the Back-Yard Chicken Forum (*www.backyardchickens.com*). This is a forum with many experienced chicken farmers who are willing to share their knowledge with beginners.

ALERT

When you receive your day-old chicks, dip the beak of the chicks in the water before you turn them loose. A baby bird will not instinctively go to the water and can die of dehydration standing right next to a waterer.

Turkeys

Today's turkeys fall into two distinct categories—Broad Breasted and not Broad Breasted. The biggest of the breeds is the Broad Breasted. These birds grow quickly and have remarkably meaty breasts. The tom turkeys (males) can actually end up dressing out (ready for consumption) at 45 pounds, and hen turkeys (females) at 25 pounds. Their breast meat often extends above the breastbone, giving them a busty look. Because these birds have been bred to be so broad-breasted, it limits their natural ability to reproduce and brood. But, unlike the Cornish Rock, their hearts won't give out after a few months. If you want to create a flock of this breed, you will need to artificially inseminate the hens and incubate the eggs.

When you picture the traditional Thanksgiving turkey, you are actually thinking of the Bronze Turkey, one of the not Broad Breasted turkey breeds. This breed is being left behind by the turkey industry because it does not grow as quickly as its Broad Breasted counterpart. Yet these turkeys are better mothers and can be fertilized naturally. Their feed-to-flesh conversion ratio is not as high as the Broad Breasted, but they can still dress out to 10 to 25 pounds.

Turkey eggs are actually good to eat, but because the cost of purchasing turkey poults (newborn turkeys) is fairly high, the eggs should be incubated so you can grow your own flock.

Duck and Geese

Ducks and geese are the guard dogs of farmyard poultry. Geese are much more aggressive than ducks and can produce a nasty bruise on the leg or arm of the unaware. Both are classified as waterfowl, but you don't need a pond or river to raise them. You do, however, need a small tub or child's swimming pool for them that will hold at least 8 inches of water. The water has to be frequently changed so it remains clean and fresh. Because both ducks and geese create a considerable amount of messy droppings, this is not always an easy task. The abundance of droppings is also why it is not a good idea to share the family swimming hole with your waterfowl.

You can raise ducks for either eggs or meat, but geese are raised primarily for their meat. Duck eggs have a particular flavor to them that is unlike chicken eggs and will often reflect what they've eaten. Waterfowl meat is quite high in fat content.

Other than needing a viable, year-round supply of clean water, ducks and geese are fairly self-sufficient. As long as ducks can forage on grain, worms, bugs, and plants—they require little or no commercial feed, which controls costs—they'll do fine. Geese can actually survive on grass; however, because of the quantity of droppings, you will want to limit their accessibility to any grass that is also used by humans.

Raising Rabbits

Rabbits have a higher feed-to-flesh conversion ratio than any other livestock. They are quiet, gentle animals that can be raised almost anywhere. They are well known for their ability to reproduce and provide mild, lean meat that tastes a lot like poultry. Perhaps you are wondering why, if you're going to raise an animal that tastes like poultry, you wouldn't just raise chickens instead. The reason is that rabbits are more efficient and productive than chickens. A female rabbit (doe) can produce up to one thousand times her body weight in food in a single year. You can process (skin and butcher) five rabbits in the same time it takes to process one chicken. Rabbits naturally live in dens and holes, so they can be raised in closer quarters than chickens. Also, rabbit fur is an additional commodity, besides the meat.

A diet of mixed grains like oat, soft wheats, and grain sorghums is a rabbit favorite. You need to supplement that with protein from good legume hay like alfalfa or timothy. Besides grain and hay, a plentiful supply of fresh water is essential for healthy rabbits.

You can raise rabbits in hutches or cages, or create rabbit runs with an outdoor fenced-in area. Letting your rabbits "run" decreases stress, increases their fur density, and gives you better meat because of the exercise. Whatever you decide, be sure that your housing is protected from predators, because that is the greatest danger to your rabbits.

FACT

One baby rabbit is called a kit; there are six to ten "kittens" in a litter. A rabbit's gestational period is one month. When they are two months old, kittens should be weaned from their mothers. You can breed the female again once her litter has been weaned. A doe potentially can give birth to forty kittens in a year's time.

Raising Pigs

The two major considerations you have when raising pigs are (1) whether you are going to buy feeders (young pigs that have been weaned and weigh about 40 pounds) or raise them yourself from your own litter, and (2) site selection.

When you purchase your pigs, look for the cream of the crop; they should be healthy and in good condition when purchased. Characteristics to look for include smooth hair coat, pink skin color, and alertness. Don't buy the runt no matter what kind of "deal" you can get for it. Runts don't have a good feed-to-flesh conversion ratio, and you will be tossing good money after bad. If you are simply raising a pig for meat, it will take from five to seven months to bring it up to the 200-pound mark, which is the optimal weight for a pig. When it gets much bigger than 200–220 pounds, you decrease efficiency (it takes more feed per pound of gain) and you increase the fat. You will obtain about 135 pounds of meat from a 200-pound pig.

If you decide to start raising your own, start out with a sow (female) and a boar (male). A sow can have two litters a year, with each litter producing five or six piglets. However, raising pigs can be difficult because pigs are prone to not only swine-based diseases, but they can also catch diseases that people carry. The more pigs you have, the higher their chances of catching something. If you are thinking about creating your own herd of pigs, be sure to talk to your local Extension agent or veterinarian about the breeds that work best in your area, and the potential diseases.

In real estate, professionals often talk about "location, location, location." Those same words should be your utmost priority once you decide to raise pigs. When air fresheners talk about "Country Fresh" they are not referring to pig manure. There is a unique and penetrating odor to pig manure. When you locate your site, you want to be sure that your home and your neighbors' homes are not downwind of the pigpen.

Truffles, a highly prized subterranean mushroom that can be sold for more than $800 per pound, are found with trained pigs. According to the Royal Philatelic Society London, French hunters of truffles have reported pigs can determine the presence of a truffle from 20 feet away.

Once you decide where, you must create the right combination of shelter for your pig. First, it needs to be secure. Pigs are strong and can easily break through insufficient fences. They also root (digging in the soil with their noses) and can dig underneath a fence line and escape. So, you have to be sure that your fence line extends below the ground about six inches and is of high-quality. In warm weather, pigs need a place that is dry and provides shade; pigs have sweat glands on their snouts only and will sunburn and overheat quickly. This is why pigs enjoy rolling in the mud; the mud not only protects their skin, it also helps to cool them down. If you can create a space in their pen for a dip in the mud, your pigs will be very happy. In cold weather, pigs need a dry place that is protected from the cold and wind.

Although pigs will eat large quantities of just about anything (that's where we get the term "eating like a pig"), they also need a balanced diet of grains (not just corn) in order to gain weight and have the correct meat-to-fat ratio. Pigs can be fed leftovers from your kitchen, the local vegetable processing plant, and even the local cheese processing plant. You just want to be sure that what you feed your pig is healthy and natural. Research what's available in your area and talk to your local Extension agent for more information.

Raising Goats

Goats are wonderfully social animals. They are intelligent, curious, and friendly. They are herd animals, so you should always have more than one goat or you might end up being drafted into their herd. Goats have developed a bad reputation for eating everything in sight, when, in fact, they are fairly picky eaters. Goats are closely related to the deer family and like to nibble on tree branches and brush. Goats can actually starve if just fed grass. They need a combination of grass, brush, weeds, grain, and, of course, clean, fresh water.

Goats' intelligence and curiosity can often get them into trouble. They will find any weakness you have in your fencing. They will sneak into your orchard and nibble off the new growth on your apple trees. They will eat your prized rose bushes. They will also eat things that are not good for them, such as milkweed, azaleas, and laurel, which are actually poisonous to goats. Be sure that you research plants in your area that are hazardous to goats and either eliminate them or be sure that you have a strong fencing system.

You can raise goats for meat, dairy, or fiber. Goat meat is called *chevon*. Young goats (kids) can be sold for meat at Easter time, especially in areas that have a large Greek Orthodox population. Goat milk, goat cheese, goat milk curd, and goat yogurt are excellent commodities and can bring in extra income. Angora and Cashmere goats produce fleece that is highly prized, and you can earn as much from their fleece as from sheep's wool.

Raising Cows

When you decide to raise a cow, you need to understand that you are looking at a long-term commitment. A cow can potentially live twenty years. During that lifespan, she can produce a calf every year and be milked for most of that time. The calves can be raised either for meat or to increase your herd.

The factors you need to consider before purchasing a cow are (1) space, (2) feed, and (3) your needs. A cow will need at least two acres of good pasture. During the time that she can't graze, you will need about 30 pounds of hay per day per cow. If you need to feed your cow hay from the beginning of November to the beginning of April, you could easily need 2½ tons of hay per cow. You will need a place to store the hay, as well as straw for bedding. Your cow will also need grain supplements throughout the year.

Depending on the breed you choose, an average cow can produce about six gallons of milk per day. After giving birth to a calf, a cow can produce milk for over a year. However, a cow is generally rebred sixty to ninety days after the birth of her last calf and only milked for seven months while she is pregnant. The total gestation (the length of a pregnancy) time for a cow is 9½ months. A newborn calf will weigh about a hundred pounds, depending on the breed, and will be able to walk within an hour of being born.

Dairy cattle tend to be gentler animals than beef cattle and are better suited for a family farm. Within the dairy breeds, Jerseys, Guernseys, Brown Swiss, and Holsteins are the friendliest. Because of their smaller size and the high butterfat content of their milk, Jerseys can be the perfect cow for someone just starting out.

Raising Sheep

If you have ever driven by a sheep farm in the spring and seen new lambs frolicking in the green pastures, you will understand the attraction of sheep. Sheep are generally docile animals and are easily handled. They produce both a wool crop and a meat crop. However, you need to get in touch with a local sheep association before you purchase your sheep to better understand the local market.

Like goats, sheep are herd animals, so it is better to buy more than one. Unlike goats, sheep, for the most part, are not highly intelligent. In *The Encyclopedia of Country Living*, Carla Emery writes, "Of all the big domestic animals, sheep are the most vulnerable to catastrophe. They have no natural defense against predators, not much good sense about things in general, and a frequently disastrous instinct to follow the leader, no matter what. If you have one sheep in trouble, you likely have more than one in trouble."

You can raise sheep for wool, meat, and milk. Fine-stranded wool comes from breeds suited to warmer climates; medium-stranded wool from breeds suited to temperate zones, like England; and coarse-stranded wool from breeds that come from cooler, damper climates. White sheep wool is the standard and has a higher market value. When you raise sheep with black wool you need to find alternate markets, like specialty spinners, in order to make any money. Meat breeds produce wool, too. However, if you are raising sheep for your family to eat, be sure they like the unique flavor of lamb and mutton.

If you are looking for an animal specifically for milk production, you are better off getting a goat or a cow. But if you are raising sheep for meat or wool, milk is an extra benefit. Sheep's teats are short and they have a limited lactation (milk production) period, but they can produce up to a quart of milk a day during that time. Because of the higher amount of solids in sheep milk, you will get two or three times more cheese than you would from cow's milk, and it makes superior ice cream and yogurt.

Because of their warm coats, shelter isn't as much of an issue for sheep, unless you live in a polar region. Pregnant ewes (females) will need shelter during cold weather and at lambing time. Also, sheep will need shelter after they are sheared if you live in a colder climate.

Sheep can live entirely on green grass, but check with you local Extension agent to see if there are any plants in your area that are poisonous to sheep.

CHAPTER 14

Hunting

Hunting is simply harvesting wild food. In most places, an experienced hunter is as important to the ecosystem as are food, water, and shelter. A hunter limits the size of a herd or flock, so animals don't overpopulate an area and end up starving to death or becoming diseased. You need to understand, however, that just as you consider the needs of your own domestic livestock, wild animals need to be shown respect and consideration when you hunt.

Know Your Quarry

To be a successful hunter, you need to educate yourself about the game you are hunting. One way to learn about your quarry is to understand its specific characteristics. Animals can be identified by four basic characteristics: markings, sounds, movement, and group behavior.

- **Markings:** the distinctive colors or patterns found on the body of the animal. For example, a male mallard duck (drake) has a teal-colored head, and the female mallard duck (hen) has a light brown–colored head. A male lion has a mane, and the female does not. It is important for you to be able to clearly distinguish your prey, not only by male and female, but also by species, to ensure you are not hunting out of season or hunting an endangered animal.
- **Sounds:** you are probably very familiar with the sounds of a cardinal or a woodpecker. Their distinct calls and sounds alert you to their proximity. Knowing the sounds of your prey will help you track them.
- **Movement:** does your prey leap or burrow when startled? Does it fly straight upward, or start low and then gain altitude? Knowing what to expect from your prey will help you to be ready when you aim your weapon.
- **Group behavior:** you have probably seen geese fly in a V-formation. Understanding group behavior like this will help you place yourself in an optimal position when hunting.

Although these basic characteristics are the most important, studying other animal traits, such as migratory and feeding patterns, animal prints, animal droppings, behavior, and how your quarry protects itself from natural predators will only increase your chance of a successful hunt.

Preparation

The first thing you should do before you plan to hunt is to become educated. Hunter education programs are not only about safety; they also include information to help produce responsible and knowledgeable hunters. There is so much more to hunting than buying a gun and some ammunition. Hunter education programs give beginning hunters a good foundation, and they also can help veteran hunters by reminding them of safe hunting practices.

The four areas most hunter education programs stress are responsibility, safety skills, knowledge, and getting involved to keep hunting a respected sport.

- **Responsibility:** A true hunter behaves responsibly. This includes courtesy to other hunters, landowners, and those who are charged with maintaining lawful hunting. A responsible hunter will never poach, act carelessly, consume alcohol (or any other mind- or behavior-altering substance) before or during shooting, or endanger those around him. Responsible hunters will also learn and obey local hunting laws, practice gun and hunting safety, and wait for a good chance at a clean kill before shooting. A clean kill is when you are able to kill an animal with the least amount of pain and suffering.
- **Safety skills:** A firearm is a very useful tool, but it can be a dangerous weapon in the hands of those who do not know how to correctly use it. Safety skills for hunting are gained through hands-on training and practice. It is important to learn these skills from an experienced hunter or a hunter education program.

QUESTION

Is hunting safe?
According to the National Safety Council, Injury Facts 2008 edition, hunting is by far the safest sport. Figures show that while football players suffer 2,585 injuries per 100,000 participants, baseball players suffer 1,122 injuries per 100,000, and even billiards players suffer 15 injuries per 100,000 participants, the incidence of injuries suffered during hunting activities was only 2 per 100,000.

- **Knowledge:** Hunting isn't only about knowing your quarry, it's also about understanding the limits and uses of your gun, safe gun handling, and hunting skills. No single firearm will be able to meet all of your hunting needs, and each unique firearm has its own strengths and limitations.

- **Involvement:** Because hunting is often a misunderstood sport, part of becoming a good hunter is supporting organizations that work to promote understanding and mutual respect. Organizations like the International Hunter Education Association (IHEA) work to "continue the heritage of hunting worldwide by developing safe, responsible, and knowledgeable hunters." Through these types of organizations, hunters work together to educate others and work with landowners and game wardens to encourage good relationships as well. There are also organizations that are specifically conservation-minded, working to help preserve wildlife habitat and promote wildlife management.

ESSENTIAL

The International Hunter Education Association (IHEA) is the professional association for 67 state and provincial wildlife conservation agencies as well as the 70,000 volunteer instructors who teach hunter education in North America. Hunter education classes reach more than 750,000 students annually. Since 1949, more than 35 million students have been trained.

Equipment

There are several different kinds of equipment that you can use for hunting—firearms, bows, rod and reel, and snares and traps. The most common piece of equipment used for hunting is a firearm.

Firearms

A firearm is a mechanical device that is designed to force a projectile through and out of a metal tube by using pressure from a small explosion. All contemporary firearms have three basic sections—the action, the stock, and the barrel.

- The action consists of the moving parts that load, fire, and eject the cartridges or shells.

- The stock is the body of the firearm. It is generally made from hard-wood or a sturdy synthetic material. It can be produced as a single unit or as two pieces.
- The barrel is the metal tube the ammunition travels through.

The three general categories of hunting firearms are rifles, shotguns, and handguns. The main differences between them are their barrels and the kind of ammunition you use in them.

- The rifle barrel is long and has thick walls with spiraling grooves cut into the bore. The grooved pattern is called *rifling*.
- The shotgun barrel is long and made of thinner steel that is smooth on the inside, as opposed to the spiraling grooves of the rifle. This smooth finish allows the shot and wad to glide down the barrel without friction. The shotgun barrel is thinner than a rifle barrel because it doesn't have to withstand as much pressure.
- The handgun's barrel is shorter than the barrel of a rifle or shotgun because a handgun is designed to be shot while being held with one or two hands, rather than being placed against the hunter's shoulder. The bores of most handgun barrels are similar to those of a rifle, having a grooved pattern.

Caliber is the measurement of the diameter of the inside of a barrel (bore) and is expressed in hundredths of an inch, thousandths of an inch, or millimeters. The caliber is used to describe not only the size of the rifle or handgun bore, but also the size of the ammunition cartridge.

FACT

Caliber designations sometimes have a second number that has nothing to do with the diameter. For example, the popular .30-30 is a .30-caliber cartridge, but the second number is a holdover from the days when the cartridge took 30 grains of powder. The "06" in .30-06 refers to the year (1906) it became adopted by the U.S. military.

Every rifle or handgun is designed for a specific cartridge. The ammunition *must match* the data stamp on the firearm. There are several .30-caliber firearms that use the same bullet size but are designed for different cartridges. If, for some reason, you cannot find the caliber stamped on your firearm, don't try to guess the right caliber; take it to a qualified gunsmith to find out your exact needs.

Rather than caliber, shotguns are classified by gauge. *Gauge* is a measurement, like caliber, that relates to the inside diameter of the shotgun bore and the size of shell designed for that specific bore. Common shotgun gauges are 10 gauge, 12 gauge, 16 gauge, 20 gauge, and 28 gauge.

The smaller the gauge number, the larger the shotgun bore. Gauge used to be determined by the number of lead balls sized equal to the approximate diameter of the bore it took to weigh one pound. For example, if it took ten lead balls, with the same diameter as the bore, to weigh one pound, the gun would be classified as a 10 gauge. Today, however, gauge is measured like caliber, by measuring the inside bore diameter.

The .410-bore shotgun is the only exception to the gauge designation for shotguns. It has an actual bore diameter of 410/1000ths of an inch, which is approximately equivalent to a 67½ gauge.

The gauge of the shotgun is always equal to the gauge of the shell, i.e., a 12-gauge shell for a 12-gauge shotgun. The gauge of a shotgun is usually marked on the rear of the barrel, and the gauge of a shell is marked on the shell as well as on the factory box.

ALERT

Carry only the correct ammunition for the firearm you're using. A common mistake involves putting a 20-gauge shotshell into a 12-gauge shotgun. The smaller-gauge shell will slide through the 12-gauge chamber and partly down the barrel, causing an obstruction. The hunter, especially when excited by the presence of game, then might insert a 12-gauge shotgun shell behind the 20-gauge shell. This can cause injury to the hunter or damage to the firearm.

Your firearm's maximum projectile range is the distance at which your firearm's projectile (or ammunition) can cause injury or damage to persons, animals, or objects in your area. Knowing this range is essential in order to be a safe and responsible hunter. Your firearm also has an effective killing range, which is the distance at which your firearm is at its most efficient and effective for hunting your prey. This is the range where you will most likely have a clean kill. Understanding these ranges and becoming proficient at estimating distances are important parts of hunting.

The storage of firearms and ammunition is very important, not only for the long life of your firearm, but also for the safety of your family. Firearms must be stored unloaded and in a locked location, separate from ammunition. The storage area should be cool, clean, and dry.

Firearms should be stored vertically, or with the muzzle pointed down. Ideally, guns should be hidden from view and locked, in a place away from curious children and potential thieves.

Ammunition should be stored in a secure, cool, dry place in order to prevent corrosion, which can cause jamming and misfiring. Ammunition should be stored away from flammables.

ALERT

Nontoxic shot is required throughout the United States for waterfowl hunting. Studies showed that many waterfowl died each year because of lead poisoning contracted when they picked up and ingested lead pellets from traditional shotshells. The toxic effect spread to other birds, such as the bald eagle, that consumed the poisoned waterfowl. To reduce this problem, conservationists worked with shotshell manufacturers to produce effective alternatives to lead shot.

Bowhunting

Bowhunting is another popular method of hunting. You can define bowhunting as the act of pursuing or taking wild game animals by use of a bow and arrow. You might be surprised to learn that bowhunting is an important aspect of life for many Americans. A 1998 survey by the U.S. Fish & Wildlife Service found that:

- More than 14 million Americans hunt, which represents about 7 percent of the population.
- Forty-four percent of hunters report that they have hunted with a bow.
- Bowhunting continues to grow in popularity, especially in recent years.
- Most bowhunters are between the ages of thirty-five and fifty-four.
- The average age at which an active bowhunter begins hunting is twenty-three.

Unlike hunting with firearms, bowhunting presents a number of challenges:

- Bowhunters need to become proficient archers before attempting to hunt with a bow and arrow. Becoming an archer requires hard work, dedication, practice, and the development of distance-judging skills.
- You need to learn and practice close-range hunting skills, which include scouting, tracking, stalking, and recovering game. Like the early American Indians, a practiced bowhunter needs to learn to walk quietly through the woods to take his quarry unaware. While some may consider this too challenging, others find that the elements of bowhunting add to the pleasure of the hunt. Because you are so close to the game, you gain a different perspective and respect for the animal you are pursuing.
- A critical skill for a bowhunter is mastering bowhunting techniques and animal anatomy and behavior, so you can achieve a quick, clean, and, most important, a humane kill.

Bowhunters must comply with state or provincial legal requirements. These requirements are passed by boards or commissions. Often, these boards are open to public hearings in order to give bowhunters and others an opportunity to provide input. You should remember that hunting is a privilege that can be taken away if you violate the hunting laws in your area. Your hunting license can be revoked if you are convicted of a serious violation or if you have repeated offenses.

Hunting regulations can be found in booklets published by every jurisdiction. These booklets are often found at the places that sell hunting licenses and sporting goods. If you are going to hunt, you need to become familiar with the requirements. Ignorance of a law is no excuse.

FACT

The "rule of first blood" establishes a fair way to determine who can claim an animal shot by two bowhunters. Although the rule may not have legal grounds, its strength and enforcement lie directly with the understanding and true sportsmanship of all responsible bowhunters. The first hunter to place an arrow in an animal's vital area, which draws enough blood to leave a trackable trail and thus has a good chance of bringing the animal to his or her possession, may claim the animal.

Rod and Reel

Angling, or fishing, is one of the most popular forms of recreation in the world. One reason for its popularity is how simple and inexpensive it is to fish. You can fish from a shoreline, from a boat, or from the middle of a river and have great success. You can also fish all year-round, although ice-fishing requires some special equipment. Fishing equipment is called *tackle*. The basic tools are a rod, a reel, fishing line, and hooks and lures.

A fishing rod is a long, straight, flexible pole that can be made of bamboo, fiberglass, or graphite. Rods are used by anglers (fishermen) to cast bait, or lures into the water. Inexpensive rods, like some bamboo and fiberglass, are often popular with beginners. Due to the low maintenance and flexibility, fiberglass rods have become the most popular rods. Graphite rods, though more expensive, are sought by experienced anglers because they are light and strong.

You should choose the length of your fishing rod depending on several factors—the type of fish you are trying to catch, the kind of water you are fishing in, and the surrounding landscape.

If you are fishing in an area where overhanging tree limbs could catch your line and lure, a short, flexible rod might be your best choice. If you are casting in moderate winds, a long, thin rod may be used. If you are planning to fish for heavy game fish in large lakes or in the ocean, you will want to use a shorter, sturdier rod.

The body of the rod is made up of a grip, or handle, that is usually made of high-quality cork or foam. In order to thread your line from your reel to your lure, there are a number of small metal rings called *eyes* attached along the rod to the tip. The eyes help your line flow smoothly when you cast your lure and retrieve it.

A fishing reel stores your line on a spool. The drag, an adjustable friction device found inside the reel, helps create tension on the line as you pull in your catch. When a fish bites your hook, then pulls back on the line, the tension of the line tires the fish and keeps the line untangled. Without a drag system, the fish would take out too much line, causing the line to tangle. And if no line was released, the line would snap. Most reels have adjustable drag settings that you can set depending upon the fish you want to catch.

There are four basic categories of reels: bait casting, spinning, spin casting, and fly.

- A bait casting reel has a covered frame and a horizontal spool that revolves and winds in line when you turn the handle. One handle turn revolves the spool four or five times, which brings in the line quickly.
- Spinning reels have a stationary spool of line set on the underside of the rod. On the outer lip of the spool sits a curved bar, called a bail. The bail acts as a guide for retrieving the line. As the handle is turned, the bail turns too, winding the line tidily onto the spool.
- The spin casting reel is a variation of the spinning reel. But the spin casting reel has a cover over the spool and the line is fed out of a hole. Instead of a bail, metal teeth attached to the spool gather in the line.
- The most basic fishing reel is the fly reel. It only has a frame, which holds a narrow revolving spool. A small handle turns the spool one rotation at a time.

The most popular fishing line used is monofilament nylon line. Not only is most monofilament clear, which makes it difficult for the fish to see, it also is strong, durable, and can stretch a little. Monofilament line comes in a variety of strengths, depending on your needs. The strengths are calculated by "pound test," which is the amount of pressure that can be put on the line before it snaps.

One end of your line is on the reel. At the other end you'll have a baited hook, lure, or fly. The hook is a pointed piece of metal shaped like a question mark. At one end is a loop that attaches to your line. At the other end is a sharp point that can pierce the fish's mouth. Once the hook has pierced the mouth, a small reverse piece, called a barb, keeps the fish from pulling away from the hook. A hook is generally hidden by a piece of bait, so the fish swallows the bait and the hook at the same time. Once the fish takes the bait, the angler pulls sharply on the line and sets the hook. A lure is artificial bait, designed to look like a worm or other object that would attract a fish. A fly is a type of lure made specifically for fly-fishing that imitates either an insect drifting or lying on top of the water (dry fly) or a larva or small fish lying just below the water surface (wet fly).

Snares and Traps

Trapping and snaring animals is a basic skill in survival strategies for several reasons. You can place a number of traps in various areas and check them regularly, so your traps "work" while you are occupied with other responsibilities; you don't have to stalk or flush out quarry; you don't need firearms; and traps can be used over and over again.

Trapping is a regulated sport, so you need to be aware of the laws about trapping in your location. However, trapping is actually an important tool for managing natural resources, for several reasons:

- As with any other kind of hunting, trapping helps control animal population. By controlling over-population you minimize problems like starvation, disease, and the destruction of natural habitat.
- Many animals that are traditionally trapped, like beavers, coyotes, and foxes, can damage personal property or livestock. For example, trapping can prevent flooding caused by beaver dams or the killing of livestock by coyotes and foxes.
- Trapping can also protect other animals, especially endangered or threatened species, from the more populated and common predatory furbearers.

Traps and snares are designed to choke, crush, hang, or entangle the animals. There are three basic types of traps:

- Body-grip traps catch the animal's entire body. These are generally killing devices.
- Foothold traps, enclosed foothold devices, and cage traps catch the animal when it steps on the trap. These are considered live-restraining devices. With these traps, you can release non-target animals.
- Snares use a loop of cable or wire to catch a furbearer by the neck, body, or leg. Some of these traps are also live-restraining devices.

You should learn about the type of traps appropriate for the animal you are hunting. You should also be aware of the trapper's code of ethics:

- Obtain the landowner's permission.
- Avoid setting traps in areas where domestic animals may be caught.
- Set traps to capture the target animal in the most humane way possible.
- Check traps at least once every twenty-four hours, preferably in the early morning.
- Record trap locations accurately.
- Identify all traps with waterproof name and address tags.
- Use as much of the animal as possible. Dispose of animal carcasses properly.
- Make an effort to trap only the surplus animals from each habitat.
- Assist landowners who are having damage problems with wildlife.
- Kill trapped furbearers in a humane manner, like a hard blow to the head, neck, or body, the same way a mousetrap kills a mouse.
- Obtain all required licenses, tags, and permits. Since trapping laws vary by state, check the state's regulations before you go trapping.

Obtaining a License

It is a requirement for hunters, trappers, and anglers to obtain a license for legal hunting in the United States, with the possible exception of property owners in certain states. Each state has a department that oversees natural resources and wildlife management and generally creates the laws and requirements that regulate hunting, fishing, and trapping within that state. In most cases, a license is obtained in the state where you want to pursue these sports and is valid for a year. You can hold licenses in several states at the same time, but if you are not a resident of the state, you will generally pay a higher fee for a nonresident hunting license.

Be sure you check your license, as often a separate license is needed for hunting, trapping, and/or fishing. However, in some states you can purchase a combination license. If you have a child under the age of fourteen, in most states you will not need to purchase a license for him or her, provided the child is with an adult who does have a license. Check with your specific state licenser to learn the regulations in your state.

When you purchase your license, you will also receive a copy of the current regulations. You should consult the regulations to be sure you are following the laws of the state.

FACT

In Florida, the cost of an alligator trapping license and alligator harvest tag is $271.50 for Florida residents, and nonresidents pay $1,021.50. The cost for each additional alligator hunting permit is $61.50, regardless of residency. All fees are nonrefundable.

Often, as in the case of deer hunting, in addition to a hunting license, other requirements must be met. In many states, when you hunt deer you also have to purchase a deer tag. In states where you may hunt more than one deer, you will need a tag for each kill.

Most sporting goods stores or your state's department of natural resources will sell licenses. Remember, a hunting license is not a firearm permit. If your state requires a firearm permit, you will have to obtain that separately, prior to purchasing your hunting license.

During the Hunt

Planning, preparation, and strategy are the three keys to a successful hunt. Often, planning a good hunt takes longer than the hunt itself. Be sure you are equipped with not only appropriate clothing and gear for the environment, but also information about your quarry, knowledge about the hunting site, and the most current state and federal regulations. Hunting techniques or strategies are skills honed through education and experience. The most ideal situation for a beginning hunter is to have an experienced hunter as a mentor and guide.

Still Hunting

Still hunting is when you walk slowly through your hunting site, stopping frequently to scan and listen for game, and, after a long period of time, moving forward again. This type of hunting is often used for big-game hunting or in areas where stands cannot be used. Generally, when you still hunt, you spend at least ten times longer being still and observing than you do moving around. The trick to still hunting is keeping a low profile and using binoculars to identify movement. Remember that a human silhouette will scare off many animals. However, be sure to wear fluorescent orange so you are not mistaken for game by other hunters.

Stalking

Stalking is very similar to still hunting, except when you are stalking, you are following signs leading to a particular type of quarry. The signs could be tracks, a morning dew trail through the grass, or even the sound or smell of an animal. Stalking is also done during the final phase of still hunting after you have spotted your quarry and need to close the distance in order to get a better shot.

ALERT

If you are hunting turkeys, remember that the turkey calls you hear may be another hunter "calling" to his quarry. For your safety and the safety of the hunters around you, you should not stalk turkeys.

Stalking requires concentration. You must remember to keep downwind, stay quiet, stay alert, and remain patient.

Posting

Posting is when you sit or stand in one spot and wait for your quarry. When you post, you want to find a vantage point near the animal's trails. Posting is best used when you know where the game travels daily and you are not able to use a blind or a stand (see the following section). Be sure when you pick your posting spot that you have enough room all around you so you are able to freely swing your firearm or draw your bow.

Blinds and Stands

Blinds and stands are structures that conceal the hunter from his prey. A ground blind is a temporary structure on the ground that is often made of branches or plywood. The most important factor is that it hides the hunter. Ground blinds should be downwind and out of the sun. An elevated stand can be constructed from wood or any heavy-duty weatherproof material that can hold up to exposure and hold the weight of a hunter. You can purchase elevated stands, or build one of your own. Elevated stands offer you an advantage because you are concealed above the level of the quarry, and your vantage point is superior to ground level. You should not only check the condition of elevated stands routinely, but also be sure before you enter the stand that you are not sharing it with insects, owls, and small mammals.

Game Calling

Calling is imitating animal sounds in order to attract an animal close enough for an effective shot. You can use a variety of different sounds to draw your quarry toward you:

- Territorial sounds: like a deer "rattling," an elk "bugling," or a turkey "gobbling"
- Feeding sounds: like a duck's feeding "chuckle"
- Distress sounds: they invite coyotes, bobcats, or foxes to feed

With practice, you can actually make hunting calls using your own hands and mouth. You can also purchase hunting call devices.

Driving

You need a group of hunters in order to "drive" your quarry. Some of the hunters are drivers and some are posters. Drivers spread out across a field or woods and move through the area, pushing the game out of the cover. Posters take positions at the sides and end of the cover to intercept the quarry being pushed out. Good organization and familiarity with the terrain are essential in order for driving to work. Also, for safety reasons, you must always wear fluorescent orange (hunter orange) and make sure everyone involved is aware of the positions of the other drivers and posters. Never shoot in the direction of another hunter!

Flushing

When you "flush" game, you are using noise, movement, or dogs to cause the game to become nervous and leave the safety of cover. Frequent pauses in your flushing activity often confuse your quarry and encourage it to leave cover.

Taking the Shot

Of course your goal is to bring home the game you are seeking. But a responsible hunter will strive to down his game by inflicting the least amount of suffering possible. In order to achieve this goal, you need to understand the anatomy of your quarry and how to position a shot for a clean kill.

Where to Shoot

You want your shot to be the most efficient, and those shots delivered to an animal's vital organs—the heart and lungs—are the most effective shots for a clean kill. In large game animals, the vital organs lie in the chest cavity behind the front shoulder. For big game, the most effective shot is actually a lung shot.

The major blood vessels and arteries are also in the area of the vital organs. If you shoot an animal in this area, you will cause considerable bleeding, so if the animal doesn't die immediately, it will be easy to track.

There are two important points to getting a clean kill: being an excellent marksman and having patience. If you can't get a shot to the vital organs, wait until the animal presents you with a better shot.

The Proper Angle

The angle of the shot can make the difference between a clean kill, and therefore hunter success, and injuring an animal and having it escape. Part of being a responsible hunter is understanding which angles offer the most effective shots.

- **Broadside:** The broadside shot angle, in which the side of your quarry is facing you, is the preferred angle for both firearm and bow hunters for larger game animals, such as elk, deer, and bear.
- **Quartering-Away:** This angle describes your quarry facing away from you, but at an angle that still allows you to shoot its vital organs behind its shoulder and into the chest. This shot is fine for firearm hunters, and in most cases for bowhunters too. The exception for bowhunters would be larger game, in which massive stomachs and intestines would block a clean shot to the vital organs.
- **Quartering-Toward:** In this case your quarry is facing you, but at an angle. Although this often gives you a clean shot to the vital organs, the animal is looking your way and will most likely spot your movements. A shot can be taken at this angle, if the gun is already trained on the animal. Bowhunters should not take a shot at this angle.
- **Head-On:** This is when your quarry is facing you directly. Your quarry will detect your movements with a head-on shot angle. If your firearm is already positioned for the shot, you should aim at the center of the chest to hit the vital organs. You should note that head-on shots rarely result in a clean kill, and much of the meat is often ruined. Bowhunters should not attempt a head-on shot.

145

- **Rear-End:** This angle, in which the rear end of your quarry faces you, should never be taken by hunters using firearms or bow. Rather than risk crippling the animal and ruining the meat, you should wait for a better shot.

Trailing Wounded Game

If you shoot and only wound an animal, it is your responsibility to stop the hunt and search for that animal. Carefully observe every movement of your quarry after you shoot it. You should investigate the ground and trail after shooting an animal before you assume you missed. Once at the site, you should look for blood on the ground or on vegetation; broken twigs or branches; tracks, hair, meat, or bone fragments left by the animal; or downhill trails—especially toward water. You should search the area in a circular or grid pattern if you lose a trail in order to pick it up again. As you follow the trail, use fluorescent orange flagging to mark the blood trail in case weather or the lack of daylight forces you to suspend the search and take it up the next day. Remember, you should remove the orange flagging once you've located your quarry.

Approaching Downed Game

A wounded animal can be very dangerous. Before you approach your quarry, you want to be sure that the animal is dead. Any downed large animal should be approached carefully from above and behind the head. If the quarry appears to be dead, you should wait a short distance away and watch the chest cavity for any rise and fall. Wait for at least a few minutes. The eyes of a dead animal are usually open—try to see if the eyes are open or closed. One way to be certain an animal is dead is if the eye does not blink when touched with a stick.

If you find that your quarry is still alive, you should finish the kill with a quick shot to the base of the ear. Bowhunters should shoot an arrow into the vital organ area.

Once you have ascertained the animal is dead, you should follow the state regulations for reporting or recording a kill. Some states require you to tag the animal immediately and indicate the date of the kill.

After the Hunt

A wounded animal that is chased down yields strong-flavored meat because waste products, produced when the animal is in stress, accumulate in the flesh. So a clean kill improves the flavor of your meat. However, the way you handle your game after you harvest it can also have a significant impact on the quality and taste of the meat.

Field Care

Part of your preparation for hunting is to have a well-stocked game care kit. This kit is what you will use to dress out your kill in the field. The reason you need to dress your kill immediately is to prevent the growth of bacteria, which is the cause of spoiled meat. Bacteria grow in the presence of heat, moisture, and dirt. When you field dress, you cool the game by removing the entrails, which lowers the body heat by allowing air into the body cavity.

Your game care kit should include the following:

- Hatchet
- Small saw
- Knife and sharpening stone
- Game bags
- License tag
- Nylon rope (at least 25 feet)
- Black pepper to repel insects
- Cheesecloth bags for organs you plan to use as meat (heart, liver)
- Cooler and ice
- Disposable plastic gloves
- Fluorescent orange flagging
- Foil
- Gambrel and pulley system
- Hand towels
- Large bag for caped or trophy head
- Plastic bags for cleanup
- Salt (noniodized) for hide care

Field Dressing Larger Game and Transporting Game

Large animals, like deer and moose, have to be bled out. Shots to the head, neck, and spine don't allow enough bleeding, and shots to the chest or abdomen will probably cause internal bleeding into the animal's body cavities. You should cut the throat as soon as you can get to a downed animal. If you are a novice hunter, the easiest way to do this is to make a side-to-side cut at the base of the neck. More experienced hunters might prefer a breastbone-to-upward cut. Position the animal so the head is in a downhill position, so as much blood as possible can drain from the animal.

In many cases, especially with larger animals, you may have to skin and quarter the game in order to pack it out to your waiting vehicle. The most ideal situation is to be able to hang your quarry from its back legs from a substantial tree limb. If that's not possible, lay the animal on its back with it's hind legs spread.

Remember to do everything you can to keep dirt off the meat. You can use the inside of the removed hide as a protective mat as you quarter the animal.

Using a very sharp knife, you should cut the skin in a straight line from the lower end of the breastbone down to the anus. Cut with the blade of the knife inserted into the skin and facing up. This will help you avoid cutting into internal organs, like the intestines. To be sure that you don't cut into the intestines, once the opening is large enough to get your other hand inside, hold the intestines away from the edge of the blade.

If your animal is female, with milk-filled mammary glands, cut around those and continue cutting to the rectum, but not into it. Then you can lift and cut away the mammary portion.

Cut around each side of the sexual organ of a male and around each side of the rectum. Because you don't want anything to spill from either of these openings, be careful not to cut into either. If you do have some spillage, the contaminated meat will have to be cut away and disposed of. Tie off the rectum, so no contents can escape.

With the first cut complete, you will now have to cut around the edge of the muscular diaphragm, which separates the abdominal cavity from the chest cavity, to get to the lungs and heart. The windpipe and the gullet are in the front of the lungs; you need to carefully cut those in order to be able to pull the heart and lungs out of the chest cavity.

When you have freed the contents of the chest and abdominal cavities, turn the animal on its side. Split the pelvic bone by inserting your knife blade into the seam between the two halves of the pelvis, tapping on the end of the handle and prying downward. You should then carefully roll out all the intestines, bladder, and genital organs. Then wipe away any blood. Slit the muscles that hold the gullet and windpipe and pull them out.

ESSENTIAL

To minimize a meat's wild flavor, hunt early in the season or kill a female. The meat of the male larger game animals becomes stronger in taste as the mating season advances.

There are some organs that are edible and you will want to save them. You should cut the heart free from the membrane pouch. If you want to save the liver, you need to cut the gallbladder from it. In order to do this without cutting into the gallbladder, you will have to throw away part of the liver. Once it's removed, you can remove both the liver and the kidneys. Put the organ meats in a clean, waterproof bag.

It's important to keep the dressed game cool and free of insects by covering it in breathable game bags or cheesecloth in the field. With a quartered animal, you can pack the meat in ice chests, in game bags, or by leaving the animal's hide on and cutting hand-holds in it to carry the meat . See the next chapter for detailed information about quartering your game. You don't want to process the meat beyond quartering until you are home or until you reach a butcher. You should be sure to keep proper "evidence of sex," because this is often required by state game laws.

CHAPTER 15

Processing Your Own Meat

Whether you have harvested wild meat or raised your own, the next step is learning how to properly process your meat. How do you skin a deer or dress a rabbit or a squirrel? How do you process a pig, chicken, or beef? How do you get rid of a "gamey" taste to your meat? What's the best way to freeze, can, or dry the meat? This next chapter will walk you through all of these questions and more.

Skinning Large Game

The most basic thing you should remember about skinning large game is that you want to get the hide off without getting dirt and hair on the meat. If the animal has horns, you may want to skin the animal while it hangs from its antlers, which is the method many hunters prefer. However, if there are no horns, it's easier to tie a bar or pole to the back legs, just above the lowest joint between the tendon and leg bone, and hang the animal from a tree using the bar. Be sure you choose a strong enough branch or beam to hold the weight of the animal.

You can also skin large game on the ground. In this case, you will skin one side and then roll the animal over to the other side. In this case, you need to have extra help in order to move the animal, and plenty of space for maneuvering. If you decide to skin your animal on the ground, it's best to use a clean ground cover or tarp underneath the animal in order to keep the meat clean.

A sharp knife and either a sharpener or second knife are essential tools for proper skinning. A "skinning knife" has a curved blade that makes it easier to maneuver your blade around the contours of the animal, but any sharp knife will do. Skinning any large game takes the edge off a blade in a short amount of time. If you skin with a dull blade, you will be putting a lot of extra effort into the process. To help preserve the sharpness of the blade tip, try to use the full blade length as you skin.

Skinning should be done as soon after the kill as possible. On a warm, freshly killed carcass, the skin can almost be just pulled away, and it only takes a few minutes. If you allow the carcass to cool, the skin will set and you will have a harder job separating it from the rest of the animal. You want to skin the animal without making cuts in either the hide or the meat. If you do slice into the meat and blood starts to get on the hide, you can apply flour or cornmeal to the cut to stop the blood.

Start by cutting all the way around the four knee joints of the animal. Then carefully slit along the inside of the leg all the way to the incision you made to initially dress the animal. The initial dressing incision was made by using a very sharp knife to cut the skin in a straight line from the lower end of the breastbone down to the anus. Remember to always cut with the blade of the knife inserted into the skin and facing up. This will help you avoid cutting into internal organs, like the intestines.

Extend the belly incision to just below the lower jaw. You can remove the head by cutting completely around the ears, jaws, and antlers. (If you are hanging the meat from the head, be sure to only cut the hide layer.) Slit the skin on the underside of the tail. Now you are ready to start removing the hide from the animal.

ESSENTIAL

Cleaning an animal requires contact with blood, bone, internal soft muscle tissue, and possibly fecal material. You can also nick your hands on bone shards and the blade of your skinning knife. To protect your hands you can use gloves for dressing and skinning your animal. Elbow-length gloves colored hunter orange for extra visibility are essential tools for a hunter. You can buy them from many major retailers, as well as from major hunting retail catalogs.

As you work, pull the skin away from the meat with your hand while carefully slicing through the white layer that lies between the meat and the hide. Watch the angle of your blade to be sure you are not slicing into the meat or hide. Determine the length of your cuts by the ease with which the hide is peeling back from the meat. In some cases, like around the chest, you will be able to pull large sections away without much cutting at all. Other places, like around the butt, will require careful, more precise work.

Quartering and Cutting Large Game

To further process your large game, the first thing you want to do is cut off the head. If you are planning on mounting the head, you will need detailed instructions from your taxidermist about how to not only process, but skin your animal. However, if you are hunting to feed your family, you will want to use all of the meat for food, not decoration.

After you have removed the head, saw the carcass down the center of the backbone. This will divide the carcass into two halves. Lay one half on a table and locate the last two ribs. Cut between the last two ribs in order to quarter it.

Chill the meat before you cut it, because cold fat is firmer. Trim off the fat because wild game fat can go rancid quickly. You can save the fat for soap making or candle making if you wish. Unless you were able to shoot the animal in the head, there will be areas of "bloodshot" meat. This is where the bullet passed through. The meat will be torn and there will be hard black bits in it. All this meat should be trimmed out and thrown away. Also get rid of any other black bits. If you bled your animal well, you shouldn't find too many of these.

FACT

You will generally get about 50 percent of the original weight of an animal in meat once it's butchered. For example, an average mule deer weighs about 150 pounds, so you could harvest about 75 pounds of meat. Other animals and their average weights: antelope—80 pounds; white-tailed deer—125 pounds; bighorn sheep—175 pounds; black bear—200 pounds; caribou—250 pounds; grizzly bear—500 pounds; elk—500 pounds; moose—650 pounds. These are male weights; females weigh approximately one-third less.

The Hindquarter

The hindquarter, or haunch, is one of the back halves of the carcass. The haunch is the whole hind leg and loin of the animal. You need to cut the haunch off ahead of the hip joint. Begin just below where the ribs end. You'll need to use a meat saw to cut through the bone. Once you've separated the haunch from the rest of the carcass, cut the haunch in two places to make thirds from top to bottom.

The top third is where you will get your round steak. Cut right across the grain and through the bone to the other end of the haunch. Another way you can process this cut is by separating the bundles of muscles. This option allows you to get the meat without having to cut through the bone for every steak. The largest bundle consists of the top round and the bottom round cuts. You can either separate them into top and bottom and cut into steaks, or leave them attached to each other and cut into steaks. The remaining bundle is the sirloin. You need to cut across the grain for your sirloin steaks.

The middle third of the haunch is generally made into roasts. If you would prefer, however, you can make it into extra round deer (like hamburger) or save it for jerky.

The bottom third of the haunch is used for hamburger or jerky, and the bone is used for soup.

Once the haunch is processed, the remainder of the hindquarter is ribs and the two strips of meat along the backbone. The strip on the outside is the most tender meat in the animal. This meat is what would be considered tenderloin, and is used to make T-bone and sirloin steaks. If you have a smaller-sized animal, like a deer, you will generally want to bone it out and make "tips" of meat.

You can then saw the ribs and the backbone to your preference. You can use this meat for soup bones, spareribs, and dog food.

ESSENTIAL

If your venison has a strong, gamey taste, there are several ways to tone it down. You can soak the meat in salt, vinegar, and water for several hours before cooking to help make the flavor milder. Use long, slow cooking methods and cook in sauces, gravies, etc. Use seasonings and marinades. Try combinations of thyme, parsley, garlic, onions, soup mixes, etc. Marinades tenderize the meat and disguise the gamey flavor.

Front Quarter

Just as you removed the haunch for the hindquarter, you will want to remove the leg of the front quarter, also known as the arm. Cut the arm away by pulling the bone away from the body at the joint and then cutting the bone at the joint until it is detached across the line where it joins the chest.

Saw the arm into three pieces, just as you did the haunch. The upper portion can be used for either roasts or hamburger. The middle third is generally made into an "arm roast," and you can use the bottom third for hamburger, jerky, and soup bones.

The remaining meat in the front quarter can be divided into two kinds of meat. The meat along the backbone is an extension of the tenderloin you had in the hindquarters. You can slice that into steaks or tips depending on your preference and the size of your animal. The other meat is basically bone, and can be made into soup bones. You can use the rib area for stew meat or spareribs.

Small Game

If you are truly relying on hunting to supply you and your family with food, the most plentiful animals to hunt are small game like rabbits, squirrels, raccoon, and opossum. There are some basic rules for harvesting small game.

- Never eat a small animal that is already dead. You don't know if the animal died of a disease that can be passed on to you and your family.
- If an animal isn't active and healthy looking, don't hunt it.
- If you hunt and kill small game, examine it closely to ensure that it doesn't look sickly. If there is any question in your mind, discard it.
- There are some infections that small animals carry that can be passed on to hunters. The likelihood is less in the winter, but whenever you handle small game you should wear gloves when you process it in order to protect yourself.
- When processing a small animal, it is important that you check the health of the liver. Small, white cystlike spots in the liver, pea-sized or smaller, signify tularemia or other infectious diseases. If you find that you have processed an infected animal, discard the meat and wash your hands and the surfaces the animal was exposed to with a strong disinfectant.

ALERT

Tularemia, also known as "rabbit fever," is a disease caused by the bacterium *Francisella tularensis*. Tularemia is typically found in animals, especially rodents, rabbits, and hares. Tularemia is usually a rural disease and has been reported in all U.S. states except Hawaii. About 200 human cases of tularemia are reported each year in the United States. Most cases occur in the south-central and western states.

Scent Glands

The scent glands are the first item you should be aware of when you process small game. These are small waxy or reddish (depending on the animal) nubs that can be situated under the forelegs, along the lower part of the backbone, and/or under the lower part of the abdomen. Often, when you skin the animal, they are pulled away with the skin. However, if they remain, they must be very carefully cut out of the meat. You need to remove them intact, because if you don't, they will release a very strong musky scent that will taint the meat.

Dressing Small Game

You need to dress small game immediately and then allow it to cool completely. The first step is to make an incision down the belly. Start near the lower portion of the abdomen. Be sure you don't puncture the stomach or the intestines with your knife. After making the incision, hold on to the front feet and the head and swing the animal sharply downward in order to snap the entrails out of the body cavity. At this point, you can remove the lungs, heart, and liver. The next step is to remove the head and wipe out the inside of the body cavity.

Skinning Small Game

The skin of many small animals is highly prized for warmth and texture. Rabbit fur and hide, for example, makes very warm mittens. If you want to use the skin of the small animals, you should first cut off the head, tail, and forepaws. In order for you to have better access, hang the animal by its hind legs, stretching the legs far enough apart to work between them.

Using a sharp knife, cut on the backside of the leg from the hock or area just above the foot to the hole made when you removed the tail, and then repeat this process on the other side. Now you need something that can grip the skin, like pliers. Starting from the hind end, peel the skin forward. You should pull it forward until you peel it over the neck and front feet.

Processing Small Game

How much meat you will obtain from your small game harvest depends on two things: the size of the animal and your ability to get as much meat as you can from the carcass. You can actually freeze a small animal whole, once it's been dressed and skinned. However, you can also process the animal for convenience and to save freezer space. To save the most space, you can debone the meat before freezing.

Is eating small game safe?
The most important thing to remember when eating small game is to make sure you have cooked it completely. Thoroughly cooking meat is important to reduce the likelihood of any bacterial disease. All meat, including venison, should be cooked until the meat is no longer pink and the juices run clear. This means cooking to a minimum internal temperature of 165°F for all types of meat, 170°F for the breast of game birds and waterfowl, and 180°F for a whole bird. If cooked according to these guidelines, the likelihood of any disease transmission to individuals consuming the meat is extremely small.

First, you need to cut the limbs from the animal at the joints. Then you should cut alongside the backbone through the ribs on both sides to free the breast meat. There is also back meat that can be harvested. On rabbits, the big meat pieces are actually found on the hind legs and haunches. The tenderloins on a rabbit are the choicest pieces of meat and are great for soups and stews. It's best to remove the bone from the thigh meat. The forelegs of a rabbit have little meat, but they can be used for soup.

After processing, wash and chill the meat. Then you can freeze it, can it, or even make jerky.

Processing Poultry

Most poultry can be processed in very similar ways. You will find that the biggest differentiating factor is size. A duck can probably be butchered by the same process as a chicken; however, when you are dealing with turkeys and geese, you need to consider their weight and size.

You need to "starve" your birds for up to twenty-four hours before you butcher them. This way their intestines are fairly empty, so there is less chance of contamination when you are processing them. This does not mean, however, that you should not give them water. A bird that is dehydrated does not bleed out as well.

Butchering Your Poultry

You have probably heard the phrase, "Running around like a chicken with its head cut off" as an apt description of someone who doesn't know what to do. Were you to cut the head off a chicken and then let go of the bird, it would flop around and scatter blood over quite a large area. This is certainly not the optimal way to butcher a chicken. However, no matter how you kill your chickens, there is going to be a certain amount of movement after the head is off and before the chicken in totally bled out, so be sure to wear old clothing and have a container ready to catch the blood. It's a good idea to have some water in the container, so the blood doesn't coagulate in it and make cleanup harder. Keep in mind that even though the body may still be moving, the bird doesn't feel anything. What you're seeing is simply a nerve reaction.

The basic idea of killing a bird is to either wring its neck or chop the head off. Then, make sure you hang it until it bleeds out, because bleeding out not only improves the flavor of the meat, but also increases its ability to be kept.

Here are several different methods for killing a bird. Those described for chickens will work well for ducks, too, and those described for turkeys will work well with geese:

- **Chopping block and a sharp ax—chicken or turkey:** Lay the bird on a chopping block (you can pound two long nails about an inch apart halfway into the block as a stanchion for the head; just be careful you don't hit the nails with your ax) and with one quick hit, bring the ax down and sever the head from the body. Then hang the chicken over a bucket to bleed out.
- **Wringing the neck—chicken:** Take hold of the chicken's head or upper neck and then swing the chicken around, as you would a heavy object on the end of a string. Swing several times until you hear or feel the "snap" of the chicken's neck breaking and separating from the body. You will then need to cut off the head and bleed the chicken.

- **Hanging—chicken:** Tie a piece of string or twine around a low-hanging tree branch. Take the other end of the string and loop it around the chicken's legs, so it hangs head down. Take a sharp knife in one hand and grasp the chicken's head in your other hand. Pull slightly on the head and then cut the head off at the top of the neck. Have a container ready to catch the blood.
- **A killing cone—chicken or turkey:** A killing cone is one of the easiest ways to process your poultry. You can purchase a killing cone or make one of your own. You need a cone-shaped object, like a one-gallon bleach bottle or a road cone (depending on the size of poultry you are processing) with both ends cut out. On one end, the opening should be about 2 inches in diameter: large enough for the bird's head and neck to slip through, but small enough so the rest of the bird doesn't follow. The other end needs to be large enough for you to be able to slip the bird inside, head first, but small enough so the bird's wings are pinned. The cone should be attached to a tree about four feet above the ground, or whatever is comfortable for your height. It can be attached with nails or screws, but it needs to be secure. You can create a cone stand with three- to four-foot lengths of two-by-fours fitted together like a pyramid with the cone held in the center for easy access. The cone should be attached so the smaller end, for the head, is closest to the ground. Place the bird in the cone, pull the head and neck through the cone and then, using a very sharp knife, sever the jugular vein and carotid artery. The cut should be made just behind the tendon attachment for the beak and tongue. Cut deeply behind the jaw, pressing firmly with your knife while using a slicing motion. Cut down and toward the front of the neck, traveling under the jaw, and then cut the other side of the neck in the same location behind the jaw to sever the opposite blood vessel. Be aware that blood will spill onto your hands, and if you only knick the artery instead of cutting through it, blood will squirt out. Have a container ready for blood.

For larger birds you can hook a metal weight to the lower beak of the bird after you have slit the throat. This holds the head, so the blood is not sprayed around the butchering area. Once the blood pressure drops, the bird will go into shock. As it dies, it will convulse and flap. Again, this is a nerve reaction to the loss of blood. At this point, the bird does not feel anything. The cone method helps to keep the bird relatively still during this process, so the meat is not bruised. You should spray the bird with water from a hose as it bleeds out to ensure the blood does not coagulate at the neck.

Picking the Poultry

You can choose, if you like, to just skin your poultry. This means you don't have to deal with scalding, plucking, or any of the traditional chores associated with dressing poultry. You can skin your poultry using a process similar to what was discussed for small animals.

If you choose to keep the skin on the meat, you will need a large container of hot water. A clean metal garbage can works well for this process. You will also need a gas burner to place under the can to keep the water at a constant temperature, between 135°F and 140°F. If the water is colder than that, the scald doesn't work; if it is warmer than that, the skin can be damaged and the bird can be partially cooked.

ESSENTIAL

When processing turkeys, you should pluck the main tail feathers and the larger tail coverts before you dunk the bird in the scalding water. This makes it easier to see the bird as you work in the scald tank.

Holding the bird by its feet, you should lower it, head first, into the scalding water. Do this slowly so you don't splash the hot water on yourself. Once the bird is in the water, you should move it up and down, swirling the water all around the bird. Make sure you keep the bird under the water to ensure even scalding, especially in the legs. Continue this process for about thirty seconds, and then pull the bird out and test the scald by rubbing your thumb against the grain of the feathers on the bird's leg. If you have scalded correctly, these feathers should come off easily. If your bird passes this test, pluck a large feather from the wing section. If this too comes out easily, you are ready to pluck the bird.

If the feathers don't come out easily, you need to scald the bird for a bit longer. However, remember that you don't want to expose the bird to too much heat, because it will damage the skin and make it easier to tear.

Move your bird to a processing table. Using your thumb and fingers in a rubbing motion like sandpaper, remove the feathers by rubbing against the grain. This works much better than trying to pull out each individual feather. Don't yank a handful of feathers; this will only tear the skin.

The first feathers you pick should be the primary wing feathers. These will not be feathers that you are able to rub free. If you aren't able to grasp a feather and twist it until it breaks free, you might need to use a pair of pliers to get a good grip.

Clean all of the feathers off the body, paying attention to the "wing pits" and any other crevices that might have hidden feathers, as well as any pin feathers that lie just under the skin. When you have thoroughly cleaned the bird, spray it down with cold water from a hose and then submerse it in a clean container of very cold water in order to cool down the body very quickly.

FACT

The average mature domestic turkey has approximately 3,500 feathers. Feathers cover most of a turkey's body, with the exception of the head and neck. These feathers can be cleaned and used to make a feather quilt or mattress.

Dressing the Poultry

At this point, you are ready to clean the bird, which means that you remove the head, feet, and internal organs. Be sure you have a clean surface for this process, a very sharp knife, some clean water handy for rinsing, and a container for the discarded pieces.

Start by removing the feet. You need to hold the leg straight, and, with just a little pressure, cut between the joints. You want to cut the tendons between the bones, not through the bone itself. The drumsticks will have some scaled skin on them; this won't affect the quality when you cook them.

Next, cut off the head. Cut the head with a sharp knife above the cuts you made to bleed out the bird. With a sharp knife, you should be able to cut right through a chicken's neck bone. However, with a turkey, you might need to use a cleaver.

After the head is removed, you should turn the bird onto its chest, so you have access to the back. Insert your knife just under the skin at the base of the neck at the shoulders and slit the skin up the neck. Sliding the skin down, you will be able to see the trachea, esophagus, and glandular tissue next to the neck. You need to carefully separate the neck from the trachea and esophagus and gently loosen them all the way to where they enter the bird's body. If you follow the esophagus further, it will widen into a pouch called a crop. Carefully separate the crop from under the skin and next to the breast meat. Then follow the trachea and pull off the fatty tissue from around the trachea and under the skin. Leave all of these items hanging free for now.

Turn the bird over, so it is lying on its back. Locate the vent between the legs. (The vent is the area where the bird emits eggs or droppings.) Insert just the tip of your knife into the skin about an inch above the vent. If you insert your knife too far you risk cutting the intestines.

Carefully cut up to the breastbone. Then carefully cut the area underneath the vent. You will want to take your time and not cut too deep. The vent has thin, tough tissue holding it in place, and you might need to work it loose with your fingers. If the bird was properly starved, there should be no feces inside the intestines; however, never take this for granted and keep the bird slightly over the edge of the table to avoid fecal matter dropping on your work surface. Immediately clean up any spilled fecal matter.

With the vent cut free and loose from the body, you can gently pull the intestines free from the carcass. Once they're removed, you can reach into the bird and move your hand along the sides of the ribs to break the entrails free of the body cavity. Once you locate the gizzard—a round, hard organ—pull it out. The rest of the entrails with come with it. Often, the esophagus and crop, as well as the trachea, will also follow the entrails when you pull the gizzard out.

Next, insert your hand back into the bird and follow the ribs to the spine. This is where you will find the lungs. They are quite spongy, so you need to carefully lift them out with your hands. Unfortunately, they don't always come out in one piece, so you need to continue until you don't feel any lung tissue anymore.

Once the cavity is clean, turn the bird back on its chest and remove the neck. You should first cut the muscle tissue around the bone as far as you can. Then you need to bend the neck backward and break it off. It is better to break the neck than cut it because the remaining edges will be less sharp, reducing the risk of puncturing the wrapping you will store your bird in when you freeze it.

Finally, on the other end of the bird are two small yellow oil glands, or preen glands. These glands should be carefully removed from the carcass. They are located inside the lump above the tail. Make an incision above the glands, cutting all the way to the bone, and then slide your knife along the bone, coming out at the tail. Be sure there is no yellow glandular tissue left, because it can foul the meat.

Rinse the bird thoroughly, inside and out. Put the bird into a tank of ice and water and let it chill for thirty minutes. Be sure the ice water also gets inside the body cavity so the entire bird is chilled.

Giblets

The giblets are the parts of the innards that you generally save and use for food. These usually include the heart, liver, gizzard, and neck. You've already harvested the neck, so just make sure it is rinsed thoroughly and placed in a plastic bag or container.

ESSENTIAL

Chicken or turkey giblets are usually simmered in water for use in soups, gravies, or poultry stuffing. Once cooked, the liver will become crumbly, and the heart and gizzard will soften and become easy to chop. Cooked giblets should have a firm texture, and their juices should run clear. Casseroles containing giblets should be cooked to 160°F. Stuffing should be cooked to 165°F. Chicken giblets also are commonly fried or broiled.

The liver needs to be separated from the gallbladder. The gallbladder contains bile, an extremely bitter green fluid. You need to handle this carefully because if you break the gallbladder, the bile can contaminate the meat and cause it to be inedible. Cut the gallbladder away from liver, being generous with the amount of liver you leave on the cut, just to be sure. Then rinse the remaining liver and package it with the neck.

You should cut the gizzard open along its narrow edge. Slice down until you see a white lining. Try not to nick the yellow inner lining. Pull the gizzard apart with your fingers and remove the inner sac and white gizzard membrane and discard. If you cut into the lining, you will find grit and even rocks. The gizzard is how birds chew their food. Simply remove the grit and peel the lining away from the muscle.

Cut the heart away from the attached arteries. Then you can slice the top off the heart, push out any coagulated blood, and rinse any out any blood remaining in the heart chambers.

Rinse all giblets thoroughly, package them, and chill them in ice water for at least thirty minutes. Then dry them and package them with the bird.

Butchering Large Domestic Animals

When you are considering butchering large domestic animals like cows and hogs, you need to be sure you have the right equipment, the space to work, and an experienced friend to work with you. If you don't have someone with experience, you can either send your animals to a butcher who will kill them and then cut and wrap the meat for you, or you can buy a DVD that shows you the process in great detail. Because you have invested time and money into raising your domestic animals, you want to be sure that you are able to harvest the greatest amount of meat possible.

You should butcher when the weather is cool, like a fall day. Pick a location for butchering that has clean running water handy. Here are some items you will need if you are going to butcher your own meat:

- A .22- or higher-caliber rifle or pistol (with cartridges) and good aim
- A block-and-tackle or strong rope and hoist to raise the animal, along with a large tree that has a strong limb to hang the carcass from
- Some good sharp knives, a whetstone, and meat saw
- A clean wood saw for cutting the animal in half
- Several five-gallon buckets to hold the liver, heart, and any other organ meat you want to save
- A 50-gallon vat for scalding a pig

- A clean tarp or cloth to cover the animal after the carcass has been skinned
- A place to store the meat so it can age before it's cut
- A place to store the meat, like a freezer or pantry, after it's been processed or canned
- Butcher paper, freezer bags, or freezer paper to store the meat in
- A marker or labels to label the date, cut of meat, and kind of meat on the package
- A garbage can with liner for the butchering residue

You should butcher only healthy animals. If your animal seems unhealthy to you, have your veterinarian check it and treat it until it is healthy again. Don't eat an animal that has died unless the animal has died of an injury, like getting hit by a car. Even in that case, if the animal has been dead for a while, don't eat it.

FACT

After you process meat, you can use the hide to create skins and pelts for your own use. "Tanning" is a procedure that cures the hide and makes is soft, malleable, and beautiful. You can tan the skin of deer, rabbits, pigs, goats, and cattle.

After your animal is butchered, check the meat carefully. Look for local bruises and injuries, abscesses, and single tumors. Those you can cut away from the meat and discard. However, if you find inflammation of the lungs, intestines, kidneys, inner surface of the chest or abdominal cavity, or numerous yellowish or pearl-like growths scattered throughout the organs (more likely in the case of sheep than cows or hogs), call your veterinarian and find out whether or not your meat is tainted.

When butchering hogs you have a unique slaughtering decision to make. Because hog rind or skin is edible and generally considered a valued part of the meat you eat, hogs are scalded and then the hide is scraped. You scrape to not only get rid of the hair, but also dirt and scarfskin, or the top layer of skin. Keep in mind the size of the hog and the logistics of getting it into the scalding water, turning it over, and getting it out of the water. In order to scale the pig, you lower it into boiling water for about a minute, pull it up and scrape it. You might need to lower it back into the water several times in order to complete the entire carcass.

The other option for a hog is to skin it, like other animals. However, you tend to lose much of the valuable fat used to make bacon and lard. Whichever option you choose, remember that you can still use the pigskin as not only a food source, but also for gloves and clothing. Once scraped or skinned, follow the procedures described above for cutting large game in order to process your pig.

CHAPTER 16

Your Pantry

When you are living off-grid, you generally don't have the ability to just run out to the corner supermarket. You need a well-stocked pantry that can not only create a foundation for the things you like to eat, but also provide as a resource for you and your family during harsh weather and lean times.

Grains

Grains are both an essential part of a healthy diet and a basic staple as an emergency food. Mankind has been harvesting grain for thousands of years. There have been archeological digs dating back to 9000 B.C. that have found evidence of the use of grains. For many cultures, grains are a dietary staple.

Wheat

If you were ever looking for one source that could be a survival food, it would be wheat. Wheat is not only a nutty-tasting grain that makes wonderful bread and muffins; you can also use wheat as a meat substitute, a vegetable, and a source of vitamin C and antioxidants. That is why wheat should be part of your family's long-term food storage plan.

You can store whole-kernel grain for a long time in a dry, cool area, but once you grind it, you should store it in your refrigerator because the oil in the kernel can spoil and the flour can turn rancid. Wheat is classified in three ways—the season of growth (winter or spring), whether it has a soft or hard kernel, and whether the bran layer is colored red or white. Generally, hard wheat is higher in protein and can store longer than soft wheat, although soft wheat is the wheat of choice for pastry flour.

When you purchase wheat you should buy it from a reputable mill. The protein count should be no less than 12 to 14 percent and the moisture count should be under 10 percent. Make sure you store your wheat in a cool location in tightly sealed containers.

Wheat can be used in a variety of ways:

- Cooked unground wheat
- Flour
- Gluten
- Sprouts
- Wheat grass

Cooked unground wheat

To get the goodness from the whole grain, you can add boiling water and whole-kernel wheat to a thermos and let it sit overnight. In the morning, the wheat will have swelled to double in bulk and softened. You can eat it like a hot breakfast cereal with honey, dried fruit, and milk. You can also use wheat as a meat substitute in a casserole. Just make sure you add additional water and allow the casserole to bake until the wheat is tender.

FACT

Bulgur is white or red, hard or soft whole-wheat kernels that have been boiled, dried, slightly scoured, cracked, and sifted for sizing. The result is par-cooked cracked wheat. Bulgur may be sold as a pilaf or tabouli mix and may be called tabouli wheat. In stores, bulgur can be found near the pasta, rice, or hot cereal, or in a specialty food aisle.

Flour

When you are going to use wheat for flour, you need a grain mill. An electric mill makes the job easier; however, it is wise to also purchase a hand mill in case of emergencies. Whole-wheat flour has more nutrients, protein, and fiber than bleached white flour. It can be substituted for part or all of the all-purpose flour in most recipes. You should experiment with your favorite recipes by substituting more whole-wheat flour for all-purpose each time. Because whole-wheat flour is denser, if you are going to replace the all-purpose flour completely, use ⅞ cup whole-wheat in place of 1 cup white. If you grind the wheat coarsely, you have cracked wheat. Cracked wheat can be used as a hot cereal and can be added to bread recipes to give the bread a nuttier taste.

ESSENTIAL

All-purpose flour is white flour milled from hard wheats or a blend of hard and soft wheats. It gives the best results for many kinds of products, including some yeast breads, quick breads, cakes, cookies, pastries, and noodles. All-purpose flour is usually enriched and may be bleached or unbleached. Bleaching will not affect nutrient value. Different brands will vary in performance. Protein varies from 8 to 11 percent.

Gluten

Gluten is the protein substance left when the starch has been taken out of the wheat. Gluten is often used as a meat substitute and can be flavored to taste like meat, fish, or poultry. Gluten is made by grinding the wheat, adding water to form a dough, and kneading and rinsing the dough to wash away the starch. Gluten is rich in protein just like beef, but it doesn't have any of the animal fat and the cholesterol. It is a great meat substitute, especially in casseroles.

FACT

Seitan (say-TAHN) is made from gluten. Known as *seitan* in Japan, *kofu* in China, and *wheat meat* (gluten) in the United States, seitan is a low-fat, high-protein, firm-textured meat substitute. It has been eaten in China, Japan, Korea, Russia, and the Middle East for thousands of years. Gluten is often referred to in Chinese restaurants as "Buddha food," because of the claim that it was developed by pacifist, vegetarian Buddhist monks as a meat substitute.

Sprouts

Wheat can also be sprouted. This turns wheat from a simple grain to a vitamin-packed vegetable. HealthRecipes.com (*http://healthrecipes.com /growing_sprouts.htm*) describes it this way:

> *As water is introduced, enzyme inhibitors are disabled and the seed explodes to life. Germination unfolds, and enzymes trigger elaborate biochemical changes. Proteins break into amino acids. Water-soluble vitamins such as B complex and vitamin C are created. Fats and carbohydrates are converted into simple sugars. . . . Through the miracle of germination, thiamin increases five-fold and niacin content doubles. Vitamin C, E, and carotene increase. In fact, the vitamin C content becomes as rich as tomatoes.*

Wheat Grass

When you "sow" wheat, just like you would any seed, the plant that grows looks like regular grass you would find on any lawn in the Midwest. But wheatgrass is not just any grass. You can grind wheatgrass to make a juice that contains chlorophyll, ninety minerals, and vitamins A, B complex,

C, E, and K. Wheatgrass is extremely rich in protein, and contains seventeen amino acids, the building blocks of protein. Wheatgrass helps to build your immune system and maintain a good metabolism. Although the most popular way to use wheatgrass is to turn it into juice, it can also be used in salads.

Barley

Barley can be purchased in two forms: pearl barley, which has had the hull removed and has been polished; and pot or hulled barley, which has been processed, but not as much as pearled barley. The hulled barley retains more of the nutritious germ and bran. But, just as with wheat, the oils in the germ can spoil over time, so hulled barley does not keep as well or as long as pearled barley. Whole barley is commonly used to add thickness to soups and stews.

ESSENTIAL

Barley is one of the most ancient of cultivated grains. Grains found in pits and pyramids in Egypt indicate that barley was cultivated there more than 5,000 years ago. The most ancient glyph or pictograph found for barley dates from about 3000 B.C. Numerous references to barley and beer are found in the earliest Egyptian and Sumerian writings.

Corn

Corn is the largest grain crop in the United States, but the majority is used for animal feed or sold to food processors to make corn sweeteners. Corn can be purchased as kernels or ground (cornmeal), but the kernels will last longer in storage. Popcorn can either be used for snacking or it can be ground into a meal, but you should check with your mill manufacturer to be sure that your mill will grind popcorn.

Millet

Millet is less known in the United States, but is a staple grain in North China and India. The grain kernels are small, round, and usually ivory colored or yellow. When cooked like rice, millet makes an excellent breakfast cereal. Millet mixes well with other flours and adds a pleasant crunch when you add it to your homemade breads.

FACT

New evidence suggests that millet was being consumed in western China as early as 5900 B.C. Analysis of dog and pig bones show that both were fed a millet-rich diet, and their human masters were very likely eating the same.

Oats

Although most people often think of oats or oatmeal as a breakfast food, it is much more versatile than just porridge. Oats make an excellent thickener of soups and stews and good fillers in meatloafs and casseroles. Cookies, granola, and granola bars are the next most typical ways oatmeal is used. All oats are processed to at least some extent before you can use them. The most common way to purchase oats is as rolled oats, which have been cut and rolled using special equipment; however, you also can purchase oat groats, which are the whole oat with the hulls removed, and steel cut oats, which are groats that have been cut into smaller pieces with steel blades. Both take longer to cook that traditional rolled oats, but they add fiber and nutrients in the trade.

Rice

Rice is the staple in the diet for much of the world. It produces more food energy per acre than other cereal grains, and is second only to wheat in importance as a food cereal and in terms of protein per acre produced. Rice is classified in two ways: the way the grain is processed and the length of the grain. The processing methods affect the nutritional value of the rice:

- **Brown rice** is the whole grain with only the hull removed. Brown rice keeps all of the nutrition of the grain and has a nutty flavor. It's the best choice as far as nutrition is concerned. However, the oil in the rice germ can become rancid, so brown rice only has a shelf life of about six months. There are distributors who can provide special packaging that seals the rice for long-term storage. However, once opened, the rice needs to be used within six months.

- **Converted rice** is soaked, steamed, and partially cooked before it is dried, hulled, and polished to remove the bran and the germ. It is more nutritious than polished white rice, and its storage life is the same as regular white rice.
- **White rice** has had its outer layers milled off. This process takes about 10 percent of the protein and most of the fat and mineral content. That's why white rice sold in the United States has to be "enriched" with vitamins to partially replace what was lost through processing. White rice has a long shelf life as long as it is stored in a cool, dry place.
- **Instant rice** is fully cooked and then dehydrated, so all you need to do is reconstitute it. Instant rice has fewer calories and carbohydrates and less protein than does regular rice.

Rice grain length is classified in these three ways:

- **Short grain rice** is softer and moister when it cooks and tends to stick together. It is a little sweeter and has a stronger flavor than long grain rice.
- **Medium grain rice** has a flavor similar to the short grain, but with a texture closer to long grain.
- **Long grain rice** cooks up dried and flakier. The flavor is blander than short grain. It is the most common rice found in grocery stores.

FACT

In Japan and Indonesia, rice has its own god. The Chinese devote a whole day of their New Year celebration to the crop. In some Asian cultures, rice is considered a link between heaven and earth. The people of India believe rice is important to fertility, which explains the long-standing tradition of throwing rice at a wedding.

Rye

Rye has dark brown kernels that are longer and thinner than wheat kernels, but it also has less gluten and less protein. The flavor of rye flour is richer than wheat and, although you might associate rye with pumpernickel or black bread, it can be found in versions ranging from dark whole-grain flour to a lighter, more processed flour.

Sorghum

Although sorghum might be more familiar in the United States as a cousin to molasses, it is actually a principal cereal grain in South Africa. The small, round brown seeds can be cooked and used like rice or as a hot cereal. Although sorghum is low in gluten, the seeds can be milled into flour and mixed with higher-gluten flours for use in baking, or used alone for flat breads, pancakes, or cookies.

Legumes

Few nonanimal foods contain the amount of protein found in legumes. However, it's not a complete protein, and needs to be combined with the proteins found in grains. This is why you will find that throughout many cultures, legumes and grains (such as beans and rice) are traditionally served together. Legumes include beans, peas, lentils, and peanuts. Legumes can also be ground and the flour can be added to breads and soups to increase the protein. Legumes generally have a long shelf life as long as they are kept in an area that is cool and dry.

Adzuki Beans

These small, deep red beans are popular in Asia. You might have tasted them if you have ever had sweet bean paste in Chinese buns and other dishes. To cook, it's best to presoak them and then boil. Their flavor is milder than kidney beans, but they can be used in chili or other dishes that traditionally use kidney beans.

Black Beans

Black beans are common in Central and South American cuisine. They are small, dark brownish-black, and oval shaped. Because of their tendency to "bleed" once cooked, the beans should be rinsed before they're added to other recipes to avoid a "muddy" appearance in the dish.

ALERT

Because legumes contain small amounts of certain uric-acid-forming substances (chemically known as *purins*), they should be avoided by people with gout. However, soybeans, garbanzo beans (chickpeas), etc., contain flavonoids, which work as the female hormone estrogen, providing women some relief from menopausal symptoms, such as hot flashes.

Black-eyed Peas

Popular in the southern part of the United States, black-eyed peas are also known as cowpeas or field peas. They are small and cream colored, with a distinctive black spot on them. They cook quickly, and traditionally are combined with rice or cornbread.

Chickpeas

The primary ingredient in hummus and falafel, chickpeas, also known as garbanzo beans, are one of the oldest cultivated legumes. They are tan or cream colored and larger than most beans. Their unusual round, kernel shape and nutty flavor make them a favorite ingredient in salads. They retain their firmness even after cooking and are often used in Indian cooking.

Great Northern Beans

These white, mild-tasting beans take on the flavor of the other ingredients with which they're prepared. Often used in soups, salads, and baked beans, the Great Northern is versatile and one of the most commonly eaten beans in the United States.

Kidney Beans

Although most people think of kidney beans as reddish-brown, they also can be white, mottled, or light red. One thing won't change—the familiar kidney bean shape. Kidney beans are meaty and have a distinct taste. Kidney beans are used in three-bean salad, chili, and many soups.

Lentils

Lentils are not a bean and not a pea—they have their own distinct classification in the legume family. They are high in protein and fiber, and can be a substitute for meat. They are also high in folate and potassium. Unlike other legumes, lentils cook quickly without presoaking. Be sure to rinse them well before adding them to recipes. You can also just boil them until tender and add seasonings of your choice. They are delicious over rice or mixed with vegetables.

Lentils come in three main varieties: brown, green, and red.

- Brown lentils are the least expensive and are best used for soups because they soften when they are cooked and can get mushy.
- Green lentils are also known as French lentils. They have a nuttier taste. They are a good choice for salads because they stay firm after they've been cooked.
- Red lentils are the fastest-cooking lentil. Although they start out red, when cooked they quickly lose their shape and turn golden yellow. Their taste is sweeter and milder than their counterparts, and they are often used in Indian cooking.

Lima Beans

Also known as "butter beans," lima beans are another common legume. Their shape is flat and broad and rounded. They have a slightly sweet flavor that is a little bland, and are one of the main ingredients in succotash. Their color can range from pale green to speckled cream and purple.

Mung Beans

Mung beans are best known as sprouts, but they are also common in Indian and Asian dishes. They are related to the field pea, with a similar shape but a darker color, ranging from medium green to nearly black.

Navy Beans

Navy beans are similar to Great Northern beans, but they are smaller and retain their shape well when they are cooked. They are often used commercially for pork and beans. They received their name because they were a staple food of the United States Navy in the early twentieth century.

Peanuts

Peanuts are not traditional nuts, like walnuts, pecans, etc. They actually grow underground, like potatoes, and are considered a legume. Peanuts have high protein and a good deal of fat. Peanuts can be ground for peanut butter, roasted, or baked, and in some regions of the United States, they are boiled.

Peas

Yellow or green, dried peas are often used in soups and also in Indian cuisine. If the peas are whole, they will need to be soaked before you cook them; however, dried split peas can be used without soaking. Split peas are best known for their use in split-pea soup.

Pinto Beans

Pinto beans are the most widely consumed legume in the southwestern area of the United States. Small, oval, and reddish-tan, pinto beans are used for refried beans, soups, and many Tex-Mex dishes.

Cooking Supplies

Many of the foods you might have purchased at the local supermarket before you started living off the grid will now be homemade—more delicious and definitely better for you. To ensure that your cooking efforts aren't frustrated, be sure you have a pantry that is stocked with the essentials you need. You can go to a warehouse store and buy many of these items in bulk. There are also wonderful cookbooks, like *Urban Pantry: Tips and Recipes for a Thrifty, Sustainable and Seasonal Kitchen* by Amy Pennington, that show you how to make some of your favorite items at home. The following list just suggests supplies you should keep on hand; be sure to create your own list to include the things your family likes.

- Spices and extracts
- Baking powder, baking soda, and yeast
- Salt—iodized, pickling, kosher, and sea salt
- Dry milk
- Dry buttermilk
- Dutch cocoa
- Cornstarch
- Cream of tartar
- Shortening
- Oil
- Sugar, brown sugar, confectioner's sugar, honey, molasses
- Nuts
- Raisins, dates, and other dried fruits
- Worcestershire sauce
- Soy sauce
- Vinegar
- Condiments
- Parchment paper, aluminum foil, plastic wrap, and plastic storage bags
- Bouillon cubes (beef and chicken)

Other helpful items you might want to have on hand are muffin and pancake mixes, gravy and seasoning mixes, various types of pasta, potato flakes, and peanut butter and jelly.

ESSENTIAL

Moving off-grid is no reason to deprive yourself of your favorite comfort foods. Whether you want something that reminds you of happy childhood times or you simply want to indulge, comfort food is important. Family favorites can really help as you make the transition to living off the grid. Make a list of the foods your family loves and can't do without, and make sure you keep some in your pantry.

Helpful Equipment

The most important items a tradesman has are the tools of his trade. You wouldn't want to be a carpenter, plumber, or electrician without the proper specialized equipment that makes the job run smoother and helps you to be more efficient. The same could be said about the tools around a kitchen, especially a kitchen that is going to be an essential part of your daily life.

Since you are living off-grid, you'll want to take into account the energy you are going to be able to produce as you look at appliances for your kitchen. That being said, even though some appliances might pull a great deal of electricity for a short amount of time, the savings in labor might be very well worth it. Keep in mind, too, that your basic kitchen appliances—refrigerator, chest freezer, oven, stovetop, and dishwasher—should be Energy Star rated.

The next level of kitchen appliances—mixer, grinder, and food processor—should be of the best quality you can afford because you will use them often. However, cost does not always equate to quality, so be sure to look at reviews of the items you want to purchase. A stand mixer with a dough hook and other attachments is an item you will use every day. If you can find one that has attachments for other kitchen tasks, like grinding, slicing, or juicing, so much the better.

Canning supplies are essential. You can purchase them new or find them at garage sales, estate auctions, and online auctions. When buying used supplies, look for items like steam juicers, cherry pitters, food strainers, and large water-bath canners. The items you will want to purchase new are pressure cookers and your canning tool set. You can buy new jars or pick them up at auctions or garage sales; just be sure they aren't chipped. You will need to buy new rings and lids.

ALERT

Think twice before buying a highly specialized appliance like a bread machine. Often you will be baking more bread than the machine can handle, and you will be wasting both money and space for a machine that can only do one thing.

Buy good-quality cookware, and be sure you also have cast-iron cookware. Cast iron is not only solid and dependable, and can take a lot of abuse, but the iron also leaches into the food you cook, increasing your iron intake.

You should have a good-quality hand-operated can opener. If you now use an electric model, you can continue to use it. But, in the event of a power outage, you will want to have a nonelectric opener close by.

Buy quality kitchen hand tools that will last and won't melt when exposed to hot surfaces. Imagine doing your everyday cooking and baking without electricity, and then buy the tools that would make that job easier.

Have at least one good set of measuring cups and spoons and several larger Pyrex multicup measuring cups. Purchase good-quality mixing bowls and bakeware. Be sure you have enough so you can bake several loaves of bread or sheets of cookies at the same time.

Survival Essentials

If there were a national emergency and daily life as you know it was suspended, if trucks could no longer deliver goods, if the grid went down, if martial law were imposed and you and your family were basically on your own, what are the things you would need to survive?

Of course, you don't need an emergency or a disaster to have to live in survival mode. What would happen if you lost your job and weren't able to get employment for months or years? What would happen if you were sick for an extended period of time? How would you care for your family?

There are basic foods and concepts you can learn in order to be prepared for these eventualities. In this small section, you will learn about the basics you need to have in your pantry. However, there are many other excellent ideas about preparedness that should be incorporated into your off-grid lifestyle. Two excellent books that go into great detail about this kind of preparedness are *The New Passport to Survival* by Rita Bingham and *Making the Best of Basics* by James Talmage Stevens.

According to Rita Bingham, there are seven survival foods—grains, legumes, sprouting seeds, honey, salt, oil, and powdered milk. Grains and legumes have already been covered in this chapter, and you've also learned a little about sprouts, but there is still more to learn.

Sprouts

Unless you can bottle or freeze them, it's hard to store leafy green vegetables for a long period of time. You have probably pulled a bag of lettuce out of your refrigerator only to find that it has gone bad between the time you purchased it and the time you wanted to use it. But those green vegetables are essential to your health. So, how are you able to offer your family a supplement of high-powered greens? Sprouts.

From their original state as seeds, beans, or grains, sprouts actually increase in vitamins A, B, C, E, and K as they grow. Riboflavin and folic acid increase up to thirteen times, and vitamin C increases up to 600 percent.

You will want to offer your family a variety of sprouts in order to ensure a balanced diet. Many of the legumes and grains discussed in this chapter are excellent choices for sprouting, including wheat, barley, chickpeas, mung beans, adzuki beans, peas, and lentils. Other good choices for sprouts are alfalfa, buckwheat, clover, and quinoa. It's suggested that a one-month supply of beans for one adult would be about five pounds.

Nonfat Dry Milk

Nonfat dry milk or powdered milk is an excellent source of protein, calcium, and nutrition. It provides about 80 calories per serving. Most vitamins in dried milks are present in levels comparable to those of whole milk. However, vitamins A and D are not present in nonfat milk and must be supplemented.

Nonfat powdered milk can be used not only in cooking and baking, but also to create other dairy products, like yogurt, cheese, and sour cream. Dried whole milk and dried buttermilk contain milkfat and are not suitable for long-term storage.

If you have milk allergies, consider other options. If your family enjoys soy milk, you can actually learn how to make your own with stored soy beans.

A month's supply of dry milk for one adult would be about 1½ pounds.

Honey

For over 10,000 years, honey has been considered a basic survival food. It was considered as such both for its food qualities and for its medicinal purposes. Honey is a natural and healthy sweetener. It will store almost indefinitely, and comes in a variety of flavors depending on what plants the bees were exposed to as they gathered nectar and pollens.

ESSENTIAL

Greeks and Romans referred to honey as a food fit for the gods. Greek custom was to offer honey to the gods and deceased spirits. This tribute kept one out of harm's way and in a spirit's or god's good graces.

Because honey isn't processed like sugar, it retains its nutrients and mineral content. And, since it is a natural food, it is digested more easily than sugar.

Honey also provides natural antioxidants that can boost your immune system. In addition, honey produced locally may help inhibit allergies.

Honey can be substituted in recipes calling for sugar. Simply use ¾ cup honey for every cup of sugar in the recipe. Because honey is liquid, as opposed to sugar, you should reduce the amount of liquid called for in the recipe by one-quarter. Honey will also give your foods a sweeter taste than sugar.

Honey can be stored in any clean container, from plastic food-grade buckets to glass jars. Honey should be stored at about 75°F, but if it is stored at a cooler temperature, the crystallization that occurs can be reversed by placing the container in warm water.

You should be aware that honey is not recommended for infants under the age of twelve months.

You should store about five pounds of honey or sugar per adult per month.

Salt

Salt improves the flavor of foods and is essential in many recipes for baked goods (it helps bread rise) and in canning and preserving food. The recommended amount of salt to store for a year's use is eight pounds per person per year. Salt can be stored long term and, if it cakes up, can be dried at a low temperature (250°F) in an oven until you can break it up so it is granulized again. It is recommended to use and store iodized salt to prevent goiter.

Oil

Fats are essential to your survival and for the structure and healthy functioning of your body. The body needs two essential fatty acids—linoleic acid, which is better known as omega-6 fatty acid, and linolenic acid, also known as alpha-linolenic, ALA, a type of omega-3 fatty acid. For general health, there should be a balance between omega-6 and omega-3 fatty acids. The ratio should be in the range of 2:1—4:1, omega-6 to omega-3.

Omega-3 fatty acid can be found in deepwater fish, fish oil, canola oil, flaxseed oil, and walnut oil. You can also find it in nuts, like almonds, hazelnuts, pecans, cashews, walnuts, and macadamia nuts. Omega-6 fatty acids are found in raw nuts, seeds, legumes, and vegetable oils like borage oil, grape seed oil, evening primrose oil, sesame oil, and soybean oil. When you store oil, be sure that you choose an oil that will help you meet your requirements of fatty acids.

It is suggested that for one month's storage you have about one quart of oil per adult.

CHAPTER 17

The Importance of Herbs

Herbs are the leaves or other parts of aromatic plants that are grown in a temperate climate. There are herbs you can use for everyday living, like cleaning, sachets, and laundry, herbs to flavor food, and herbs for medicinal purposes. Herbs can offer you a natural and healthier alternative to many of the products you might currently be using in your home.

Your Herb Garden

Traditionally, herb gardens were laid out in geometric patterns. From simple kitchen gardens to extravagant formal gardens, the plants were organized by use, relationships to other plants, or appearance. In more contemporary times, gardeners still enjoy unique herb gardens, but approach them with a more organic point of view, where appearance, color, and texture dictate the direction of the garden over use. Many times, herb gardens have elements that contrast with the plants. This is not only for aesthetics, but also to keep the herbs confined. You will find many herb gardens with brick paths, stone walls, containers of various shapes and sizes, and even statues like sundials or cherubs.

FACT

The Egyptians studied herbs and used them in medicinal and religious functions as far back as 3,500 B.C. The Chinese began the organized study of herbs in 2,500 B.C. Written records in China enumerate the uses of herbs dating from 100 B.C.

Your herb garden should be designed to suit your needs. But keep in mind that a well-thought-out plan in terms of planting, weeding, and collecting your herbs will go a long way in ensuring that your garden does not become such a cumbersome job that you neglect it.

Most herbs like full sun with well-drained soil and constant moisture. The plants that are originally from warmer areas, like rosemary, lavender, and sage, are more tolerant of dry conditions and flourish in warm weather.

You can start many of your herb seeds indoors in the winter and plant them in the garden in the spring, once all danger of frost is past. You'll want to start the seeds eight to twelve weeks before the last frost date for your region.

Herbs are not only good for you, they are also good for your garden. Herbs attract bees and other pollinating insects. Some herbs are bug repellents. And some herbs actually have large root systems that help break up the soil.

An herb garden's greatest reward is for you personally, both in using the final product and enjoying the whole experience of nurturing an herb garden, which is a unique pleasure. You will find that as you take care of these plants, you will receive the benefits. There is nothing you will find quite as calming as weeding around chamomile plants after a stressful day.

ESSENTIAL

If you don't have space for an herb garden, create a container garden of herbs. Many herbs flourish in a window box or in pots on a sunny window ledge. Even a sunny kitchen window is a wonderful place to grow a collection of kitchen herbs.

Herbs in Food

Herbs that have historically been used for food have also played a vital role in your health, but it was often hidden under their excellent taste. Originally, herbs were added to cooking for their digestive and preservative properties, rather than their unique tastes and smells. Herbs in the mint family aid digestion; members of that family include marjoram, rosemary, and peppermint. Herbs like parsley and caraway soothe the walls of the digestive tract and reduce flatulence.

QUESTION

How many pounds of herbs are sold in the United States?
In the United States alone, 200 million pounds of herbs and spices are consumed annually, with black pepper, cinnamon, nutmeg, garlic, paprika, chili powder, oregano, celery (seeds and salt), onions, and parsley heading the list.

Adding herbs to food enhances flavor and, in many cases, adds to the vitamins and minerals you receive. When you use herbs to season foods, you should use them sparingly. You want the herb to enhance the flavor of the food, not overwhelm it.

Harvesting Herbs

You should harvest herbs in the morning, just after the dew has evaporated and before the sun can warm the leaves. Because the oils that give the herbs their distinct aromas are volatile, you want to handle the plants carefully as you pick them, taking care not to bruise or injure the leaves. You should pick only the amount you need, unless you are getting to the end of the season and need to dry them for use during the winter months.

You should pick only healthy-looking herbs that are clean and blemish free.

Both the flavor and aroma of herbs declines soon after picking, so you need to be ready to use them immediately. You can store them for a short period of time in a perforated plastic bag inside your refrigerator.

Tips for Using Herbs

You can experiment with herbs to see what you and your family like. There are no rules about using herbs, but here are some suggestions.

- Herbs should be at room temperature when using them in cold foods.
- Prepare a bouquet garni (a bundle of herbs containing parsley, bay leaf, thyme, and other herbs) when preparing stock, stews, or soups.
- Herbs can be used in three ways—fresh, dried, and crumbled. Dried herbs are more concentrated than fresh, and powdered herbs are more concentrated than crumbled. Generally, ¼ teaspoon of powdered herbs is equal to ¾ to 1 teaspoon crumbled or 2 to 4 teaspoons fresh.
- You should chop the leaves of fresh herbs very fine because more of the oils and, therefore, more of the flavor will be released.
- When using an herb for the first time, you should use a small amount until you become familiar with it.
- Extended cooking will reduce the flavor of the herb. To enhance the flavor of the dish, add fresh herbs close to the completed cooking time.
- Because a cold temperature often inhibits the release of oils, fresh herbs used in refrigerated foods should be added at least several hours before serving.

Common Culinary Herbs

Some basic culinary herbs include:

- **Basil** is most commonly used in Italian recipes and tomato-based recipes such as spaghetti sauces, pizza, and pesto. However, it is a very versatile herb, and you can also use it in soups and bread as well as with fish, eggs, poultry, lamb, beef, pork, vegetables, and even desserts.
- **Chives** look like tall, thin pieces of grass caught up in a bunch. They have a delicate onion flavor. You can chop the leaves and sprinkle them on salads, cottage cheese, or eggs. Chives are best known as a garnish for potatoes along with sour cream.
- **Dill** is a very delicate plant with tall, thin stalks and feathery foliage. It's best known for its use in pickles and dips, but you can also use it for soups, sauces, fish, eggs, meat, and poultry.
- **Mint** is available in many varieties, including spearmint, peppermint, and even applemint. You can use mint leaves for teas, in desserts, and in Mediterranean cooking. Mint leaves are also used to make mint jelly, which is used as an accompaniment to lamb, and can be used in herbal vinegars.
- **Oregano** is used in Italian cooking. You can add it to tomato sauces for pasta and also use it in yeast breads, marinated vegetables, black beans, zucchini, eggplant, roasted meats, and fish.
- **Parsley** grows in two varieties—curly leaf and flat leaf. The flat leaf is the Italian type. Parsley is a versatile herb and can be used chopped or whole. Chopped parsley can be used in soups, breads, eggs, beef, and vegetables. The whole leaf can be used as a garnish.
- **Rosemary** is an evergreen plant in its native setting. You can use its green needlelike leaves in soups, breads, fish, eggs, shellfish, lamb, beef, and pork.
- **Sage** is a dusty green–colored herb that is used most frequently with poultry, especially in stuffing. Sage can be used with pork dishes too.
- **Tarragon** is an herb that is often used in French cooking. The leaves are long and narrow and it has a distinctive aniselike flavor. You can use tarragon to flavor soups, fish, shellfish, beef, pork, salad dressings, and eggs.

- **Thyme** is another herb that is generally used with poultry, especially in stuffing. You can also use thyme in sauces, breads, fish, eggs, shellfish, lamb, beef, pork, soups, and stews.

How to Use Herbs for Health

There are five basic herbal preparations used primarily in home herbal medicine—infusions, decoctions, compresses, poultices, and tinctures. You are probably very familiar with several of these preparations. Most herb teas are infusions. Decoctions are woodier than infusions and have larger pieces of herbs in them. They are also sold as herb teas, but you must brew them for a longer period of time. Your grandmother probably used poultices on a regular basis for anything from a chest cold to a spider bite.

Infusions

Infusions are usually made using the leaves or the flowers of a plant. Making an infusion is very similar to making tea. Place the suggested amount of herbs in a large bowl, and pour boiling water over them. Let the herbs steep in the water for ten to fifteen minutes. Strain the used herbs from the infused water and store the water in a clean jar or bottle until needed.

Decoctions

Decoctions are similar to infusions, except with a decoction you are using the woodier parts of the plant and often the root of the plant. These parts of the herbs should be chopped into small prices. Place the pieces in a pan and add water. Bring the herbs and water to a boil and then turn down and simmer for ten to fifteen minutes. Strain the liquid while hot and store in a clean jar or bottle.

Compresses

Compresses are small bundles of material that have been soaked in an infusion or decoction and applied to the skin. Linen, gauze, or cotton are often used for compresses. Be sure that the infusion or decoction is hot when you soak the material. You should apply the compress to the affected area and change it when it has cooled down.

Poultice

When you make a poultice, you wrap the herbs themselves in a piece of gauze and soak it in the infusion or decoction, then apply it to the skin. You can also use cider vinegar in place of the usual water when you create an infusion or decoction for poultice use. You should apply it to the affected area and change it when it cools down.

Tincture

A tincture is a mixture of herbs and sometimes alcohol to preserve the benefits of the herb. Generally vodka is used in many of the tincture recipes, but other types of alcohol can be used. Generally, the ratio of herb to fluid is one to five. Measure the required amount of herb and place it in a dark, screw-top jar. Pour the alcohol over the herbs, remembering the one to five ratio. If you don't have a dark jar, be sure you store your bottled tincture in a paper sack in a dark pantry. Keep the tincture tightly covered in a warm place, like a pantry, and shake it twice a day. In two weeks, open the bottle and strain the contents through cheesecloth, saving the liquid. Store the liquid in a dark, tightly sealed bottle until you need it.

Herbs for Beauty and Home Care

When you think about personal care or even home-care products, you might think of heavy perfumed or antiseptic-scented concoctions. If you substitute herbal products, those heavy, artificial scents are replaced with lemon balm, rose, basil, and lavender.

Body Care

Herbal products not only cleanse your body with gentle, natural methods, they can also offer additional healing benefits not found with traditional manufactured products. You should pick the herb that works best with your skin type. Dry skin needs an emollient herb that will soften and lubricate the skin. Oily skin should use a more astringent herb. Here are some examples of types of herbs and their body-care properties:

- **Comfrey:** emollient
- **Marigold (calendula):** astringent, cleansing, and promotes healing of wounds
- **Chamomile:** cleansing, soothing
- **Lavender:** antiseptic, stimulating
- **Yarrow:** cleansing, toning
- **Lady's mantle:** astringent

These are only a few of the herbs you can use for body care.

FACT

The amazing properties of lavender essential oil were discovered before World War I. When a French chemist named Rene-Maurice Gattefosse burned himself in the family perfumery, the only liquid available was a vat of lavender essential oil, so he stuck his hand into it. The burn healed very quickly, and the chemist devoted the rest of his life to studying the medicinal properties of essential oils.

Hair Care

There are herbs that will help dry hair, dull hair, oily hair, and even prevent dandruff. You can use specific herbs depending on the color of your hair. Here are a few examples:

- **Burdock root:** prevents dandruff
- **Stinging nettle:** helps dull hair
- **Lavender:** good for oily hair
- **Marigold:** good for red hair
- **Chamomile:** good for blonde hair
- **Sage:** good for dark hair
- **Catnip:** encourages hair growth

Oral Hygiene

You might already use herbs to freshen your mouth; peppermint or even parsley work to sweeten your breath. Some other herbs that can be used for oral hygiene are cloves, sage, thyme, and marjoram; you can either steep these in a tea or chew on them like parsley.

Relaxation/Aromatherapy

Herbs are wonderful to aid in relaxation. A hot bath sprinkled with herbs can not only soothe and calm, it can soften and clean your skin. Herbs that are well known for their soothing qualities are lemon balm, chamomile, vervain, skullcap, bergamot, and lavender. You can use these herbs in compresses, herbal baths, in soaps and shower gels, and even in rubs. You can also take larger pieces of the dried herb and use them as a potpourri throughout your home.

Herbs for Medicinal Purposes

Using herbs as a way to treat ailments can be dated all the way back to the ancient Egyptians. Herbal medicine also uses natural plant substances to prevent illness. Today, 80 percent of the population of the United States uses some type of herbal medicine. In China, herbal medicine has been used for over 2,500 years and is considered the primary means of health care.

ESSENTIAL

Natural herbs, herbal medicines, and natural supplements represent the most popular area of complementary and alternative medicine, according to the National Center for Complementary and Alternative Medicine (NCCAM). Herbal supplements are sometimes referred to as "botanicals."

Herbal medicines can be found in everyday options like teas or herbal extracts. But many herbs can also be found in the medications you use. A quarter of the prescriptions today are plant based, and many of the over-the-counter remedies find their base in herbal medicine.

Here is a list of common ailments and a sampling of herbs that have medicinal properties for those problems:

- **Digestive problems:** angelica, bee balm, cilantro, ginger, lavender, parsley, sage, and spearmint
- **Migraines/headaches:** angelica, marjoram, and rosemary
- **Ulcers:** angelica and periwinkle
- **Colds and sore throats:** bee balm, cilantro, dill, ginger, marjoram, periwinkle, spearmint, and thyme
- **Fevers:** cilantro, lavender, and safflower
- **Wounds/muscle aches:** comfrey, garlic, and thyme
- **Flatulence:** dill, fennel, and sage
- **Bug bites:** safflower and sage
- **Anxiety:** ginger, marjoram, rosemary, spearmint, and St. John's Wort
- **Bladder problems:** lavender and St. John's Wort

ALERT

Turmeric is one of nature's most powerful healers. The active ingredient in turmeric is curcumin. Turmeric may prevent and slow the progression of Alzheimer's disease by removing amyloid plaque buildup in the brain. It is a potent natural anti-inflammatory that works as well as many anti-inflammatory drugs, but without the side effects.

Wild Herbs

From dandelions to stinging nettle to sumac, there are wild herbs all around you, and collecting them is not only a pleasant way for you to get closer to nature, it also allows you to find herbs in their purest form. Your first step is to learn which herbs grow in your area. By knowing what does and does not grow naturally, you can save yourself time and possible misidentification. You should arm yourself with good information before you start. There are field guides with color photos and descriptions that can help you, or you can search the Internet and create your own booklet. Remember that some plants change their appearance throughout the different stages of their growth, so be sure to familiarize yourself with all of the stages. The best help you can get is to go with someone who has experience hunting wild herbs.

ESSENTIAL

Cattail pollen is equal to bee pollen in terms of minerals, enzymes, and protein. Native Americans have used cattails as herbal remedies for a variety of ailments for centuries. Most commonly, a gel is made from the young leaves of the immature cattail for healing wounds, sores, boils, etc. It also has some pain reduction properties.

As you familiarize yourself with the herbs in the area, especially when you are hunting for the first time, it's a good idea to have a notebook where you can draw a map of your journey and identify the areas where you located the various herbs you found. Take samplings of the herbs—stems, flowers, leaves, and roots—and place them in a plastic bag. Label what you found and where you found it. (Often, those who hunt for herbs carry baskets for transporting them.) These samplings will help you successfully identify the herb, and your map will help you find it again.

When you do go back to harvest some of the herb, you need to remember that you should never take all of the plants from an area. You always want to leave enough for the plant to reseed for the next year.

CHAPTER 18

Water, Water, Everywhere

Access to water is essential for your off-grid homestead. You need water for drinking, bathing, cleaning, cooking, feeding your livestock, watering your garden, and canning your produce. Your first step is to make sure you will have the water rights before you buy your piece of property. The next step is learning how to make the best use of the water you have.

Harvesting Water

Harvesting rainwater is one of the oldest known methods of capturing and storing water to use for irrigating your garden or supplying your household or your livestock with water. These methods are still used by many people in third-world countries and are growing more common in the United States, especially in the Southwest, where water is very scarce.

FACT

The earth's total amount of water has a volume of about 344 million cubic miles. Of this, 315 million cubic miles is seawater, 9 million cubic miles is groundwater in aquifers, 7 million cubic miles is frozen in polar ice caps, 53,000 cubic miles of water pass through the planet's lakes and streams, 4,000 cubic miles of water is atmospheric moisture, and 3,400 cubic miles of water are locked within the bodies of living things.

The basic foundation of a water harvesting system is the means to direct rainfall where you want it to go. Water harvest can entail a series of small trenches or contoured areas that begin just below the downspouts of your house or your barn and run into your garden. Or, it can be a more sophisticated system with water running from your downspout into some kind of storage container for future use.

ESSENTIAL

The average American household consumes about 127,400 gallons of water during a year. Homeowners in Washington, DC, pay about $350 for that amount of water. Buying that same amount from a vendor in Guatemala City would cost more than $1,700.

Your roof is not the only surface or "catchment" that can capture rainfall. Any large surface that can capture and/or carry water to where it can be used or stored is also considered a catchment. Think about the catchments on your property—the barn roof, the outhouse roof, the patio, or even the driveway. All of these hard surfaces allow water to run off and have the potential of being part of your water harvest system.

Now, not all of these catchments have to direct water to the same place. Your roof could have a system that directs the water to barrels attached to your downspouts. Your driveway could have a series of dikes, berms, or contouring to direct the water to irrigate your garden.

Planning Your System

In order to determine how you should store your water, you need to develop a site plan. Using graph paper, draw a scale model of your property with the location of your house, outbuildings, and any other areas that you think might be catchments. Then indicate water flow by drawing arrows to indicate water flow direction across each surface; i.e., your roof will have arrows from the peak going down each side. Add to the drawing those areas that will need water, such as your garden, your livestock area, and your orchard, and even areas in your house that could use graywater, like your toilets.

Now you can calculate the approximate amount of water you will harvest using the designated catchments. Using your graph paper, calculate the number of square feet in each catchment area. The next thing you need to do is determine the runoff coefficient for the different surfaces of your catchment. The runoff coefficient roughly calculates the percentage of water that will not be absorbed or evaporated from the surface. If the surface is smooth, use the higher coefficient from the following list; if the surface is rough, the lower one. For example, the runoff coefficient for a smooth metal roof is 0.95. Here is a list of the runoff coefficients:

- **Roof:** metal, gravel, asphalt, shingle, fiberglass, mineral paper—high coefficient 0.95, low coefficient 0.90
- **Paving:** concrete, asphalt—high coefficient 1.00, low coefficient 0.90
- **Gravel:** high coefficient 0.70, low coefficient 0.25
- **Soil:** flat, bare—high coefficient 0.75, low coefficient 0.20
- **Soil:** flat, with vegetation—high coefficient 0.60, low coefficient 0.10
- **Lawns:** flat, sandy soil—high coefficient 0.10, low coefficient 0.05
- **Lawns:** flat, heavy soil—high coefficient 0.17, low coefficient 0.13

With all of this information in hand, you can use the formula that follows to calculate your water capture:

A = average monthly rainfall amount (this can vary greatly from month to month, so you may need to calculate each month's potential water capture)

B = 0.623 (converts inches into gallons per square foot)

C = square footage of the catchment surface

D = the runoff coefficient from the preceding list

$A \times B \times C \times D$ = *monthly yield of harvested water in gallons*

Once you have calculated the monthly yield from your catchment surfaces, you can determine where you want the water to go.

Preparing Your Site

Your potential harvested water needs somewhere to go. Do you want to divert it all into the garden or orchard, do you want to store it in holding tanks near your home, or do you want to build a cistern and store the water there? These are the next decisions you have to make.

Keep in mind that you need to size your storage container(s) large enough to hold your calculated supply. Water collected from any catchment area can be distributed anywhere on your property through a series of PVC pipes and hoses. However, it will save you time, effort, and money if you are able to locate water storage *close* to the areas needing water, and *higher* than the area to take advantage of gravity flow.

If you live in an area that has minimal rainfall, there are some things you can do to optimize your water harvest:

- Create depressions around trees and line them with rocks or mulch to retain moisture.
- If you are designing a new home site for water harvesting, arrange brick or flagstone paving to direct water to plants.
- Dig furrows and channels to direct water to a garden.
- Make sure your gutters and downspouts are free of trash, dirt, and leaves.

Storing Rainwater

Having water surplus available to you at the right time of year makes storage well worth the time and effort. But when water is stored for more than several months, it can stagnate and present a health hazard because it could become a breeding area for mosquitoes.

To determine whether storage should be part of your harvesting system, compare the total amount of water available in a given month (estimated rainfall) to the estimated water usage in the same month. If you find that you have a surplus that can be used in a reasonable amount of time, you should consider a storage system.

A Simple Storage System

You can create a simple water storage system consisting of a plastic barrel placed on a raised platform under a rain-gutter downspout. There should be an opening on top of the barrel for the water to be fed in through the downspout and some kind of filtering system above the opening. The barrel should also have an external pipe with a shutoff valve to control the amount of water withdrawn. If you have designed your system properly, gravity will enable you to send water from the barrel to a drip irrigation system without a pump.

Wells and Pumps

When you move off-grid, another thing you don't have access to is municipal water systems. If you are living in a rural area with a private well, you will find that owning an electric pump is a necessity. You will find that most pumping needs will be met with a low-voltage DC-powered pump.

General Purpose/Intermittent Pumping

If you have stored the water for your home in a water tank that is a gravity-driven system, a small DC-powered pump might be just what you need. An intermittent-use pump operates in an "always on" style, with removable wiring clips that attach to the power source. When you attach the pump to the source, it will run. When you disconnect the clips, the pump turns

off. Because the pump would only be used to move water from one holding tank to another, or from a transport tank to a holding tank, connecting
and disconnecting the wiring clips should prove convenient. Many of these
pumps can be attached inline in a transfer hose, or can be submerged in
the transfer tank, with a hose attached only to the outlet. Using an intermit-
tent pump is much more convenient that siphoning water from one container to another.

Water Pressure Systems

If you don't have a gravity-fed water system, chances are you have a pressure system, which is the most common type of off-grid household water
supply system. If your household runs on a holding-tank water system or a low-
yield well, you will boost water pressure at the household faucets if you set up a
pressure system. You can operate a water pressure system with an on-demand
pressure pump, a pressurized water tank, or a combination of the two.

On-demand pumps are equipped with built-in pressure switches, which
automatically turn on when water pressure drops. Once the pressure builds
back up, the switch will shut down. If you have a system that uses a holding
tank, an on-demand pump is ideal for moving water from the holding tank
into the household water system. If your system is running on a private well,
you can install a holding tank with a float switch between the well and the
household water system, and the pressure pump can be installed between
the holding tank and the household water system.

You can use either a well pump or an on-demand pump with a pressure tank system. If you use a well system, the pressure switch would be
installed between the well and the pressure tank, cycling the well pump
only as needed to keep the pressure tank filled above a certain pressure
level. If you are using a holding tank, an on-demand pump can be installed
between the holding tank and the pressure tank. This way, the on-demand
pump can fill the pressure tank from the holding tank, and the pressure tank
will supply water pressure to the household.

Surface/Shallow Well Pumps

If your house is located near any kind of fresh water, a surface pump can
be used to transfer water from the stream, river, lake, or pond to a top-inlet

holding tank equipped with a float switch. Whenever the holding tank water level drops below a set level, the float switch will run the pump. If you have a shallow water well and the water level is within twenty feet of ground level, you can also use a surface pump.

Designed to push water over long distances, surface pumps are well suited for supplying water to outlying buildings, fields, or a house situated on a hill above an available water source. And with the use of special pumping controllers, DC pumps can be run directly from solar panels or wind generators. This allows you to install them in remote locations like livestock watering stations or even in the middle of a garden.

ESSENTIAL

There are more than 17 million homes in the United States that get their water from private wells. The principle is simple—a hole is dug or drilled deep into the ground and a pump draws out the water. There are many regulations that apply to private wells, so you should only use a licensed well driller. It's easy for harmful contaminants to leak into your well if it's not installed properly.

Submersible/Deep Well Pumps

If your home is in an area where water tables are far underground, submersible pumps are the only choice for running a well water system. Although not suited for situations in which water is required to be pumped over long distances or up considerable heights, a deep well pump will operate quite well on its own for a household system. You can supplement this system with a holding tank and a pressure tank. This way, the pump can fill the pressure tank from the holding tank, and the pressure tank will supply water pressure to the household.

Irrigation

There are several options for irrigating your garden and orchard area when you live off-grid. As discussed earlier in the chapter, if water harvesting is an option, you can create a system of trenches and furrows to move rainwater from one area of your property to your garden. You can also collect rainwater in containers and use a gravity-fed drip-irrigation system.

Another option is to dig a channel from a nearby stream or river to your garden area. You should check with you local government entity to ensure this is legal in your area. At the mouth of the channel, next to the water source, create a gate that can be opened or closed manually. Then dig a series of connecting channels from the main channel that separate into smaller furrows throughout your garden and orchard. At the head of each of these connecting channels, create a gate to stop the water flow. When you are ready to irrigate, open the main gate to allow the water from the water source to stream down the main channel. By opening and closing the gates to the connecting channels, you can divert water to the areas of your garden and orchard that you want to irrigate.

Finally, using a solar- or wind-powered surface pump, you can push water through a series of larger PVC pipes to either drip through an irrigation system at ground level or be sprayed from an irrigation system built above the garden.

Graywater Use

The term "graywater" is used when you are talking about water that has already been used once. This doesn't include water from the toilet, which is known as "blackwater," but does include water from the sink, the washing machine, the shower, and the bathtub. Graywater comprises about 50 to 80 percent of all residential water use.

Graywater systems are used for several reasons:

- To promote a green lifestyle by using fewer resources
- To conserve water in an arid area
- To place less stress on a septic system
- To save money, when the cost of pumping water is more expensive than the cost of reusing water

When you build a graywater system you separate the graywater from the blackwater and send the graywater through a separate treatment system.

Blackwater will go into your septic system and graywater will pass through a filtering or purification system and then be reused. Ideally, after the graywater passes through a purification process it can then be reused. Graywater systems are particularly appropriate in off-grid locations. They reduce use of fresh water, place less stress on existing conventional septic tanks, have a highly effective purification process, and there is less chemical and energy use.

ALERT

If you plan on using graywater for irrigation, avoid using laundry powders. These powders often contain high levels of salt as a bulking agent, and this has the same effect on your soil as a drought. Use an organic liquid laundry detergent instead.

If you create a system that will separate blackwater from graywater, the graywater can be recycled back into the home and garden. Graywater can be used to flush toilets or irrigate the garden. Although there are systems that filter graywater enough to purify it to a state of drinking water, most graywater systems do not allow that degree of filtering. For that reason, graywater should not be used for drinking, cooking, or cleaning.

Because graywater still carries particles from food, your skin, and cleaning agents, and is often discharged warm, it is important not to store it before using it for irrigation purposes. Storing graywater would allow bacteria to grow in the water and transfer to your plants.

There are many ways you can filter graywater. The systems that allow you to feed the water back into the home for use in toilet flushing are more complex than those that simply filter the graywater and pressurize it for irrigation purposes. Some building designs, like the Earthships, have an entire graywater system built into their blueprints.

Septic Systems

The most common system you can use to dispose of wastewater is a septic system. Whether or not you decide to recycle graywater, you will still need a septic system to get rid of the blackwater from your home.

There are four main components to a typical septic system:

- A pipe to carry the waste from the home
- The actual septic tank to start the digestion process
- The drain field to spread out the wastewater
- The soil with microbes to do the final filtering and cleaning of the water

Once the used water enters the system, the pipe carries the water and accompanying waste out of your home and into the working parts of your septic system. The septic tank is actually a watertight tank that is buried several feet underground. Septic tanks have concrete manhole-size lids that generally sit at ground level, providing easy access for cleaning, inspection, and pumping the tanks.

Tanks can be made of concrete, fiberglass, or polyethylene. When wastewater comes into the tank, the solids settle to the bottom. This material is known as *sludge*. The oil, grease, and other nonsolid components rise to the top and are known as *scum*. This separation allows for a partial decomposition of the solid material. This decomposition is aided by a variety of different bacteria and enzymes that naturally break down the human waste in the tank and help it dissolve back into the earth, so you are not just accumulating a massive amount of refuse.

Sludge and scum are prevented from leeching out of the septic tank by a T-shaped outlet design that holds in the more solid materials and allows the water to seep into the drain field. You should use additional screens throughout the system to ensure that the solids do not make it into the drain field.

Once wastewater has been separated from the solids, it exits the septic tank into a drain field to complete its treatment in the soil. Wastewater is fed into the drain field every time new blackwater and graywater are introduced into the tank.

The soil surrounding the drain field is essential in removing contaminants from your wastewater before it is returned to the groundwater. The microbes in the soil remove harmful bacteria, viruses, and nutrients from the wastewater. This is accomplished by the wastewater filtering through the drain field.

Have your soil tested to be sure it is porous enough to allow natural filtration. Once installed, your septic system should be inspected every three years and pumped out every three to five years. However, maintenance of the septic system should be an ongoing process.

ESSENTIAL

The death of beneficial bacterial colonies in your septic tank can be lessened by changing from potent chemical cleaners to organic cleaning products, which are not quite as harsh on the bacteria that work in the tank.

Unfortunately, the bacteria and enzymes that eat away the sludge and scum are easily destroyed by bleach or paint thinner entering the system. You can restore the natural enzymes in the system quickly and inexpensively. All you have to do is buy a box or package of the enzymes made for septic systems and flush it down one of the toilets in your home. Some have found that adding brown sugar with the enzymes helps to increase their viability. You should add enzymes to stimulate the function of your septic tank about once a month for optimal performance.

Water Storage

When you are living off-grid you need to think of supplying water for more than just household purposes; you also need to think about extra water for fire protection or emergencies. And, if you have livestock, you need to be sure you have enough water to care for them as well.

Your ideal off-grid water storage system would be a sparkling spring that had plenty of water all year round. Then you would never have to worry about your water supply at all. Unfortunately, you probably can't count on that kind of source for your off-grid property unless you are very lucky. For most, some kind of water storage is critical to ensure a safe, reliable supply of water. Even if you have a plentiful supply, you still might want to consider extra water storage for fire protection or emergency preparedness.

In the September/October 2001 issue of *Backwoods Home Magazine*, found at *www.backwoodshome.com/articles2/yago71.html*, Jeffrey Yago, a licensed professional engineer and certified energy manager with over twenty-five years' experience in the energy conservation field, described the water storage system in his off-grid home. After the pump system he installed at a nearby stream was swept away after a storm surge, Jeff realized that he needed a more reliable source for water, but one that could be viable under the limitations of his solar-powered home. Jeff put a 500-gallon water tank into the basement of his home and set up an array of two pumps, installed near a shallow well. The first pump was a slow-flow 24-volt DC solar pump that would supply a slow but constant water supply into the tank during the day. The other pump was a 120-volt AC pump that was powered by a generator and could pull in large quantities of water in case of emergency, like a forest fire.

He installed a ball float switch to activate the DC well pump when the water level in the tank is low, and turn it off when full. Jeff found that 300 gallons a day would supply his family for several days. With an "on-demand" water heater, he could also meet the household needs for hot water.

If you decide that a well and a solar pump will meet your water needs, you still might want to consider some kind of emergency water storage. Should a natural or national disaster strike, water would be key to your survival. The average person can survive several weeks without food, but only a few days without water.

QUESTION

Does stored water taste bad?
Stored water is merely lacking oxygen. You can get it back to tasting great simply by pouring it back and forth a couple of times between a couple of pitchers, or glasses. This will infuse oxygen back into the water.

Your water storage plans should be based on having enough water to supply each person with one gallon per day. This amount is only for general drinking purposes. You should store more water for cooking and hygiene. If you are able to have a 150-gallon water tank or a number of 50-gallon water barrels, you would be able to serve the basic needs of a family of four for about a month. If you want to store more than one month's worth of water, you will need to multiply the number of containers.

Often you can find used plastic 50-gallon barrels for a reduced price through soft-drink bottlers, who use the barrels for concentrated syrup. You would have to thoroughly clean the buckets to remove the lingering taste, but they would offer you an inexpensive way to store water for your family.

For long-term water storage, tap water should be chemically disinfected by treating each gallon with sixteen drops (⅛ teaspoon) of liquid chlorine bleach containing 4 percent to 6 percent sodium hypochlorite. Scented bleach will perfume the water, so don't use it. One teaspoon of bleach disinfects five gallons of water. Three tablespoons will disinfect 55 gallons. If you add this to your water, you will kill bacteria and viruses and prevent the growth of microorganisms during storage.

CHAPTER 19

Dealing with Rodents, Critters, and Pests of All Kinds

When you move off the grid you will be exposed to "new neighbors." Depending on where your move takes you, these neighbors could be as innocuous as white-tailed deer and rabbits, or as predatory as badgers and coyotes. Learning how to recognize and deal with these critters that will share your space is imperative.

Man's Best Friend

A dog will not only provide companionship, he will also provide protection for you, your family, and your livestock. If you already have a dog as part of your family, remember that moving off the grid is going to be a culture shock for him too. Don't let your dog run loose; he may not be able to find his way home. And, if your new property is close to farmers with livestock, be sure to keep your dog on your property until you've had a chance to introduce him to your neighbors, because most farmers have no qualms about shooting an unknown dog that wanders close to their property.

FACT

Dogs are descended from a small, weasel-like mammal called Miacis, which was a tree-dwelling creature that existed about 40 million years ago. The domestic dog of today first appeared in Eurasia about 13,000 years ago, and was probably a direct descendant of a small, gray wolf.

Dogs, like people, have their own unique temperaments, but there are certain breeds that are more suited to living on a farm than others. These breeds, which tend to be the herding dogs and the working dogs, somehow understand that your chickens are not playthings, but are part of their pack and need to be protected. However, even these breeds need to be trained properly to respect the other livestock and understand that you and your family members are the alpha in his pack, which means you need to be obeyed. Most of these kinds of dogs are large, and a large, untrained dog is a danger to himself and the people around him. Don't feel as though you have to get a purebred dog. Lots of breed mixes make excellent farm dogs, and they often are readily available at shelters, rescues, or through "free-to-a-good home" advertisements in local newspapers.

Here is a list of dog breeds recommended for farms:

- **Border collie** is one of several herding breeds popular as farm dogs. Weighing between 27 and 45 pounds, the border collie is a medium-size dog with high energy. They are very smart and easy to train, but they need lots of activity to keep them happy.

- **Scotch collie** is also known as the farm collie or old farm collie. The Scotch collie is larger than the Border collie and not quite as energetic, but is devoted to its master and delighted to do his bidding.
- **Australian shepherd** is another herding breed popular for farms. Also known as an Aussie, they are natural herders as well as good watchdogs. They are medium-size dogs with friendly dispositions, and they interact well with children and other dogs.
- **Australian cattle dog** is also called a blue heeler. They are smart and easily trained. Because they are territorial they are good watchdogs, but they also have a hard time sharing their territory with other animals.
- **Corgis** are small herding dogs that are good farm dogs. Their bodies are similar in size to medium-size dogs, but their extremely short legs classify them as small herding dogs. They are intelligent and very energetic. They were originally bred to drive cattle, hunt vermin, and guard farms in the United Kingdom. Because of its close-to-the-ground stature, the corgi herds by barking and nipping at the heels of livestock.
- **German shepherds**, although often used as guard dogs, are actually a herding breed. German shepherds are loyal and intelligent and can be trained as sheepdogs. Full grown, they can weigh between 75 and 85 pounds.
- **Bernese Mountain Dog** is a large working breed. These dogs were bred to guard sheep in the Swiss Alps, and also to pull milk carts. They were bred to warn of intruders, but not to be aggressive, because they lived with the animals they protected. They will grow to be 80 to 100 pounds and, because of their heavy coat, may not be suited to warmer climates.
- **Great Pyrenees** is a non-herding dog well suited for life in colder climates. Like its cousin, the Bernese Mountain Dog, the Great Pyrenees was bred to protect flocks of sheep and goats. It is considered to be a guardian of family, farm, and livestock. Calm and loyal, this breed is also fiercely independent, which can create problems while training.
- **Old English sheepdog** is another herding breed that is popular on farms. Made popular by many movies, like *The Shaggy Dog* and *Peter Pan*, the family-friendly temperament is well known. Old English sheepdogs herd by bumping rather than nipping. And with an average weight of 60 to 100 pounds, when they bump you, you feel it.

How to Identify Rodents

One of the biggest problems you can encounter when you have your own farm is rodent infestation. The main issue with rats and mice is not the things they eat; it is the destruction they create when finding food. Rodents chew through items in your home or in your storage buildings. They will chew through plastic, wood, cardboard, and even electrical wires. Rats have even been found to chew through lead pipes and concrete dams. When they find a food source, they will leave feces throughout the food they don't consume. This includes grain supplies for your livestock and even food supplies for your family.

There is never just one rodent. A pair of rats and their offspring can produce 1,500 more rats within a twelve-month period. Because rodents are nocturnal, you need to look for the signs of infestation, rather than assume that if you don't see it, it's not there.

ALERT

The feces and urine that rodents leave in food supplies are often very dangerous. Salmonellosis and E. coli are two gastrointestinal infections that have been linked to rodent infestation. Other diseases that are linked with rodents are hantavirus, a respiratory disease, as well as the plague and murine typhus.

Holes and Nests

The difference between rat holes and mice holes is size. A rat hole is about three inches in diameter. A mouse hole is one-quarter of that size, or about three-quarters of an inch. Rodent holes can be found outdoors under sheds, in outbuildings, around haystacks, and in refuse heaps. Inside, holes may be gnawed in floors, between walls, behind counters, and at baseboards. Both rats and mice make nests using whatever kind of material is available to them, like paper, cloth, grass, leaves, cardboard, and insulation material.

Runs

Rodents tend to travel using an established route. Outdoors you may be able to see the pathway or run in the vegetation around the outbuildings. Inside, unless the route travels through a dusty area, it is hard to locate.

Smears

Rats like to move with their bodies in contact with a solid object, like a wall. This contact will often create a greasy stain or smear on the wall. They also leave smears from their backs when they scramble under joists or other obstructions.

ALERT

Even though most people consider mice less disgusting than rats, mice are much more common and cause more damage. Mice are prolific breeders, producing offspring in great abundance. There are approximately five to ten babies per litter, with a new litter born every forty-five days or so. At eight weeks of age, the pups are capable of mating.

Droppings

Droppings are a sure indicator you have a rodent issue. The number of droppings, their position, and age will give you an idea of how many rodents you have and where they are moving and feeding. Fresh droppings are shiny, soft, and moist for a few hours. As they start to age they become duller and harder. Rat droppings are capsule-shaped and about a half-inch long; they are often found in groups on runs. Mice droppings are rod-shaped, less than a quarter-inch long, and are generally scattered.

Signs of Damage

The more rodents you have, the more extensive and obvious the damage. Damage can include holes gnawed through wood, plastic, cables, pipes, silage bags, and sacks. Rat damage will be larger than that done by a mouse.

Rodent Control

Successful rodent control involves three different facets: (1) sanitation, (2) rodent-proofing, and (3) rodent killing. Though the first two methods are most important, they also require the most effort and therefore are frequently neglected.

You must use tight lids on garbage cans, get rid of refuse, remove junk, and properly store food and construction materials. These steps will limit the food supply and nesting sites for rodents.

You should store food products in sealed cabinets or in glass or metal containers. Store feed for your livestock in metal containers, like metal garbage cans, with tight-fitting lids. Be sure to clean up any spilled food. A well-swept floor makes it easier to detect signs of rodent activity.

Rodent-proofing also involves looking at your home and your outbuildings to see how you can keep them out. Inspect these areas thoroughly to find any trouble spots. Some areas you might consider are:

- All openings where water pipes, drain spouts, and vents enter a building. These should be tightly sealed with sheet-metal patches or filled with concrete.
- Doors, windows, and screens should close tightly to ensure that rodents cannot enter through them. Check to see if window frames fit tightly against the foundation in the basement, especially in older homes.
- Install 24- to 26-gauge galvanized sheet-metal flashing around wooden door jambs and metal kick plates on the outside of doors to prevent rats from gnawing entrances under or around doors.
- Floor drains and fan openings should be tightly covered with galvanized hardware cloth, 19-gauge, ¼-inch mesh, so the rodents can't enter through them.

- Remove materials that are stacked against the outside of an otherwise rodent-proof building. This will stop rats and mice from gaining entry into upper stories.
- Nonconcrete basement floors, especially dirt floors, and shallow foundations should be protected from burrowing rats with a cement curtain wall around the outer edge extending three feet into the ground, or in an L shape two feet into the ground, with a one-foot lip extending outward.
- Check for any other possible entrances that are larger than one-quarter inch, and seal or block them so a rodent cannot get in.

If your rodent infestations are severe, you should work to kill the rodents first, before you remove their safe havens, to prevent them from just migrating to other nearby areas.

Killing Rodents

Trapping is the most common method of killing rodents. Traps may or may not be baited, but should always be placed in areas of rodent activity. Look for signs of droppings or runs and set up the traps there. Bacon, peanut butter, bread, and nutmeats are good baits for the traps.

Place mouse traps at intervals of about three to four feet. Rat traps should be set father apart, about fifteen to thirty feet. The most effective way to situate the trap is with the bait toward the wall and the spring away from the wall, because mice and rats tend to follow the wall line. Check the traps often, discard dead rodents, and reset the traps.

Rodenticides, or rat poison, is an alternative method of killing rodents. The rodent eats the poison and then goes back to the nest and dies. If you have rodents in your home, having the rodent die in the wall can create an unpleasant smell. Poison can be used effectively if you have rats in your outbuildings. However, do not use poison if you have small children or other animals on your property that might accidentally ingest the poison.

There are also traps on the market that consist of a sticky surface that attracts mice and rats. Once the rodent steps onto the surface, it is caught and cannot get away. Unlike a spring trap, which kills the rodent immediately by breaking its neck, these traps prolong death. Often you will come across live rodents stuck to the trap and screaming. To put them out of their misery, you can pick up the trap carefully and put it in a bucket of water, so the rodent drowns.

Barn Cats

One of most natural ways to prevent rodent infestation and even keep the population of other small animals like rabbits to a minimum is to have some barn cats. Barn cats are not your Great-Aunt Ida's spoiled lap cat. They are usually at least partially feral cats who take the role of hunter and protector seriously.

QUESTION

What is the greatest number of mice killed by one cat?
Towser, a tortoiseshell tabby in charge of rodent control in Scotland, killed 28,899 mice in her twenty-one years. This is about four mice per day, every day, for twenty-one years. Towser died in 1987.

You might have already inherited barn cats when you purchased your property. If not, ask around; someone is usually in need of a home for some new barn kittens.

Although these are not pets, you have a responsibility to care for them, just like any other animal on your property. Here are some of the things you should consider to ensure that you have healthy and helpful barn cats:

Deworming

Because the main job of your barn cat is to catch and kill mice, they are susceptible to transmission of the worms that reside inside the rodent. Your veterinarian can prescribe a broad spectrum dewormer. Ask your veterinarian how often you should administer the medicine to your cat.

Heartworms are carried by mosquitoes, so if you live in an area where mosquitoes are plentiful, you will want to give your barn cat a monthly heartworm preventive. Be sure to have your cat tested before you begin preventative measures, because if your cat already had heartworms, they must be eliminated from the cat's system first.

Vaccination for Feline Diseases

There are a number of diseases that are considered the "core" cat diseases: feline herpes virus, calichi virus, and panleukopenia virus. Your veterinarian can give your cat a combination vaccination when the cat is still young and then annually to continue protection. Rabies virus vaccine is also necessary for your barn cat, especially if there are bats that are infected with rabies in your area. Rabies-infected bats eventually become paralyzed and fall to the ground. Before they die, they twitch around, and could attract the attention of your barn cat.

FeLV/FIV Testing and Vaccination

Feline leukemia, or feline immunodeficiency virus, is the equivalent of HIV in cats. If your veterinarian performs a simple blood test on your cat, she will be able to determine whether your cat is a carrier. Many cats with FeLV/FIV do fine, but about one-third become very ill. If your barn cat has FeLV/FIV, you will want to vaccinate the uninfected cats, so they don't become sick.

Nutrition

Just because your barn cat catches mice, rabbits, and even squirrels does not mean that it doesn't need a supplemental diet. You want to maintain a healthy barn cat, and a good-quality dry diet is all your cat requires. Keep a bowl full of dry food and another bowl filled with fresh water for your cats.

ALERT

Antifreeze poisoning is fatal in cats and dogs, if left untreated. Unfortunately, antifreeze also tastes good to these animals. In addition, you need to be sure that chemicals, pesticides, insecticides, rat poison, and even moldy feed are disposed of in closed containers where your animals cannot gain access to them.

Check On Your Barn Cats

Barn cats will usually remain healthy if they have high-quality food and clean water. But when cats become ill, they often try to hide it. Barn cats will usually greet you as you go about your morning chores, but you should remember to do a quick check on your cats once a week to see if you notice any signs of illness. If you suspect something, call your local veterinarian and explain the problem to her. She will be able to let you know what your options are for treatment.

Learning the Habits of Your New "Neighbors"

The first thing you should learn when you move to your new location is what kinds of predators are common in the area. Your local Extension agent will likely be an excellent source of information to get you started. The agent can give you an idea of what animals are prevalent in your area, help you with any legal questions you may have about whether any of the predators are protected, and may also be able to help you find a reputable, knowledgeable trapper in your area. Here are a few of the predators that might be on your list:

Weasels

Weasels are found throughout the United States and are very destructive. Because weasels can enter a chicken coop through even a mouse-sized hole, they are almost impossible to keep out. As a preventive measure, you can nail hardware cloth over small holes to prevent them from getting into your chicken coop. A weasel will kill everything it can catch unless it is interrupted. You can tell that a weasel is the predator by a bite mark on the back of the prey's neck near the base of the skull. Weasels like to eat the entrails of poultry—the heart, liver, and kidneys.

However, your poultry is not the food of choice for weasels; they much prefer mice and rats. Weasels are also very bold, curious animals and therefore are easy to trap. If you have pet mice (gerbils, hamsters, etc.) you can save the cage cleanings and use those instead of bait. If you don't have cage cleanings, use fresh liver as bait in a rat-sized snap trap. Set the traps near the holes and along the outside walls of outbuildings next to weeds that can provide cover.

Mink

The favorite hunting ground for mink is near water, although the males tend to travel longer distances than the females, especially during the winter breeding season. If you live in the country or anywhere near water, you need to be on guard against mink. Mink will kill poultry and small animals like rabbits. You'll know if you've been visited by a mink because it will leave a distinctive musky smell. Mink eat large amounts of food and then den up for a period of time. If you don't catch it, a mink will be back in ten to fourteen days to kill again. Mink can be quite vicious, so if you suspect you have one attacking your livestock, contact a local trapper to catch this predator.

Skunks

You can generally tell when a skunk has been surprised; the unique skunk smell can permeate the air for miles. Skunks are generally not a huge predator, but, if they can get into your coop, they will eat eggs and small chicks. The biggest problem is accidentally walking in on a skunk in your chicken coop. Skunks are easily caught in a cage trap baited with cat food. To calm the skunk before you move it, lay an old blanket slowly over the trap.

Opossums

Opossums are scavengers, and they often visit human homes or settlements to raid garbage cans, dumpsters, and other containers. They are attracted to carrion and can often be spotted near roadkill. Opossums will eat eggs, chicks, and adult birds. They have razor-sharp teeth and they use their long rat-like tail as a fifth limb. When cornered, opossums will often "play dead," but they have also been known to be aggressive. They are easily caught in cage traps, and any food, even pet food, will work as bait. Opossums also carry a disease that is spread through their feces that can be fatal to horses, so extra care should be taken in and around stables.

Foxes

The best clue that a fox has raided your henhouse is that there will be little evidence other than a missing bird. You may find a few feathers or a wing, but a fox will usually take the bird with it unless it has been disturbed during the kill. A good dog or lights around the building will likely deter foxes, since foxes are normally quite shy. The term "clever as a fox" was coined for good reason. If you suspect a fox to be your predator, you should call an experienced trapper to help you catch it.

FACT

Foxes are omnivores. They are solitary hunters and eat rodents, insects, worms, fruit, birds, eggs, and all other kinds of small animals. About 60 percent of a red fox's diet is made up of rabbits and mice. Foxes are very fast animals and usually catch their prey by outrunning them.

Raccoons

Raccoons are strong and intelligent animals with paws that are very dexterous. Raccoons are able to tear through poultry netting and will even pull a bird right through larger, heavier fencing if they can grab on to any part of the bird. Finding a head that was bitten off a bird is a sure sign that your predator is a raccoon. A female with kits can destroy large numbers of birds in a short period of time. There are also several raccoon-specific traps that are safe to use around dogs and cats. Raccoons are not afraid of traps and are easily caught using fish baits, such as wet or dry cat food.

Coyotes

Coyotes return often to good hunting grounds. If one of these predators has raided your farm, you can bet they will be back for more. The best sign that coyotes are around are the howls you hear in the evening. A large dog can deter a coyote, but coyotes often travel in packs and know how to work together to overpower a dog. The best means to rid yourself of this kind of predator is calling an experienced trapper, securing your livestock, and adding an electric fence.

ALERT

Coyotes use a wide variety of vocalizations in order to communicate with one another. Howls, yelps, and high-pitched cries are best known, but they also bark, growl, wail, and squeal sometimes. Family groups, that can range from five to fourteen coyotes, yelping in unison can create the illusion of a dozen or more performing together. Coyotes are most often heard around dawn and dusk. However, they may respond to sirens and fire whistles at any time of day or night.

Hawks, Eagles, and Owls

One of the few predators that hunt during the day, raptors—hawks and eagles—will capture a bird and tear the breast out of it. Hawks have even been known to attack through netting if they can push it down far enough to get to the chicken. In many states, raptors are protected by law. Check with your state department of natural resources or wildlife management before you try to capture this predator. If you have chickens vanish at night without a trace, you have most likely been visited by an owl. Bringing your birds into a secure coop at night is the best deterrent against owls.

FACT

Larger owls catch rabbits and squirrels, and smaller ones catch mice, rats, and shrews. Some owls also hunt birds and insects; others have been known to take fish from shallow waters. Owls tear large prey into pieces when they eat it. If the prey is small enough, they swallow it whole. They later cough up pellets of undigested bones, fur, scales, and feathers. These owl pellets are found under their nests and roosting areas.

Larger Predators

In some areas of the country it is not unusual to lose livestock to mountain lions, bears, and wolves. These predators can kill larger livestock and endanger you and your family. If you suspect that a larger predator is hunting on your property, contact your local department of natural resources or wildlife management to learn about your options for removing the animal.

Canine Distemper

On occasion, you might come across an animal "acting strangely" on your property; for example, a nocturnal animal may be out during the day, or an animal that is generally timid might wander into your dog run. When animals display characteristics that are unnatural, you need to suspect rabies or canine distemper.

Canine distemper is actually caused by a virus. The virus is related to rubella (the measles virus), but canine distemper poses no threat to humans. However, your domestic animals are at risk because the disease is highly contagious. Distemper affects a large variety of carnivores in North America. These animals include raccoons, foxes, skunks, weasels, and coyotes.

The majority of distemper cases are seen in the spring and summer because young animals are the most susceptible to the disease, but distemper can appear year-round. Cases of distemper can appear as widespread outbreaks or as just an isolated case.

Although the virus does not survive for very long outside the host body, a healthy animal can catch canine distemper either from direct contact with an infected animal or from its bodily secretions and waste. And because many of the symptoms an animal exhibits when it has distemper mimic the symptoms of rabies, you need to contact a physician immediately if you are bitten by an animal exhibiting any unusual behavior. The only way to be sure the animal has distemper rather than rabies is to test the brain tissue.

ALERT

Beware of bats! Most of the new cases of rabies in humans involve bats. Although rabies are a possible threat from wild mammals like raccoons and foxes, the recent increase in annual cases of rabies in humans has actually been linked to bats. Of course, not all bats have rabies, but you should handle any encounter with a bat as if it carried the disease.

The symptoms of distemper are the same in all susceptible animals. The signs you should look for are obvious distress, coughing, sneezing, loose bowels, discharge from eyes and/or nostrils, and eyelids that are crusted over and stuck together. Infected animals can also have convulsions, tremors, and chewing fits. Because of their distress, these animals may lose their fear of humans. You should be very wary because they can become aggressive when approached. An infected animal that is typically nocturnal may be seen during the day. The animal may exhibit dizziness and awkward movements.

If you suspect that an animal has distemper, you must be sure to keep your pets and children away. If you need to destroy the animal or if it dies in your yard, be sure to either bury it deep enough to discourage your pet from digging it up or place it in a secure container and dispose of it in the trash. Wear gloves when disposing of the animal. Do not try to catch a diseased animal. If the animal is threatening you, your children, or your pets, you should kill it. To keep you and your family safe, make sure your pets are vaccinated against distemper.

Natural Insecticides

Whether you are looking for a natural insect deterrent for your garden or for yourself and your family, there are many options available that don't require you to spend a lot of money and won't have your worrying about exposure to harsh chemicals.

Diatomaceous Earth

Diatomaceous earth is actually made from tiny fossilized water plants. These water plants, called *diatoms*, were once algae-like plants, but now are a sedimentary mineral. The sediment is mined and then ground up to a consistency that resembles talcum powder. However, if you were to look at diatomaceous earth through a microscope, you would see microscopic razor-sharp edges. These sharp, diamond-like particles either cut through an insect's outer layer or shred the insides of the insect if the dust is ingested.

Homemade Sprays

Many nontoxic ingredients found in your home are wonderful deterrents to insects. A simple spray consisting of liquid detergent and water will keep insects off nonedible houseplants and will also kill box-elder bugs. Bugs generally don't care for "hot" mixtures; one proven spray includes one crushed clove of garlic, one small chopped hot pepper, and one quart of water. This can be sprayed on plants to repel insects. There are many more recipes like this that include safe ingredients. Test them to see which ones work best for you.

Herbal Options

The plant world offers a wide array of options for repelling insects:

- **Fly repellents:** collect pennyroyal, rosemary, rue, southernwood, thyme, or tansy and hang them or stand them up in a vase where flies are bothersome. These plants were used during the Middle Ages to help repel flies.
- **Ant and mite repellent:** a strong decoction of walnut leaves (six handfuls of leaves boiled in one pint of water for twenty to thirty minutes) can be "painted" around floors or on work surfaces.
- **Moth repellent:** lay sprigs of dried herbs like rosemary, southernwood, santolina, and lavender among blankets or woolens.
- **Outdoor insect repellents:** rub a handful of fresh elder leaves on your arms, legs, and neck. This works for about twenty minutes and then must be renewed. You can also use strong infusions of chamomile or elder leaves dabbed on the skin to prevent insect bites.

Companion Planting

Many herbs can actually repel pests away from the plants they are planted near. Careful use of companion plants can protect your garden from pesky intruders. Here are some examples of companion plants:

HERB OR PLANT	LOCATION	BENEFIT
Pennyroyal	plant anywhere in the garden	repels ants
Nasturtium	plant near apple trees, tomatoes, broad beans	repels aphids; attracts blackflies to itself, keeping the neighboring plants safe; repels ants; and keeps the garden healthy
French marigold	plant near tomatoes	repels aphids
Chives	plant near apple trees, roses	prevents scab, prevents black spot
Garlic	plant near roses	helps the overall health of the plant
Sage	plant near cabbages, vines, rosemary, general garden use	repels cabbage moth; generally beneficial to the garden and repels a number of harmful flying insects
Summer savory	plant near beans	attracts bees and is generally beneficial
Nettle	plant anywhere in the garden	controls blackflies
Caraway, buckwheat, flax	plant anywhere in the garden	improves the condition of the soil
Basil	plant near tomatoes	repels flying insects
Borage	plant near strawberries	improves crop yield, attracts bees
Chamomile	plant anywhere in the garden, and near onions	repels flying insects, improves crop yield
Coriander	plant anywhere in the garden, and near anise	attracts bees, improves flavor
Hyssop	plant near grapevines	improves crop yield
Mint	plant anywhere in the garden, and near cabbage	repels flies and cabbage grubs
Rosemary	plant near carrots, sage	repels carrot fly; generally beneficial to sage
Dill, fennel	plant anywhere in the garden	attracts beneficial insects

Flying Pests

In the recent past, the United States has been inundated with two new species of insects that have become overwhelming in both the home and the garden. At least one of these bugs, Asian beetles, were actually brought to the United States by the government in the hope that they would be a solution for another problem. Unfortunately, the solution was worse than the initial problem. Wasps, on the other hand, have been around for a long time, but can be threatening to your family.

Asian Lady Beetles

The University of Kentucky, College of Agriculture Entomologists Michael F. Potter, Ric Bessin, and Lee Townsend fact sheet on Asian lady beetles stated:

> During the 1960s to 1990s, the U.S. Department of Agriculture attempted to establish the Asian lady beetle to control agricultural pests, especially of pecans and apples. Large numbers of the beetles were released in several states, including Georgia, South Carolina, Louisiana, Mississippi, California, Washington, Pennsylvania, Connecticut, and Maryland. . . .

> Large numbers of lady beetles (ladybugs) infesting homes and buildings in the United States were first reported in the early 1990s. Ladybugs normally are considered beneficial, since they live outdoors and feed on plant pests.

> One species of lady beetle, Harmonia axyridis, can be a nuisance however, they would fly to buildings in search of overwintering sites and end up indoors. Once inside, the Asian beetles crawl about on windows, walls, attics, etc., often emitting a noxious odor and yellowish staining fluid before dying.

Unfortunately, Asian lady beetles appear to lack natural enemies, although cold weather and freezing temperatures will kill some of them.

Asian lady beetles will start migrating into your home when autumn approaches. Swarms of lady beetles typically fly to buildings from September through November, depending on locale and weather conditions. These swarms are heaviest on sunny days following a period of cooler weather, when temperatures return to at least the mid-60s. Asian beetles tend to congregate on the sunnier, southwest sides of buildings illuminated by afternoon sun. Homes that are shaded from afternoon sun are less likely to attract beetles.

ESSENTIAL

Multicolored Asian lady beetles are beneficial insects. Their natural control of aphids in pecan orchards has decreased insecticide use against those pests. Additionally, they have controlled aphids on some ornamental plants. Still, these lady beetles are unwelcome guests for many homeowners.

Once the beetles land on your home, they begin to look for crevices and protected places to spend the winter. They often gather in attics, wall cavities, and other protected locations.

Asian lady beetles generally do not injure humans and are mainly a nuisance. However, although Asian lady beetles do not transmit diseases, recent studies suggest that infestations can cause allergies in some individuals, ranging from eye irritation to asthma.

There are several things you can do to rid your home of Asian beetles.

- Vacuum. The easiest way to remove them is with a vacuum cleaner.
- Caulk and seal entry points throughout your home.
- Place some glue traps on your windowsills. The Asian beetles will flock to the windows, get stuck on the traps, and die. You can simple replace the traps as they fill up.

Japanese Beetles

Just when you were getting used to Asian beetles, a new variety of beetle appeared on the scene in the United States, Japanese beetles. These bugs attack plants both as adults and as grubs (larvae). The adults eat the leaves and fruits of several hundred kinds of fruit trees, as well as ornamental trees, shrubs, vines, and crops, leaving behind large holes in the leaves.

As they develop, grubs attack the roots of trees and feed on the roots of various plants and grasses. Grubs have been known to destroy turf in lawns, parks, golf courses, and pastures.

Female adult beetles burrow about three inches into the ground and lay their eggs. One female can lay up to sixty eggs. The eggs hatch by mid-summer, and the young grubs begin to feed, destroying the roots of the surrounding plants. When autumn is nearly over, the grubs will burrow into the soil and remain dormant until the following spring. In the spring, the grubs return to the turf and continue to feed until they change into pupae. Within two weeks, the pupae become adult beetles and emerge from the ground. Then the cycle begins again.

Although chemical insecticides are an option for killing both the beetle and the grub, you should consult with your county Extension agent to determine what is allowed in your area. The most common way to eliminate Japanese beetles is to use commercial traps. Traps for adult beetles operate primarily with two chemical lures. A combination of a pheromone, or sex attractant, and a floral lure attract both male and female adult beetles to the trap. Then, as a result of their clumsy flying and the design of the trap, they end up caught in either the bag or funnel portion of the trap.

What you need to understand as you place your traps is that the pheromone in the trap will attract beetles from all around, so if you put the trap in the middle of your orchard you are increasing your problem, not decreasing it. The best thing to do is find an area far away from your garden and orchard and hang the trap. Remember to check the trap to empty the bag, and then be sure to eliminate any beetles that are still alive.

Wasps

A wasp's stinger is not barbed like a honeybee's stinger, so a wasp can repeatedly sting its victim. If you are stung by a wasp, wash the area with soap and water, take an antihistamine, and apply ice to the sting. If you are stung by a wasp on more than one occasion, you can develop a dangerous allergic reaction to the sting. If you are allergic to bee stings and are stung by a wasp, seek medical care immediately. Also, if you are allergic to bees or wasps, ask you doctor about a prescription for the EpiPen, which you can carry with you.

To get rid of wasps, you first must locate the nest. Wasps not only build nests in elevated areas; they can also build nests underground. Your best clue is to watch for heavy wasp traffic during dusk or dawn, when wasps return to the nest. Wait for the sun to go down, as cooler temperatures impede the wasps' movement. Dress in protective clothing, including long sleeves and gloves, and spray the nest with an insecticide designed specifically for wasps. These insecticides generally have projectile shooting abilities, so you don't have to get too close to the nest. Spray liberally, but avoid inhaling too much of the poison. Most wasp poisons kill wasps on contact, but it's best to be safe by slowly leaving the area, as sudden movements can attract the wasps' attention.

Judiciously check the nest the next day to ensure that all of the insects have been killed. If not, repeat the process in the evening.

CHAPTER 20

Emergency Preparedness

As someone who has decided to move off-grid, you understand the world you live in has no certainties. The only thing you can do to protect your family is to be prepared for whatever eventually may happen. This chapter will suggest scenarios that will cause your family to rely on themselves and the emergency preparations you have made.

72-Hour Kit

Prior to Hurricane Katrina, FEMA used to encourage people to have a 72-hour kit for each member of the family, because it was assumed that within 72 hours, government agencies would be able to get to the scene of any disaster or emergency and bring aid. Katrina proved that when there is a disaster of large scale, or one that affects a large portion of the country, you might have to rely on yourself for more than 72 hours.

ALERT

The U.S. Department of Homeland Security's Ready Campaign is designed to empower and educate citizens to prepare for the potential of an emergency, whether a terrorist attack or natural disaster, by following some basic steps. The Ready Campaign requires three simple actions: supply yourself with an emergency kit; have a plan for your family; and understand the kinds of situations that you'll need to prepare for, and how to react to them.

However, the idea of having a 72-hour kit or a "bug-out bag" is still good. If you need to leave your home quickly, whether in case of fire, flooding, or other natural disasters, each family member can quickly grab his or her 72-hour kit and have some supplies that will make being displaced a lot more tolerable. Each kit should be contained in something that is easy to grab and carry. It's best to have a container that's waterproof. Some people use five-gallon buckets for their 72-hour kits, and backpacks are also often used. The following section provides some ideas of things you could place in your kit. Be sure to customize the list in order to meet the needs your family.

Food and Water

You should have a three-day supply of food and water, per person, that requires no refrigeration or cooking. If you prefer, a small water filtration device can take the place of three days supply of bottled water, which can be heavy to carry. Some ideas for food include:

- Protein bars/granola bars
- Trail mix/dried fruit
- Hard candy
- Beef jerky
- Juice boxes

Remember to create the bags to meet the needs of your family. If you have infants and use formula, be sure to include formula and diapers in one of the 72-hour kits.

ALERT

Not every emergency happens when everyone is at home. Have a contact number that all family members should call in case of emergency. Be sure every member of your family knows the phone number and has a cell phone, coins, or a prepaid phone card to call the emergency contact.

Bedding and Clothing

Having warm and dry clothing and blankets are important during any emergency and can sometimes be the difference between life and death.

- Change of clothing: inexpensive sweatshirts and sweatpants are excellent choices—and don't forget socks!
- Undergarments
- Raincoat/Poncho: small emergency ponchos work well
- Blankets and emergency heat blankets (the kind that keep in warmth)
- Cloth sheet: to place over you
- Plastic sheet: to lie on if the ground is damp or to shield you from rain.

Fuel and Light

The ability to heat food or water or to escape from a dangerous situation at night are only two reasons to have sufficient fuel and light. Another is to provide comfort in a scary situation.

- Flashlights
- Extra batteries
- Flares
- Candles
- Lighter
- Waterproof matches

Miscellaneous Equipment

These are some of the items that will make life much easier in case of emergency.

- Can opener
- Dishes/utensils
- Shovel
- Radio (with batteries)
- Pen and paper
- Axe
- Pocket knife
- Rope
- Duct tape

Personal Supplies and Medication

You can't take your bathroom medicine cabinet with you, but you should be sure you have the life-sustaining medical supplies you need during an emergency.

- First-aid kit and supplies
- Toiletries (roll of toilet paper—remove the center tube to easily flatten into a zip-top bag—feminine hygiene, folding brush, etc.)
- Cleaning supplies (mini hand sanitizer, soap, shampoo, dish soap, etc.)
- Medicine (acetaminophen, ibuprofen, children's medication, etc.)
- Prescription medication (for three weeks or more)
- Extra pair of glasses

ALERT

The Ready Campaign, FEMA, Citizen Corps, American Red Cross, and the Humane Society of the United States have developed an emergency preparedness toolkit for your pets. This toolkit can be found at *www.ready.gov/america/toolkit_pets/index.html.*

Personal Documents and Money

If your home was devastated by a flood or fire, what are some of the legal documents you would need as you put your life back together? Here's a list of some of the items. You might think of others that are important to you. Place these items in plastic bags so they are waterproof.

- Copies of legal documents (birth/marriage certificates, wills, passports, contracts, etc.)
- Copies of vaccination papers
- Copies of insurance policies
- Cash
- Credit card

Remember to update your kits to make sure all food, water, and medication is fresh and has not expired, that the clothing still fits, that the personal documents and credit cards are up to date, and that the batteries are charged.

ALERT

If you have a cell phone, make sure you program your emergency contact as "ICE" (In Case of Emergency) in your phone. If you are in an accident, emergency personnel will often check your ICE listings in order to get ahold of someone you know. Make sure your family, especially your children, have ICE numbers in their phones.

Heat

It's the middle of winter and a major ice storm has swept through not only your state, but also an entire four- or five-state region. Electric lines are down and hundreds of thousands of people are without power. You live in a rural community, so you are among one of the last groups that get power restored. The temperatures outside are in the single digits and the wind chill is making it even colder. What are you going to do?

If you are totally off-grid, life goes on as usual. But, if your off-grid experience still relies on local utilities, some of these ideas might save your life.

Wood Stoves

If you have already installed a wood stove, you have both an alternative heat source and a way to cook for your family. Wood stoves need no electricity to run and can warm just one room or, in some cases, an entire house. With a wood stove you can also use non-electric heat-powered fans that can sit on the stove and move the heat throughout the room. As mentioned earlier in the book, wood stoves are more efficient than fireplaces because they don't pull warm air out of the house.

ALERT

When you choose a portable heater, purchase one approved by a nationally known safety-testing laboratory, such as Underwriters Laboratories or Factory Mutual Research Corporation. Look for a heater with a broad, solid base, as well as an automatic cutoff switch, which trips when a unit is tipped over. Thoroughly read all manufacturers' instructions about the installation and use of portable heaters. Keep the instructions in an accessible place, so you can reread the operating and safety precautions every year.

Propane Heaters

Portable propane heaters are another good option for emergency home heating. The advantage of a propane heater is that propane is easily stored and, if you have a propane grill, you may already have a tank on hand. Propane is clean burning with little odor, and is relatively safe. Because portable propane heaters are unvented, you must crack open a window. If you use a larger, 20-pound tank to run the stove, it is recommended you place the tank on the outside of the house and run an extension hose from the tank to the stove. A portable propane heater puts out about 9,000 BTU (British thermal units), which is enough to heat one medium-size room. There are other, larger propane heaters that can put out about 12,000 BTU.

Kerosene Heaters

Portable kerosene heaters are one of the most popular ways to provide emergency home heat. Most modern kerosene heaters are safe, but you still need to keep a window cracked open to prevent carbon monoxide buildup. Kerosene heaters are generally round, with a wick that pulls up the fuel and burns it to create heat. Newer models have an automatic shutoff system in case the heater is tipped over. Some models have a battery-powered ignition to light the wick.

There is some slight odor to kerosene heaters, mostly when they are extinguished. Floor-standing kerosene heaters can put out 20,000 BTU or more, enough to keep a modest-size home warm. If this is your choice of emergency heat, you will have to be sure you keep a supply of kerosene on hand.

Your Own Furnace with a Generator Backup

Even if you have a gas, liquid propane, or oil-fired furnace, you might still need electricity to start the pilot light or make the blower work. In order to use your furnace during a power outage, you will need a backup generator. You will need to have an electrician add a bypass switch and connection for the portable generator. At the least, you will need a 5-kW generator, which will also be able to power some other circuits, including a fridge and lights; however, it will not likely be able to power your whole house. Expect to spend at least $3,000 on a generator, plus the bypass box and electrician's fees.

Emergency Cooking

During an emergency, providing hot meals for your family can be a challenge. But in order to avoid making a stressful situation even worse, proper nutrition and some kind of routine is good for your family. In order to conserve your cooking fuel, you need to work at being as efficient as possible. Only boil the amount of water you are going to need. Put out the fire as soon as you have finished cooking. Plan your meals ahead of time to be able to consolidate as much cooking as possible. Use the top of your heating unit, if possible, to cook your meals.

Always keep enough fuel, including charcoal and LP, to allow you to cook outdoors for at least seven to ten days. Use Dutch ovens and pressure cookers to optimize the use of fuel.

Store matches in a waterproof, airtight tin with each piece of equipment that must be lit with a flame. Other options for cooking during an emergency include the following.

Camp Stove

Camp stoves provide a perfect alternative when home electric or gas stoves are inoperable. A two-burner camp stove is a compact, portable, and convenient means to provide hot meals and hot drinks for days on end if necessary. Models are available that run on propane or liquid camping fuel (sometimes called white gas). In addition, some models can run on either liquid camping fuel or unleaded gasoline. Fuel-powered camp stoves must never be used indoors.

ESSENTIAL

The Dutch oven is a part of early American history. Paul Revere is generally credited with refining the Dutch oven (namely the flanged lid) that is still the standard today. When Thomas Jefferson charged Lewis and Clark to find a water route to the Pacific in 1803, the pair carted along a Dutch oven to cook up the grub foraged along the journey.

Sterno Fuel

Sterno Fuel, a jellied petroleum product, is an excellent source of cooking fuel. Sterno is very lightweight, odorless, and can be easily ignited with a match or a spark from flint and steel. It is not explosive and it's safe for use indoors. You can also purchase Sterno stoves at any sporting goods store for a relatively small amount of money. The stoves fold up into very small, compact units.

FACT

Sterno fuel was invented around 1900. Made from ethanol, methanol, water, and a gelling agent, it also contains a dye that colors it pink. A seven-ounce container will burn for as long as two hours.

Sterno is ideal for carrying in a pack. The fuel is readily available at all sporting goods stores and many drugstores. One can of Sterno fuel about the diameter of a can of tuna fish and twice as tall will allow you to cook six meals if used frugally.

The disadvantage of Sterno is that it will evaporate very easily, even when the lid is securely fastened. If you store Sterno, you should check it every six to eight months to ensure that it has not evaporated beyond the point of usage. Because of this problem, it is not a good fuel for long-term storage. It is very expensive to use compared to other fuels available, but is extremely convenient and portable.

Charcoal

Charcoal is the least expensive fuel per BTU to store. However, charcoal can only be used outdoors because of the vast amounts of poisonous carbon monoxide it produces. Charcoal will store for extended periods of time if it is stored in airtight containers. Because it can easily absorb the moisture from the air, it should not be stored in the paper bag it comes in for more than a few months. Transfer it to airtight metal or plastic containers and it will keep almost forever. If you store $50–$60 worth of charcoal, you will have enough cooking fuel for a family for an entire year if used sparingly.

You can use charcoal in a traditional grill or you can use it with a Dutch oven. A Dutch oven is a cast-iron pot with a lid that can come in various sizes and can be used over an open fire. When you combine a Dutch oven with charcoal, you are able to create stews, soups, and even baked goods. You need to remember that each briquette will produce about 40 degrees of heat. If you are baking bread, for example, and need 400 degrees of heat for your oven, simply use ten briquettes.

Food

During emergencies you don't want to give your system a shock by eating foods you have never tried before. Your emergency supplies should include foods like peanut butter that are easy to use and offer you high protein. Make sure you try out your emergency supplies if you are going to use foods like MREs and dehydrated foods before an emergency happens.

If your activity is reduced, you can survive on half your usual food intake for an extended period and even go without any food for many days. Food, unlike water, may be rationed safely, except for children and pregnant women. If your water supply is limited, don't eat salty foods, since they will make you thirsty. Instead, eat salt-free crackers, whole-grain cereals, and canned foods with high liquid content.

MREs and Dehydrated Foods

Meals Ready to Eat (MREs) were originally government-issued dehydrated meals developed for soldiers. Although the government does not allow military MRE manufacturers to sell to civilians, there are MREs available for sale to the general public. The positive aspect of an MRE is that it is a complete meal in one package that is designed to withstand the elements. Within each package there is generally an entrée, side dish, cracker or bread, spread, dessert, candy, beverage, seasoning or hot sauce, plastic ware, and a flameless ration heater. Each MRE contains one-third of a day's nutritional value, with 1,250 calories and mineral and vitamin supplements. The downside of MREs is that they can be expensive and there are limited menus available in the retail versions.

Dehydrated foods have come a long way in the past twenty years. Originally very simple and bland, dehydrated foods comes in a great variety of offerings, including gourmet foods. You can purchase dehydrated foods in large number ten cans, the size of a coffee can, to feed your whole family, or in individualized single meals. As the name implies, all you have to do is reconstitute the food with water and then heat it. Dehydrated food can have a shelf life of eight to ten years.

Family Friendly Foods

If you have children, your emergency food stores should include food that is familiar and comforting. Peanut butter, macaroni and cheese, pudding, and powdered drink mix can lend an air of normalcy to a tense situation. Be sure to have crackers and hard candy in your emergency food supply for treats. Powdered chocolate drink mix can help turn nonfat dry milk into a more palatable drink for both children and adults.

Maintaining Your Strength

During and especially after a disaster, it is vital for you to maintain your strength. Be sure that you eat at least one well-balanced meal each day, drink enough liquid to enable your body to function properly, and take in enough calories to enable you to do any necessary work. Vitamin, mineral, and protein supplements are essential during times of high stress on your body; don't forget to take them.

Water

Having an ample supply of clean water is a top priority in an emergency. A normally active person needs to drink at least two quarts of water each day. If an emergency occurs in the summer, or if you live in a hot or arid environment, you will require more. In all cases, children, nursing mothers, and ill people will require more than two quarts of water a day. Because you will also need water for food preparation and personal hygiene, you should store one gallon per person per day. FEMA recommends that, if possible, you store a two-week supply of water for each member of your family. And if supplies run low, don't ration water. Drink the amount you need today, and try to find more for tomorrow. You can minimize the amount of water your body needs by reducing activity and staying cool.

Store drinking water in food-grade containers. Two-liter plastic soft-drink bottles work well. You can store water to be used for personal hygiene, flushing toilets, and general cleaning in old bleach and laundry detergent containers.

To prepare your own stored water supply, follow these tips, as suggested by FEMA:

- Thoroughly clean the bottles with dishwashing soap and water, and rinse completely so there is no residual soap.
- Additionally, for plastic soft-drink bottles, sanitize the bottles by adding a solution of 1 teaspoon nonscented liquid household chlorine bleach to a quart (¼ gallon) of water. Swish the sanitizing solution in the bottle so that it touches all surfaces. After sanitizing the bottle, thoroughly rinse out the sanitizing solution with clean water.
- Fill the bottle to the top with regular tap water. If your water utility company treats your tap water with chlorine, you do not need to add anything else to the water to keep it clean. If the water you are using comes from a well or water source that is not treated with chlorine, add two drops of nonscented liquid household chlorine bleach to each gallon of water.
- Tightly close the container using the original cap. Be careful not to contaminate the cap; do not touch the inside of it with your fingers. Write the date on the outside of the container so that you know when you filled it. Store in a cool, dark place.
- Replace the water every six months if not using commercially bottled water.

During an emergency, remember that you can use some of the "hidden" sources of water in your home, including your hot-water heater, accumulated water in your pipes (accessed by unscrewing a pipe in the lowest area of your home, like a basement), and water from ice cubes in your freezer. You should not drink the water from toilet flush tanks or bowls, radiators, waterbeds, or swimming pools and spas.

If you use the water in your hot-water tank, be sure the electricity or gas is shut off, and then drain the water from the bottom of the tank. When the power and/or water is restored, be sure to fill your tank back up before turning on the power.

You can also find water outside your home in case of emergency. Rainwater, streams, rivers and ponds, natural springs, and lakes are other sources for water. Be sure never to take water from places that have material floating on top, or that have an odor or dark color to them. Never drink flood water. Water that you have gathered from the outdoors needs to be treated before you can safely drink it. There are several ways to treat water:

- Use a ceramic filtration system to filter out unhealthy microorganisms.
- The safest way for you to treat water is to boil it. However, you must remember that boiling does not mean a bubble or two. When you boil water, you must bring it to a rolling boil for at least one full minute. If you are concerned about evaporation, you can place a lid on the pot to capture the steam. After boiling, place the water in a clean container and allow to cool. For better-tasting water, you can return oxygen to it. To do this, simply pour the water back and forth between two clean containers. The movement of the water between the containers will increase the oxygen content. This method also works for stored water.
- If you decide to chlorinate the water you have gathered from your water source, you should add sixteen drops (⅛ teaspoon) of bleach per gallon of water. Stir the water thoroughly and then let it stand for thirty minutes. Once the time has passed, smell the water. You should be able to smell the bleach. If you can't, add an additional ⅛ teaspoon bleach per gallon, mix thoroughly, and let it stand for another fifteen minutes. Once again, smell the water. If it still does not have a slight odor of bleach, discard it and find another source of water.

Medicines

You should not only have an ample supply of over-the-counter medicines for emergencies; if you rely on prescription drugs for your health and well-being, you should also try to have at least an additional three-month supply of them in your home. Talk to your physician about writing an additional prescription to ensure you can have an extra supply in case of emergency.

Here is a list of some of the basic over-the-counter medicines and medical equipment you should have in your home:

- Pain relievers like acetaminophen, aspirin, naproxen, and ibuprofen
- Antibiotic cream like Neosporin or Betadine
- Tweezers
- Rubbing alcohol
- Cotton balls, bandages, Ace bandages, adhesive tape
- Antacid (Tums, Rolaids)
- Thermometer
- Cotton swabs
- Sunscreen
- Hydrocortisone cream
- Anti-diarrheal medicine
- Heat pack and ice pack
- Itch medicine (calamine lotion)
- Cough syrup, cold/allergy medicine, antihistamine and decongestant
- Mild laxative
- Petroleum jelly
- Syrup of ipecac (to induce vomiting)
- Hot-water bottle
- Eye cup and over-the-counter eye wash
- Ear drops

Light

Emergencies can happen in the middle of the night, and that is not the time to start searching for flashlights, batteries, or other light sources. To be prepared, you need to have immediate light sources and potential long-term light sources.

Flashlights

Flashlights are great for a quick response to an emergency situation. The more reliable flashlights are LED flashlights because incandescent bulbs can burn out suddenly or break if you drop your flashlight. LED flashlights don't have breakable parts and actually last for about 10,000 hours of use.

If you purchase an inexpensive flashlight, the light will not be as bright and might be slightly off-color. There are many different shapes and styles of flashlights, but the major difference is the size and weight of flashlight you want to carry, as well as the brightness you desire.

- Key-ring flashlights are generally more gimmicky than useful. They can fit in your pocket or your purse and weigh next to nothing, but most give barely enough light to see a few feet in front of you.
- Pocket flashlights are a good choice for emergency. The better-quality flashlights are able to regulate voltage, so even when the battery is losing power, the light will remain bright. They are small enough to carry in a pocket, purse, or backpack, or to put in a drawer in your nightstand.
- Glove-compartment flashlights are too large to easily fit in your pocket and too heavy to carry in your purse or backpack. The best ones provide you with an adjustable high and low beam; the low beam for use inside the car, and the high beam for lighting the outside of the car in emergencies.
- Emergency crank flashlights are excellent tools for emergencies. Not limited to the charge of a battery, they are small enough to fit in a glove compartment and can run thirty to sixty minutes after one minute of cranking. Often these flashlights include other options, like weather radios.
- Large household flashlights are heavy and can be cumbersome, but they provide a great deal of light when you are trying to find your way through your home in a power outage.
- Rechargeable flashlights are great while you still have power or, if they are solar powered, while there is sun available, but they lose their power fairly quickly compared to other choices. A rechargeable flashlight is best used in areas where a sudden power outage can

be dangerous or frightening, like for small children in a bathroom, because they are easily located.

Experts recommend lithium-ion–powered flashlights for use in very cold weather and for flashlights stored in a disaster shelter because they last for a longer period of time under harsher circumstances.

Candles

Using candles for emergency lighting is one of the least expensive lighting options. Emergency candles that come in a glass container are the best kind of candles to have in case of emergencies. Regular dinner candles or even scented candles don't put out the kind of light you need and can be dangerous if left unattended. Emergency candles are long-burning. There are even some 120-hour versions, and they are constructed for safe burning.

When using any kind of candle, be sure it is situated on a stable surface that is free from clutter. Because a quick draft can cause a candle flame to jump, never put a candle near curtains or any other flammable objects.

You can also use candle lanterns to increase the safety of using candles. Lanterns provide a base, a lid, and a glass surround or chimney to place the candle into. They also provide a carrying handle, so the candle can be safely transported without fear of the flame being blown out. Some lanterns designed for camping and outdoor use can hold a standard white emergency candle, which can burn for eight or nine hours.

A Candlelier is a lantern that holds three standard emergency candles. The candles can be burned individually or simultaneously, depending on the amount of light you desire. The top of the lantern has a heat shield that can also be used as a small stove. They also produce enough heat to be a personal heat source.

Lanterns and Oil Lamps

Lanterns and oil lamps are another option for lighting your home during an emergency. Lanterns have been used for centuries to provide portable light for barns throughout the world. Generally, kerosene or specially made lamp fuels are used for lanterns. You can purchase an inexpensive oil lamp that uses paraffin oil at most department stores. These are mostly ornamental, although they give enough light to see and can be placed throughout your home when not in use as part of the décor. Both of the aforementioned fixtures generally use wicks to pull the fuel up from the base and feed the flame. Specialty lamps, like Aladdin lamps, use mantles and kerosene fuel. The light from an Aladdin lamp is equal to a 50-watt light bulb.

Storing Important Documents

From birth certificates to passports, from insurance policies to car titles, many of the documents you have in your home are very important, but could be lost during a fire, flood, or other disaster. It is a good policy to make several copies of these important documents. The original copies should be kept in a safe-deposit box in a bank; another copy could be given to family members who don't live in your household, another copy should be filed away in your home office; and the final copy should be laminated and stored in your 72-hour kit, so if an emergency arises and you have to leave your home, all of your important documents are with you.

CHAPTER 21

Starting Today

Even before reaching this final chapter, you probably were dreaming about the possibilities that exist for you in the future, when you can finally move off-grid. But you don't have to wait until you pay off your debt and purchase your piece of land. You can begin your off-grid experience right away by employing some of the concepts you've learned into your everyday life.

Urban Homesteading

Urban homesteading is a growing movement to bring some of the back-to-basics lifestyle into an urban setting—although, if you look at urban homesteading closely, you will discover that, rather than a new movement, it is basically a re-adaptation of the way our grandparents used to live. Urban homesteading is about learning to be as self-sufficient as possible while lessening your impact on the environment. It is adapting a "less is more" attitude in the things you own, the things you do, and even the careers you pursue. It is implementing a "use up, reuse, or do without" attitude that was common during the Great Depression. It is finding more happiness in simple things and taking the time to slow down and enjoy them.

The Dervaes family from Pasadena, California, has been practicing urban homesteading for more than twenty years. Their website, urbanhomestead.org (*http://urbanhomestead.org*), offers an account of the family's experiences. The Dervaes's "10 Elements of Urban Homesteading" are:

- Grow your own food on your city lot.
- Use alternative energy sources.
- Use alternative fuels and transportation.
- Keep farm animals for manure and food. Practice animal husbandry.
- Practice waste reduction.
- Reclaim graywater and collect rainwater.
- Live simply.
- Do the work yourself.
- Work at home.
- Be a good neighbor.

Grow Your Own Food

Start by assessing your home. Whether it's an apartment or a bungalow, there are places you can plant some of your own food. Whether all you can manage are some herbs on a windowsill or a couple of upside-down planters that grow tomatoes on your apartment balcony, it's a start. Get rid of the lawn and plant a garden. Get rid of houseplants and plant herbs and vegetables. Be creative, and you will be surprised at what you are able to accomplish.

FACT

Studies have shown that the average fresh food item has traveled between 1,300 and 2,000 miles before reaching the dinner plate. Because of this long-distance transport, as well as the machinery, fertilizers, pesticides, fuel, and other goods used in large-scale agricultural production, the food production system is a significant user of energy, accounting for 15.7 percent of the total national energy budget in 2007.

Use Alternative Energy Sources

Where can you replace traditional energy sources in your life? Can you use solar-powered panels anywhere in your home? How about something simple, like using rechargeable batteries or line-drying your clothes (wind and solar power combined)? If you can't find a place for adding alternative sources, how about looking at ways you can decrease consumption?

Use Alternative Fuels and Transportation

Opt for a hybrid car. Take a bus, ride a bike, or walk. When you have to drive, batch your errands. Instead of running an errand or two every day, do everything at once, planning your most efficient route to save gas and time. Also do as much bill-paying online as possible, to eliminate some errands.

Practice Animal Husbandry

You need to initially consider your city zoning ordinances or homeowners association rules before you begin to add livestock to your life. You also need to consider the needs of the animal and the impact on your neighbors before you decide that you can raise a cow in a 10' × 10' backyard. However, there are many animals that do well in confined areas and will allow you to enjoy the experience of animal husbandry. Rabbits and chickens are animals that primarily stay in coops and just need a place to run during the day. Depending on your acreage, goats can also do well on a fairly small amount of land. But before you bring any animal onto your property, make sure you have strong enough fencing to keep them where you want them to be.

Practice Waste Reduction

Now is the time to think about what you're putting in your trash. Urban homesteaders take recycling to a whole new level with composting, repurposing, garage sales, thrift stores, and bartering. One of the offshoots of this new attitude is Freecycle.org (*www.freecycle.org*), a network dedicated to keeping things out of landfills. The following is the site's welcome statement:

> *The Freecycle Network is made up of 4,934 groups with 8,352,217 members around the world. It's a grassroots and entirely nonprofit movement of people who are giving (and getting) stuff for free in their own towns. It's all about reuse and keeping good stuff out of landfills. Each local group is moderated by local volunteers (them's good people). Membership is free.*

FACT

Each ton (2,000 pounds) of recycled paper can save 17 trees, 380 gallons of oil, three cubic yards of landfill space, 4,000 kilowatts of energy, and 7,000 gallons of water. This represents a 64 percent energy savings, a 58 percent water savings, and 60 pounds less of air pollution!

Reclaim Graywater and Collect Rainwater

You can easily divert your rainspouts to rain barrels and collect rainwater for your garden and other outdoor needs. You will need to decide how you want to divert graywater in your home. If you are on a city sewer system, both your graywater and blackwater escape your home through the same system. You would need to separate the system, being sure the blackwater goes directly to the sewer system or into your septic system.

Live Simply

When you are without debt and obligations to others, you have the freedom to choose the lifestyle you want to enjoy. With a minimalist lifestyle, you can choose to work from home, because you don't need the high-powered, large income anymore.

How do you live simply? Look for ways to save money in everything you do. Here are some examples:

- Turn off the lights and open the curtains.
- Walk instead of drive.
- Cook at home rather than eat out.
- Hang your clothes on a line rather than using a dryer.
- Read a book instead of watching a movie.
- Put on a sweater instead of cranking up the thermostat.
- Buy energy-efficient appliances.
- Buy clothing at resale shops.
- Turn off your computer and spend some time outside.

As you implement these ideas, you might also find that not only do they help you save money, they help you enjoy a better lifestyle.

ESSENTIAL

Frugal tip: get your candles to last longer. Chilling the candles before you use them makes the wax burn more slowly and evenly. You can just refrigerate them for eight hours before you burn them.

Do the Work Yourself

Do you know how to change the oil in your car? Do you know how to do basic wiring or plumbing? How about carpentry? Have you ever tied a quilt? Do you know how to make a dress or bake bread? Can you cut hair?

These are some of the skills our grandparents had when they had to do everything themselves. Having these skills can move you in the direction of self-reliance. If you are not familiar with any of them, you might want to sign up for classes offered by many community colleges or craft stores so you can learn a few.

Work from Home

Early homesteaders worked the land and raised vegetables, livestock, and eggs. Some did carpentry, blacksmithing, sewing, or baking to supplement their incomes. Urban homesteaders create websites, do graphic arts, sell crafts on etsy.com, and become consultants. Their goal is to forget the nine-to-five "rat race" and find a job that frees them from conventional hours, intraoffice politics, and routine. Today, with the Internet at our fingertips, working from home is becoming a reality for many every day. And, if you can work from home, moving off-grid is a much more viable option for you.

Not everyone can just quit their job and start working at home. But you can try some part-time work from home to see if it can eventually replace your day job. Some potential home-based jobs are:

- Selling your crafts or artwork
- Selling food items, from specialty preserves to your own honey
- Selling fresh herbs or other home-grown produce
- Cutting, delivering, and selling firewood
- Being a hunting or fishing guide
- Being a computer consultant
- Offering housecleaning or janitorial services
- Writing about your urban homesteading adventure and selling the story
- Doing medical transcription

Be a Good Neighbor

You should be the neighbor you would want to have. One of the basic ideas behind urban homesteading is bringing communities back together. Being self-reliant doesn't mean being alone. There is a shared responsibility of community when you become an urban homesteader, and an opportunity to learn from each other.

Container Gardening

You don't have to give up on the idea of growing fresh vegetables just because you don't have yard space for conventional gardening. Another viable option is container gardening. Container gardening allows you to plant your vegetables or herbs in containers that can be kept on your balcony, patio, roof, or any place they can get sunshine and warmth.

In some cases, container gardening is used for herbs in order to keep them contained in one space. Some herbs, like mint, spread out and could take over an entire garden if you allow it. Also, if you plant your herbs in containers, you can bring them indoors as winter approaches and enjoy fresh herbs throughout the winter.

Container planting is also advantageous because of the mobility of the containers. You can actually move the container to follow the sun. You can also situate the containers so that weeding and, eventually, harvesting is done at a comfortable level, rather than on your knees as in a traditional garden.

You can be very creative with container gardens. Not only can you plant an eye-catching combination of vegetables, herbs, or flowers in a single container, you can also create a plant tepee for your children. Simple fill four to six medium-size containers with soil, and then place a ½-inch PVC pipe about five to six feet long in each container. Space the containers a foot or so apart in a circle. Gather the tops of the pipes together and bind them with twine about four inches from their tops. Then plant a climbing plant, like a cucumber, in each container at the base of the pipe. Train the plants to grow up the pipes by tying the vines loosely to the PVC. In a few weeks, you will have a green tepee.

You can plant just about anything in containers; you just need to have a large enough container and the space to allow the plant to grow.

Make Your Plant Selections

Decide what you would like to grow months before your growing season starts. This way you will have plenty of time to select and order your seeds, gather your containers, and even start some seeds indoors. You should choose dwarf varieties, if available, for your container plants. You should also choose vertical or climbing plants rather than bush plants to save space. Vertical plants can be trained to grow on trellises or fences. If you place a vertical plant in a large enough pot, you can actually plant a companion plant, like herbs, alongside it.

ESSENTIAL

Some plants, like pumpkins, watermelons, and winter squash, usually require quite a bit of space. If you choose the smaller varieties now available, you can plant them in containers. However, as the vines grow and develop fruit, it's wise to hang small hammocks of netting from the trellis or fencing in order to support the weight of the fruit. Trellis or fencing should be installed when you plant the seeds.

Because some vegetables prefer the colder spring weather and some enjoy the warmer weather of summer, you can often plant one variety in your container early in the growing season, harvest it, and grow a different crop in the container months later.

Containers

You can be creative as you choose your containers. Clay or plastic gardening pots are fine, but you can also look around and see what options you have in your home. Containers have to be able to hold the soil, plant, and water; hold moisture and not deteriorate; drain water from the bottom; and be the appropriate size for the plant.

Many types of containers are appropriate for container gardening: planter boxes, pails, buckets, bushel baskets, wire baskets, wooden boxes, nursery flats, gallon cans, washtubs, strawberry pots, plastic bottles and bags, large food cans, or even an old discarded bathtub filled with soil after drain holes are drilled in the bottom.

The size of the container will vary according to the plant selection and space available. Keep in mind that the size, material, and shape of the container will make a difference to your plant's health. Consider the following guidelines when choosing your container:

- Try to avoid containers with narrow openings.
- Hanging baskets can leak onto patio furniture or the floor.

- Plastic containers are lighter weight, but they can deteriorate in sunlight or become brittle in lower temperatures. They keep water over a longer period, which can be an advantage in dry areas.
- Terra-cotta containers are porous, but they are heavy and break easily.
- Glazed ceramic pots require several drainage holes because moisture can't evaporate through their glazed sides.
- Wooden containers can be built to sizes and shapes suiting the location. However, you need to find wood that is not susceptible to rot, such as redwood or cedar.
- Metal containers absorb heat from the sun and might cause root damage. If you are using a metal container, consider also using a clay or plastic pot as a liner.
- Window boxes are usually made of wood or plastic.
- Although stone containers create a natural effect, they are heavy and break easily.
- In order to restrain a plant, you can "plant" the container in the ground.
- Be sure to use containers with adequate capacity, according to the size and number of plants to be grown in them. Remember that small pots limit the root area and dry out very quickly. Deep-rooted vegetables require deeper containers. For larger vegetables like tomatoes and eggplants, use a five-gallon container for each plant.
- Be sure you match the dimensions of the grown plant to the pot. Look in the seed catalog or on the back of the seed envelope to see how large the plant is going to get at maturity, then pick a pot that gives it plenty of room to grow.

Proper drainage is important because water caught in a container can stagnate, soil can become waterlogged, and the roots of the plant can rot. Any container you use should have holes at the base or in the bottom. Once you've made holes, you should line the base of the container with something that will prevent soil loss through the holes; a layer of newspaper or coarse gravel works very well. In order for the container to drain properly, especially if the drainage holes are on the bottom, you should raise the container up on "feet." Bricks, two-by-four blocks, or any flat object will work. If you are concerned about the drainage damaging the surface below, place saucers under your pot to catch any excess water.

The color and shape of a container can have some bearing on what you plant in it and where you position it. Dark-colored containers absorb more heat; if you place them in full sun, especially if you live in a hot, arid climate, you can damage the plant roots and the plant itself. Your choices are to use light-colored containers in very sunny or hot areas, paint the dark containers a lighter color, or place them in the shade.

The size and shape of a container should be appropriate for the plant you want to grow. If you have a container, for example, that has a round shape (a small top, a larger middle, and a small bottom) and you decide to plant a root crop in it, harvesting could be problematic. Also, consider the mature size of the plant. You don't want your pot to be tipped over by the weight, height, or length of the maturing plant.

Watering

Container gardening is an excellent way to control and maximize water usage, but pots and containers do require more frequent watering than a traditional garden because there is less soil around the plants to retain the water. Small pots and those made from porous materials, like clay, dry out especially quickly. Remember, too, that containers in an exposed area, subjected to wind or heat, will lose moisture more rapidly.

ESSENTIAL

To water your plants while on vacation, save small, empty four-ounce plastic bottles. Cut the bottom off of each bottle, thoroughly water your plants, and then push the tops of the bottles with the caps off several inches into the soil. Fill the bottles with water. These tiny bottles will release water gradually as your plants need it. If you need more water, you can use sixteen-ounce water bottles for large plants, or big two-liter plastic bottles for outdoor plants.

You should also pay attention to the watering needs of your plants. Potatoes, for instance, like a moist soil, while other vegetables do better in drier conditions. Before you water your plants, allow the water to reach room temperature, especially for sensitive plants.

Your plants will of course need more water as they grow. As their root systems expand, their water needs expand too. When watering, you should pour the water directly on the soil. Watering from the top down, rather than wicking up the water from the bottom, is better for your plants. Applying mulch to the top of the soil will help retain the moisture.

Soil

You should use the best-quality organic potting soil you can afford. Good soil is what brings the nutrients to your vegetables, so excellent soil makes excellent produce. Regular garden soil does not work well for container gardening because it is heavy and does not drain as well as potting soil. You can also create your own mixture of soil that includes one part garden soil, one part peat moss or compost, and one part coarse sand. You should also add a slow-release fertilizer (such as 14-14-14), but add that just before you plant the seedling or seeds, so you can fine-tune the fertilizer amount to the needs of the specific plant.

You can use the same soil in your containers for two years, but if you had a plant that ended up diseased, replace the soil and thoroughly clean the container before you use it again.

Planting

When you fill your containers, leave at least a few inches between the top of the container and the top of the soil for mulch. For plants that need quite a bit of moisture, be sure you have at least four inches of soil in the container. Remember, once the soil has been watered, it will settle, so initially add more than you think you will need.

Take the seeds out of their container and select a few more than the number of plants you want to grow. To ensure you don't plant a container with seeds that will never germinate, you can use an easy method to test their viability. Simply soak the seeds in water for a few hours; the ones that are viable will generally sink to the bottom, while those that are dead will float to the top.

Before you plant your seeds, check the information that came with them to determine their sowing needs. Most seeds should be covered with fine planting soil to a depth that is two times the diameter of the seed. This will help provide good germination. Very small seeds and those that require light for germination should just lie on the surface of the soil. To ensure that these seeds "connect" with the soil, use your fingers to gently tap down on the seeds and the soil.

To create a greenhouse effect as your seeds begin to germinate, you can place plastic wrap over the containers. This will keep the moisture level stable and allow you to leave the seeds undisturbed. If you do need to water your new seedlings, place the container in a basin of water and allow the water to be wicked up. Once the seeds germinate, the plastic wrap should be removed, because the seedlings can develop a fungal infection.

Your seeds should be started in a warm room with sufficient sunlight. Most seeds will germinate best if they can get twelve to sixteen hours of light each day. The best way to do this is to place seed containers in a south-facing location. Make sure you give the containers a quarter turn each day to prevent seedlings from overreaching toward the light. Before planting, seedlings will need to be hardened off or acclimated to direct sunlight and changing temperatures. You can easily do this by placing them outside in direct sunlight for a few hours only and then slowly increasing their exposure.

Diseases and Insects

Unfortunately, plants grown in containers can be attacked by the same kinds of insects and infected with the same kinds of diseases as the plants in a traditional garden. You need to inspect your plants for insects or any discoloration of the foliage. If you find insects, you can use organic insecticides to discourage them. You can also use companion planting practices to discourage pests.

Container Potatoes

You might think growing potatoes in a container is impossible, but, actually, even if you do have a lot of space, you might want to consider this method of growing potatoes. When you grow potatoes in a traditional garden, the most time-consuming part is "hilling" them. Potatoes are initially planted in a trench and then covered with soil as they grow, so the potatoes themselves are never exposed to sunlight. If you grow potatoes in a container, you are able to hill them in a more convenient manner.

For potatoes you'll need a container that is at least two feet in diameter and several feet tall (even better is a container whose height can be increased when needed), potting soil, seed potatoes, and fertilizer. Make sure your container has good drainage. Cut your seed potatoes so there are at least two eyes on each piece of potato.

Place the potatoes about ten inches apart and a few inches from the outside of the container. For a container that is about two feet in diameter, you only need four to six seed potato pieces.

Put up to four inches of soil over the potatoes and water them well. Keep the soil moist, but not soaking wet. Check once a day to see if you need more water.

Once your potato plants have grown about six inches, you start the hilling process by adding a combination of compost and soil on top. You should cover about one-third of the new growth. As your plants continue to grow, you will need to continue to hill them. Potato plants grow quickly, so keep an eye on them.

The fun part is when you harvest the potatoes. Once the plant starts to dry out, you can pour the contents of your container onto a tarp and separate the potatoes from the dirt.

ESSENTIAL

Here are some edible crops that are generally easy to grow in containers: beets, beans, peas, lemon cucumbers, tomatoes, lettuce, chard, zucchinis, radishes, spinach, kale, chili peppers, mint, oregano, thyme, basil, rosemary, and strawberries.

Local Foods

About 100 years ago, most of the American population lived on farms. If you didn't grow your own food, you bought it locally. There were no chemical preservatives, and food processing was done by canning, dehydrating, smoking, or drying. Few foods were transported more than a few miles, with the exception of things like oranges, which were only purchased for special occasions. You generally ate either what was available during the season of the year or what you preserved during the summer and the fall.

After World War II, the cost of transporting goods dropped and methods of refrigeration improved, making it easier for perishable items to be shipped over long distances. People finally were able to get their food from all over the world.

But in the late 1960s, there was a desire to get back to nature. This movement, which encouraged eating more natural, locally grown foods, seemed to lose its way in the 1980s and 1990s, when many were more concerned about convenience than where their food originated.

Today, there is a resurgence of interest in local foods. Whether due to local economic factors, environmental concerns, or quality control, the desire for food that is locally raised and grown is increasing in the United States and gaining momentum.

As you contemplate your move off-grid, there are several factors in the local food movement you should consider:

- Marketing your own fresh produce
- Incorporating a local-food lifestyle in your family
- Encouraging a local-food movement in your community

Marketing Your Own Fresh Produce

In a recent national study by the Food Marketing Institute, the reasons consumers chose to buy locally were freshness (82 percent), support for the local economy (75 percent), and knowing the source of the product (58 percent). People want to buy local produce, but you need to be able to communicate to your potential buyers that your produce is locally grown.

Other studies have documented that consumers perceive local food to be fresher looking and tasting, of higher quality, and a better value for the price. Other consumers feel that locally grown foods are linked with helping the environment. Many consumers feel the term "local foods" is synonymous with small family farms and getting back to nature. Studies have also discovered that consumers are willing to pay a premium for local foods. What does this information mean to you?

If you are thinking about selling your own locally raised produce, you already have an established "brand" to stand behind. You should use that brand to your advantage as you market your produce. There are many ways to sell your goods directly to the consumer, including farmers' markets, farm stands/on-farm sales, pick-your-own operations, and community-supported agriculture (CSAs) operations.

Community-Supported Agriculture Programs

For more than twenty years, CSA programs have been a wonderful way to partner consumers with local farmers. The basic idea behind a CSA operation is this: a farmer offers a certain number of "shares" to interested consumers. The share can consist of vegetables, fruit, eggs, even meat and poultry—depending on what the farmer grows or produces. The consumer purchases a share (which can also be considered a seasonal membership to the farmer's goods), and in return receives a box of seasonal produce each week throughout the farming season. This can be a great arrangement for both farmer and consumer.

Advantages for the farmer:

- She gets to pre-sell her produce early in the year, before the growing season begins.
- She receives payment early in the season, helping cash flow.
- She creates a relationship with a consumer and encourages local food sales.

Advantages for the consumer:

- He gets to consume farm-fresh produce, at the peak of its nutritional life.
- He has peace of mind, knowing where his produce comes from.
- He generally gets a better deal than if he had purchased the food separately at a farmers' market.
- He and his family get to develop a relationship with a farmer and learn more about the process.

You might be surprised to learn that tens of thousands of families have joined CSAs, and the impact has been overpowering. In some areas of the country there is more demand for CSAs than there are farms to supply them.

There are a number of variations of the original CSA model. Some farmers allow members to come to the farm and load up their own boxes with an assortment of produce the farmer has already picked and cleaned. Often there are limits to the number of items you can take, so everyone gets a share of each item, but this way, if a consumer is not going to use a certain vegetable, he might swap it for another, or just choose to leave it. In many cases, the produce that is not selected is donated to a local food bank, so there is no waste. The consumer received what he wanted, and the community as a whole benefits.

Another theme is offering an option of more than vegetables. Farmers can add extra shares to supply eggs, cheese, meat, preserves, fruit, homemade bread, flowers, or any other farm product. Often farmers will form a coalition to provide a good variety to all of their shareholders.

Although the idea is spreading like wildfire, there are some risks associated with CSAs. If the farmer's crop is destroyed in a flood, if it's a bad growing season, or if some other natural disaster occurs, the shareholders also take part in the risk of farming. So, while they all benefit if there is a bumper crop, they can also all lose if there is a severe hailstorm.

However, most consumers understand this going into the arrangement and, if they have a long-running relationship with the farmer, it's a learning experience regarding the uncertainties and gambles that are part of the American farmer's job.

ESSENTIAL

The number of farmers' markets in the United States grew from nearly 300 in the mid-1970s to more than 3,700 in 2004. The number of community-supported agriculture programs (CSAs)—in which members pay farmers for regular deliveries of fruits and vegetables—have grown from just one in 1985 to over 1,200 today.

Adopting a Local-Food Lifestyle

People who value local as their primary food criterion are sometimes referred to as *locavores*. This term was created by Jessica Prentice from the San Francisco Bay Area for World Environment Day 2005. She used it to describe and promote the practice of eating a diet consisting of food harvested from the local area. Prentice's definition of "local area" was an area bound by a 100-mile radius. Prentice's new word became popular around the country, and in 2007, the New Oxford American Dictionary chose "locavore" as its word of the year.

How Do You Become a Locavore?

One simple way is to grow a garden and produce a lot of your vegetables in your own backyard. Another way is to locate all of the "pick-your-own" farms in your area and take advantage of the things they have to offer. You can also find local farmers and see if you can participate in a CSA. You can find a nearby, small-town processing plant and find out if it has locally raised meat for sale. Even your neighborhood grocery store might offer some local produce for the summer.

When you go shopping, buy extra quantities of your favorite local fruit or vegetable when it's in season and preserve it for a later date. Help pass along the excitement of local foods by sharing with others. Host a harvest party at your home or in your community, featuring locally available and in-season foods.

Challenge your family. See if you can only eat local foods for a weekend, and then expand from there. Obviously, there will be some exceptions to the rules—there are not many cinnamon trees in the United States—but for the most part, you will be amazed at what you find when you purchase only local foods.

FACT

Burgerville, a chain of thirty-nine fast-food restaurants in the U.S. Pacific Northwest, features a menu nearly identical to that of McDonald's, but it buys the bulk of its ingredients from farmers in Oregon and Washington.

Encouraging a Local Food Movement in Your Community

Local foods are not only good for you, they are good for the local economy. Talk to your county Extension agent to see if there are any local-food groups you can join. Ask your favorite restaurants whether they use local foods in their menus. Ask the manager of your local grocery store, if he buys produce from local farmers. Encourage your local politicians to form a food policy council to promote farmers' markets, to develop a local-food directory, and to get fresh foods into schools and other cafeterias. Visit local farmers who market regularly and talk with them to learn all you can about raising your own produce.

ALERT

Small communities reap more economic benefits from the presence of small farms than they do from large ones. Studies have shown that small farms reinvest more money into local economies by purchasing feed, seed, and other materials from local businesses. Large farms generally order in bulk from distant companies.

Preparing Physically

If you move completely off-grid you will need to be able to perform a lot of physical labor, from chopping wood to planting and harvesting gardens to dealing with the day-to-day work of a farm. One thing you can start today, as you plan for your off-grid experience, is to get yourself physically fit. The three areas you need to look at are physical activity, diet, and addictions.

Physical Activity

Physical activity simply means using energy to move your body. You participate in physical activity all the time—walking, gardening, pushing a baby stroller, climbing the stairs, playing soccer, or dancing. To improve your fitness level, your physical activity should be moderate or vigorous and last at least thirty minutes a day. In order to be considered moderate or vigorous, the activity must increase your heart rate. Such activities are considered aerobic because they increase your heart rate and breathing, thereby improving your heart and lung fitness. Here are some examples of moderate aerobic activities:

- Walking briskly (about 3½ miles per hour)
- Hiking

- Gardening/yard work
- Dancing
- Golf (walking and carrying clubs)
- Bicycling (less than 10 miles per hour)

Some vigorous aerobic activities include:

- Running/jogging (5 miles per hour)
- Bicycling (more than 10 miles per hour)
- Swimming (freestyle laps)
- Aerobic exercise classes
- Walking very fast (4½ miles per hour)
- Heavy yard work, such as chopping wood
- Basketball (competitive)

In addition to aerobic activities you should also engage in resistance training, strength building, and weight-bearing activities. These exercises include free weights, weight machines, resistance bands, or using your own weight to build muscles and strength. These exercises help build and maintain bones and muscles by working them against gravity. They are also the fastest way to improve muscle strength and endurance, which allows a person to perform everyday tasks with less effort and for longer periods of time.

Resistance/strength training can also improve circulation, coordination, balance, bone, and ligament strength. These exercises include any exercise during which muscles expand and contract against an external resistance. The idea behind resistance is to increase the strength, endurance, and tone of the muscle. The external resistance can come from a number of things—dumbbells, weight machines, elastic tubing or bands, cinder blocks, cans of soup, even your own body weight. What you are looking for is something that causes your muscles to work as you expand and contract them. The best results in resistance training come with increases in repetition and weight.

Diet

You should begin to live with a diet that will match the restrictions you will have when you move off-grid. If you want to eventually use freshly ground whole-wheat flour to make your breads and baked goods, start adding a little whole wheat to the things you make now, so your body can adapt. When you are off-grid, most of your foods will have less processing, and will be much better for you than chips and frozen pizza. But if you are used to high-carb, high-fat, and high-sodium foods, you are going to want to wean your body off those and move toward a more basic diet.

One of the principles of a basic diet is to simply eat a wide variety of foods. A variety is essential because different foods make different nutritional contributions. The foods that should make up the bulk of your healthy diet are fruits, vegetables, grains, and legumes. These are all foods that are high in complex carbohydrates, fiber, vitamins, and minerals, low in fat, and free of cholesterol. The rest of your diet should come from dairy products, meat and poultry, and fish.

The following basic guidelines will help you construct a healthy diet.

- **Eat plenty of high-fiber foods.** Concentrate on fruits, vegetables, beans, and whole grains. There are good carbohydrates and bad carbohydrates, and these are the good ones. These foods are nutritious, low in calories, and they fill you up. Your body needs 20 to 30 grams of fiber per day; eating these foods will help you meet that fiber goal.

- **Include green, orange, and yellow fruits and vegetables in your diet.** The color palette is actually important. Different colors represent some of the varied antioxidants and other nutrients in these foods that can help to protect you against developing certain types of cancer and other diseases. You should eat five or more servings a day of fruits and vegetables.

- **Avoid "bad" carbohydrates, like sugar.** Sugar actually encourages you to eat more than you should. Your body burns carbs before it burns fat. When you eat sugar you get a "sugar rush" and you feel energized. But as the sugar is burned for fuel, your body reacts and wants more sugar for another quick rush. The body doesn't turn to its own fat, as it should, because it's been trained to consume the sugar. When you begin a low-carb diet it takes several weeks before your body starts to efficiently burn fat. But once you take sugar out of your diet, you will be amazed at how much energy you have.

- **Cut the trans fats out of your diet.** These are supplied by hydrogenated vegetable oils used in most processed foods found in the supermarket, and in many fast foods.
- **Eat more fish and nuts, which contain healthy unsaturated fats.** Substitute olive or canola oil for butter or stick margarine.
- **Don't let your food get boring.** Eating a wide assortment of foods helps to ensure that you will get all the necessary nutrients.
- **Maintain an adequate calcium intake.** This is especially true for women and children. Calcium is essential for strong bones and teeth. Get your calcium from low-fat sources, such as skim milk and low-fat yogurt. If you can't get the optimal amount from foods, take supplements.
- **If you drink alcohol, do so in moderation.** That is, one drink a day for women, two a day for men. A drink is defined as 12 ounces of beer, 4 ounces of wine, or 1.5 ounces of 80-proof spirits. Excess alcohol consumption leads to a variety of health problems. And alcoholic beverages can add many calories to your diet without supplying nutrients.

Addictions

The alarm clock goes off. You reach over and shut it off and stumble to the kitchen. The automatic coffee pot is set to a timer, so your first cup is already waiting for you. You sip it tentatively, feeling the caffeine course through your body. Now you can face the day. What happens if the coffee isn't there?

It's 10:30 in the morning. You walk down the hall to the break room, the change jingling in your hand. You reach the machine, drop the quarters in, and push the button for the diet caffeinated soda. Now you can make it to lunch. What happens if the soda isn't there?

If you smoke cigarettes, you've already been told over and over again that it's bad for your health. But, if you smoke and you are going off-grid, you need to think about the cost of making sure you can always satisfy your nicotine cravings.

If there is anything in your life that you have to have in order to be a pleasant, functioning human being, whether it's caffeine, tobacco, alcohol, chocolate, or something else entirely, you need to get rid of the habit before you go completely off-grid.

The idea of being off-grid is being self-sufficient. If you are chained to an addiction, you're not free. And going through withdrawal from any addiction when people are relying on you for their welfare is never a good idea. The sooner you stop using it, the better.

A Trial Run

As you prepare for your off-grid lifestyle, it's a good idea for you and your family to experience off-grid living in a controlled situation. You want to hope your off-grid home will have all of the conveniences of your current home, but when you decide to plan a trial run, you should make the situation a little more challenging to ensure you are up to the change.

Select a weekend for your trial run. For your first one, select a weekend when the temperatures will be moderate. Make sure everyone in your family understands what is going on, so they can be prepared. Then, turn off your electricity and keep it off throughout the entire weekend. This means you will have no access to computers, television, radio, refrigeration, heat, electric lights, your washer and dryer—anything that runs on electricity. Now, your challenge is to put the skills you have been reading about and, hopefully, practicing, to good use.

You can cook on your camp stove outside and heat water on it too. If your water comes from your own well, you will have to use your stored water for drinking, cooking, and personal needs. During this experiment you cannot run to the store because you forgot to get something. The only way you are going to learn what you need to live in an off-grid manner is to try it out.

You will want to be aware of how many times the toilet is flushed. You will want to save your graywater. Remember that your pets need water, too.

Did you remember batteries for your flashlights for when it starts to get dark? Do you have candles? Do they provide enough light for your needs?

Do you have games and puzzles to provide entertainment without the television and computers? Are you able to prepare a meal that everyone enjoys? Are you eating the kind of foods you are storing for off-grid living?

If you can last the entire weekend, congratulate yourself. But take the time to assess the places where you felt less prepared than you should be. If you were lacking in any way, be sure to redouble your efforts in that area.

You might want to try another off-grid weekend in six months, when the weather is slightly different, and see how you do in those circumstances. Remember, the more you can prepare for your off-grid experience, the better.

Creating a Plan

Stephen Covey, a motivational speaker and the author of *The 7 Habits of Highly Effective People,* has said that you need to set goals with the end in mind. In other words, you need to look at what you want in your life and set goals in that context. If you do this, you will set goals that you really do want to achieve.

Visualize what you want. Do you really want to live off-grid? Do you want to have a more self-sufficient lifestyle? Do you want to escape from the nine-to-five rat race? Do you want a simpler, more environmentally friendly life? Do you really want it?

Here are some steps to help you turn your desire of living off-grid into a reality.

Begin with a Dream

All personal goals begin with a dream and a desire. You want to get out of debt. You want to live a simpler life. You want to be able to spend more time with your family. You want to be sure your children are growing up in a safe environment. You want to be able to see the stars at night. Think about your dream. Visualize your dream. And visualize yourself in the dream.

Implement

Now you have the dream and you can picture yourself living it. Your next step is to figure out how you can implement the idea. Get a notepad and start jotting down all of the ways you can realize the dream. Do you need to get out of debt? Do you need to increase your skill sets? Do you need to become more physically fit?

Once you've finished writing down your ideas, prioritize them. What really has to come first before you do anything else? Put that one at the top of the list. Then go through the list and prioritize the rest of the ideas. When you have finished prioritizing, go back to the top of the list and set a goal of when you want to have that first priority completed. You can actually set goals for the first three priorities. Set realistic goals, but goals that will make you work hard to achieve them. Set these goals as long term (six months or more), medium term (three to six months), and short term (in a matter of weeks).

Make Your Goals Personal

It's important to have family goals and you should have your family come together to discuss their ideas about living off-grid. But to begin with, you need to concentrate on your own personal goals, especially the goals in the areas where you have to make changes. Whether you need to curtail your spending habits, lose weight, or gain control of your finances, you are the only one who can decide whether your goal is important enough to make you want to change your habits. You are the one who will decide to take the first step. You will be your best cheerleader.

Write Your Goals Down

Visualization is a powerful tool. Many athletes say they use visualization when they have to accomplish a difficult task. One Olympics-winning pole-vaulter said he would always visualize himself jumping three feet higher than he needed, and he would always do well. You need to visualize yourself completing your goals. Take the time to write down your goals, but do more than just jot down a sentence. Take the time to describe how you will feel when those goals are accomplished. Take the time to write down how you will feel when you've lost the extra 25 pounds or when you've received the notice in the mail that lets you know your mortgage is paid and you own your home free and clear. Write about how important the accomplishment of these goals is to you.

Be Specific with Your Goals

When you are specific with your goals, you are letting your mind know that you are serious. "I will get out of debt" is a nice goal, but "I will have no credit card debt and all of my other payments will be up to date in six months" is much more specific and quantified. Think about the details of your goals. Write down exactly what you want and when you want it. Don't be vague—be as specific as possible.

Time Based

Make sure that each of your goals has a specific deadline for its completion. Mark those dates on your calendar, so you clearly see how many days you have left to accomplish your task. If the goal is a long-term goal, set up some shorter-term benchmark dates to see how you are doing. For example, if your goal is to lose 30 pounds in six months, have short-term goals of 5 pounds a month. This will help keep your goal manageable and will give you opportunities to succeed.

Visualize Your Goals

Have you ever seen a movie or a cartoon where someone is lost in the desert and they think they see an oasis and struggle toward it? Often, it happens when they have just about given up, then it appears on the horizon. It gives them enough renewed hope to access some inner strength when they didn't think they had any left and to move forward.

You need the same kind of motivation to access your inner strength. You need visual reminders of not only your goals, but your rewards. Use a screen saver on your computer with a picture of the off-grid home of your dreams, or the outfit you want to purchase once you've lost the 30 pounds. Have a calendar in your office with photos of gardening. Have something out in the open, whether it's your computer screen or on your refrigerator door, that reminds you of what you are trying to accomplish and why you are trying to accomplish it.

Have Faith

Decide today that you are going to accomplish your goals, and have faith that you will do it. Don't allow self-doubt to pull you back. Know that you can do this! You have the knowledge, you have the willpower, and you have the determination. You can and will succeed. Have faith and a positive attitude. The power of positive thinking is amazing! It will help you get to where you want to be.

Strategy

You have your dreams, you have your goals, and now you need to think about your strategy. Strategy encompasses the tactics you will use to achieve your goals. For example, if one of your goals is to lose weight, one strategy might be to make sure there are no snack foods in your house. Another strategy might be to park the car farther away from the office or the store, so you have to exercise a little more each day. When you plan your strategy, think about your goals and ask yourself, "How am I going to accomplish this?"

Just as you did with your goals, write down your strategies and incorporate them into your life. Soon you will have reached your goals and will move on to realize your dreams.

Remember, you can accomplish whatever you set out to do. It's within your reach—you just need to take the first step.

APPENDIX A

Recommended Reading

Although this book has touched on many different ideas to help you move off the grid, there are a number of sources that can offer you much more detail in specific areas of interest. Here are some books you should have in your library, magazines you should subscribe to or get from your library, and a list of websites to help you as you make your move off-grid.

Books

Bingham, Rita. *Passport to Survival: 12 Steps to Self-Sufficient Living.* Edmond, OK, Natural Meals Publishing, 1999.

Bubel, Mike, and Nancy Bubel. *Root Cellaring: Natural Cold Storage of Fruits & Vegetables.* North Adams, MA: Storey Publishing, 1991.

Emery, Carla. *The Encyclopedia of Country Living.* Seattle: Sasquatch Books, 2008.

Gehring, Abigail. *Back to Basics: A Complete Guide to Traditional Skills.* New York: Skyhorse Publishing, 2008.

Mabey, Richard. *The New Age Herbalist.* London: Gaia Books Ltd,. 1988.

Raymond, Dick. *Garden Way's Joy of Gardening.* Charlotte, VT: Garden Way, 1982.

Rogers, Marc. *Saving Seeds: The Gardener's Guide to Growing and Storing Vegetable and Flower Seeds.* North Adams, MA: Storey Publishing, 1990.

Sammataro, Diana, and Alphonse Avitabile. *The Beekeeper's Handbook.* Ithaca, NY: Comstock Publishing Associates, Cornell University Press, 1998.

Stevens, James Talmage. *Making the Best of Basics: Family Preparedness Handbook.* Salt Lake City: Peton Corp., 1997.

Magazines

Backwoods Home—www.backwoodshome.com

MaryJane's Farm: The Everyday Organic Lifestyle Magazine— www.maryjanesfarm.org

Hobby Farms—www.hobbyfarms.com

Websites

Timebomb2000—*www.timebomb2000.com*

The Survival Mom—*http://thesurvivalmom.com*

Provident Living—*www.providentliving.org*

Off Grid Survival—*http://offgridsurvival.com*

The Frugal Squirrel—*www.frugalsquirrels.com*

The Gentle Survivalist—*http://site.infowest.com/business/g/gentle/siteindex.html*

Prepared Society—*www.preparedsociety.com/forum*

Government Resources

The Home Safety Council

www.homesafetycouncil.org/index.asp

Center for International Disaster Information

www.cidi.org

Ready.gov

www.ready.gov

State of Washington Emergency Preparedness

www.doh.wa.gov/phepr/factsheets.htm

FEMA (Federal Emergency Management Agency)

www.fema.gov

The CDC Emergency Preparedness and Response

www.bt.cdc.gov

Natural Resources Research Information Pages

www4.ncsu.edu/~leung/agusa.html

Index

We Have
EVERYTHING®
on Anything!

With more than 19 million copies sold, the Everything® series has become one of America's favorite resources for solving problems, learning new skills, and organizing lives. Our brand is not only recognizable—it's also welcomed.

The series is a hand-in-hand partner for people who are ready to tackle new subjects—like you!

For more information on the Everything® series, please visit *www.adamsmedia.com*

The Everything® list spans a wide range of subjects, with more than 500 titles covering 25 different categories:

Business	History	Reference
Careers	Home Improvement	Religion
Children's Storybooks	Everything Kids	Self-Help
Computers	Languages	Sports & Fitness
Cooking	Music	Travel
Crafts and Hobbies	New Age	Wedding
Education/Schools	Parenting	Writing
Games and Puzzles	Personal Finance	
Health	Pets	

Made in the USA
Middletown, DE
02 December 2015